Robert Peal is joint Head Teacher and teacher of history at the West London Free School. He was awarded a double first in history from the University of Cambridge and studied for his masters at the University of Pennsylvania. He qualified as a teacher through the Teach First Programme before working as a policy advisor at the Department for Education. He is the author of a number of history textbooks for use in secondary schools.

MEET THE GEORGIANS

EPIC TALES FROM BRITAIN'S WILDEST CENTURY

ROBERT PEAL

**WILLIAM
COLLINS**

William Collins
An imprint of HarperCollins*Publishers*
1 London Bridge Street
London SE1 9GF

WilliamCollinsBooks.com

HarperCollins*Publishers*
1st Floor, Watermarque Building, Ringsend Road
Dublin 4, Ireland

First published in Great Britain in 2021 by William Collins
This William Collins paperback edition published in 2022

1

Typeset in Minion Pro by
Palimpsest Book Production Ltd, Falkirk, Stirlingshire

Printed and bound in the UK using
100% renewable electricity at CPI Group (UK) Ltd

MIX
Paper from
responsible sources
FSC C007454
www.fsc.org

This book is produced from independently certified FSC™ paper
to ensure responsible forest management.

For more information visit: www.harpercollins.co.uk/green

To mum and dad.
The best teachers I ever had.

Contents

Introduction

Mad, Bad and Dangerous to Know

'Mad, bad and dangerous to know.' That is how one of the characters in this book, the poet Lord Byron, was described by his lover, the equally nutty Lady Caroline Lamb. She was not wrong. He was the sort of man who drank wine out of a monk's skull, slept with his half-sister, and arrived at the University of Cambridge with a pet bear, having been told that students were not permitted to keep dogs.

Mad, bad and dangerous. It was a good description of Lord Byron, but it is also a good description of the Georgian period as a whole. Beginning with the coronation of King George I in 1714 and ending with the death of his great-great-grandson King George IV in 1830, the Georgian period was quite possibly the wildest era in British history. It overflows with outrageous characters, and this book introduces you to twelve of the best: a dirty dozen of wicked women, Regency rogues and fearless freedom fighters.

Sadly, the Georgian period is rather ignored these days. At school, you probably studied the seventeenth-century Stuarts, with their Civil War and Great Fire, plagues and Puritans. Everyone at some point seems to study the

Victorians, those earnest do-gooders with enormous courage but a limited sense of humour. Between these two periods come the fun-loving, devil-may-care Georgians like a burst of sun breaking through the clouds of the gloomier, more serious periods of Britain's past.

And they really did shine. If you have ever been to a fancy-dress party dressed as a dashing highwayman, swash-buckling pirate or bewigged aristocrat, you'll know how easy it is to look totally epic dressing like it's 1725. Just pull on your leather boots, billowing linen shirt, waistcoat and tricorn hat, tuck a pistol into your belt, and you're ready to roll. And it was not only the men who dressed this way, as you will discover when reading in Chapter 1 about Anne Bonny and Mary Read, two foul-mouthed, cross-dressing pirate queens of the Caribbean.

Some imagine that the Britain of the past was always a place of polite manners, Sunday church and stiff upper lips. However, this national character was a creation of the Victorian period. If you look at the riotous cartoons drawn by Georgian artists, or read their bawdy plays and comic novels, you will see how much they gloried in life's vulgar pleasures: gambling, drinking, dancing, fighting, flirting and . . . I forget what else. In the sunny uplands of the eighteenth century, the Merrie England of maypoles, country fetes, drunken squires and frol-icking farmhands still ruled.

Much of this merrymaking came from an intense relief that the seventeenth century, with all its violence and religious conflict, was over. The Georgians' predecessors, the Stuarts, had been pretty hopeless rulers, and when the last Stuart monarch, Queen Anne, died in 1714, Parliament knew the country needed a fresh start. They had been casting around Europe for a new monarch, and landed upon George I, a minor royal from the German state of Hanover. He was a curious choice for king of Great Britain, having only visited the country once in his life, being unable to speak English, and ranking fifty-seventh in line to the throne.

However, unlike the fifty-six descendants of the English royal family ahead of him, he had one redeeming feature: he was a Protestant. Catholicism in eighteenth-century England was associated with the tyranny of the Stuarts, the terrorism of Guy Fawkes, and treacherous loyalty to France. Parliament needed a Protestant king. A podgy and dim-witted German princeling was what they got.

However, the Stuarts were not going to give way to the Georgians without a fight. In Chapter 2, you will read the story of Bonnie Prince Charlie, the grandson of England's last Stuart king. He landed in Scotland in 1745, raised an army of Highland supporters, invaded England and tried to take back his family's throne. Although he made a strong start, the invasion ended in failure. King George II's army obliterated Prince Charlie's ragtag band of Highland soldiers at the Battle of Culloden on 16 April 1746. It was the last battle ever fought on Great Britain's soil.

The people of Britain could now sleep soundly at night, safe in the knowledge that the rule of their new Georgian monarchs was secure. Not that they did much ruling. George I and his equally uninspiring son George II gave their names to the period, but were essentially controlled by Parliament. Having a pair of tubby German puppets as kings – Dunce the First and Dunce the Second, in the words of one writer – suited the British quite well. They had a monarchy, but nobody had to take them seriously. When George II died in 1760, it seemed entirely fitting to his subjects that he did so on the toilet. Taking a dump. Like Elvis.

George II's grandson, George III, was next in line to the throne. Claiming to 'glory in the name of Briton', he was loved by his people and had a few good years before getting spanked in the American War of Independence and going mad. Literally. Around 1788, he began speaking in tongues, and causing acute embarrassment to all involved by attempting to make love to the Queen in public. Rumours spread that he had been seen talking to a tree and attempting to shake its hand, entirely convinced that it was the King of Prussia.

However, when George III went mad, it didn't really matter. Although his son, the Prince Regent (and later George IV), stepped in to take on royal duties, it was Parliament that was running the show. This prolonged period of political stability gave Georgian Britain its carefree, merrymaking atmosphere. With most of the nation's religious and political conflict put to bed, its people could finally focus on the good things in life. Drinking, in particular. As will be clear in the stories that follow, Georgian Britons loved the booze.

The reputation of many a young man was built on his capacity for drink: to qualify as good company, you had to be a three-bottle man. The hell-raising Irish playwright Richard Sheridan was a six-bottle man. The behaviour of Britain's boozy aristocracy gave rise to the saying 'drunk as a lord', but drunkenness ran right through society as Georgians of all social classes took pride in getting pissed. An estimate from 1737 suggested that one in every six properties in London sold alcohol, with 'brandyshops' outnumbering all the bakers, butchers, cheesemongers, fishmongers and herb stalls combined. In the Midlands village of Edwalton, you can still find the gravestone of one Rebecca Freeland, who died in 1741. Her epitaph reads:

>She drank good ale, good punch, and wine
>And lived to the age of ninety-nine.

However, if you wanted to get absolutely gazeboed in Georgian Britain, there was only one drink for you: gin. Early in the century, it was estimated that the average Londoner was drinking almost a pint of spirits a week. Nicknamed 'Madame Geneva', gin was strong, plentiful and dangerously cheap. By the 1730s, thousands of unlicensed gin cellars lined the streets of Britain's towns and cities. One reportedly had a sign which read, 'drunk for a penny, dead drunk for two-pence, clean straw for nothing'. When Parliament tried to limit the sale of gin through new licences in 1736, the proudly pissed Georgians took to the streets and rioted. They shouted their slogan 'no gin, no king!' and held mock funeral processions for their dearly beloved Madame Geneva, no doubt tanked up on lashings of her fiery liquor.

And where there was drinking, there was sex. In fact, if you go by some of the poems, plays and (frankly pornographic) pictures left behind by the Georgians, you could be forgiven for thinking that all they ever thought about, from the lowliest docker to the noblest duke, was shagging. Sex was 'the master-piece of nature ... the purest source of human felicity', according to the scientist, philosopher and occasional woman-iser Dr Erasmus Darwin, grandfather to the rather more buttoned-up Charles Darwin. The Georgians were baffled by their socially awkward Prime Minister William Pitt the Younger, who never showed the slightest interest in sexual relationships. 'Stiff to everyone but a lady', his friends liked to joke.

And just like today's London, the patch of land between Covent Garden, Leicester Square and Oxford Street was

Britain's seediest square mile. Pubs, taverns and theatres lined the West End's streets, as did shops such as the Green Canister, where a former courtesan named Teresia Constantia Phillips would sell you a packet of 'Con's preservatives': condoms made of sheep's intestine, secured with a dainty coloured ribbon around the base. Prostitution was endemic in Britain's towns and cities, with one historian putting the number of prostitutes in London alone at between 3,000 and 7,000. The most popular featured in *Harris's List of Covent Garden Ladies*, a handy guide to the working women of London published in numerous editions from 1757 to 1795. It was named after Jack Harris, head waiter at the Shakespeare's Head Tavern, a notorious inn-cum-brothel where he forged his reputation as 'Pimp-General to the People of England'.

As the prevalence of prostitution shows, sex was a man's game. However, the Georgians were not afraid of female sexuality. They enjoyed reading *Fanny Hill*, the fictionalised memoirs of a happy-go-lucky prostitute and 'woman of pleasure' who finds contentment in marriage to a former client. *Fanny Hill* was published in 1748 but banned the following year for 'corrupting the King's subjects'; it was legally republished in the UK for the first time only in 1963. The popular pregnancy guide *Aristotle's Compleat Masterpiece* ran to forty-three editions and advised women to enjoy sex in ways that seem remarkably frank to modern eyes. In 1717, an advertisement appeared in the *Nottingham Weekly Courant* from a certain Sarah Y—tes, whose husband had 'lost the use of his Peace-Maker'. She was offering half a crown a night and a pair of clean sheets to 'any able young Man, strong in the Back, and endow'd with a good Carnal Weapon'. Sadly, no record of the responses has survived.

As this candid celebration of sex suggests, the Georgians

saw having fun as their sacred right. In contrast to the era of the more housebound Victorians, Georgian Britain was an intensely sociable place, and socialising occurred through a dizzying array of clubs: political clubs, literary clubs, sporting clubs, clubs for short people, clubs for fat people, clubs for ugly people. There was even a 'farting' club, whose members met once a week in order to 'poison the neighbouring air with their unsavoury crepitations'. Members of the club ate cabbage, onions and pea-porridge until their stomachs swelled up like a 'blown bag pipe'. They then competed to see whose 'windy eruptions' were the loudest and the longest.

The infamous farting club is a reminder of one of the Georgians' most endearing traits: their unwillingness to take life too seriously. And they were pretty relaxed about death as well. Today, we are shielded from death, but during the eighteenth century, when one in three children died before the age of five, death was everywhere. In fact, it went further: death was also public entertainment. The gallows in town and city centres were a constant reminder that if you committed even minor crimes, such as forging coins or stealing sheep, you could be led to the hangman's noose. In London, the convicted were wheeled around the city in the back of a wagon for a whole morning, sometimes chatting about their fate and sharing drinks with the crowds. When the thief, jailbreaker and cult hero Jack Sheppard was taken to the gallows in 1724, some 200,000 people gathered to watch him die.

Nothing better sums up the Georgian people's indifferent attitude towards death than the duel. Over the course of George III's reign, 172 duels were recorded, resulting in 69 deaths. One of those was meted out by the 5th Baron Byron, known as the 'Wicked Lord', and great-uncle to Lord Byron. In the winter of 1765, Baron Byron got into an argument with his neighbour during a night out at the Star and Garter tavern. Both felt their honour had been insulted, so they staggered to a back room of the tavern and settled the dispute with swords. Baron Byron thrust his weapon through his neighbour's stomach, a wound from which he died the following day. The cause of the argument? A debate over who had the most game on their estate. Many Georgians were willing to die for a good cause, and often for a stupid one as well.

The Georgians seemed to be equally relaxed about losing money. During a single night playing cards, a wealthy Georgian might bet away tens of thousands of pounds, millions in today's money. Officially, the winner was the man or woman who left with the most money. But unofficially, there was always a competition for who could care the least about losing an entire fortune in a single night. That was a sign of true class.

The politician Charles James Fox was very good at this game. In an epic gambling session in 1772, he lost £11,000 at cards in his London club on day one, then stayed up all night and won back £6,000 on day two, before riding to Newmarket racecourse in the early hours of day three, where he lost £10,000 on the horses. Little surprise then that Fox, having inherited one of the largest fortunes in the country, ended up bankrupt. And this is a man who came within a whisker of becoming prime minister.

The Georgians' carefree attitude towards life was helped by a lack of religious seriousness. For the previous two centuries, the Wars of Religion had caused death and destruction across Europe on a scale never seen before in history. So, by the eighteenth century, it had become distinctly uncool to show religious enthusiasm. In 1714, there were seventy-two churches in London offering daily services, but by 1732 this had shrunk to forty-four. Most Georgians still went to church on Sunday, but for many it was a weekly chore to be got out of the way early in the day, so that the real fun could start.

In fact, for the first time in British history, it became possible to question the very existence of God. The Georgian period was not just an age of wild behaviour but of wild thoughts, and many a fashionable intellectual flirted with atheism. In 1811, Byron's buddy, the poet Percy Bysshe Shelley, wrote an essay entitled 'The Necessity of Atheism' and distributed it around the University of Oxford. This prank got him expelled. Two centuries earlier, however, it would have got him killed.

If you were to choose one person who summed up the devil-may-care atmosphere of Georgian England, it would have to be John Wilkes. Though largely forgotten today, Wilkes was the most famous politician of the 1760s. His story in Chapter 3 tells how he took on King George III's government in a series of legal and electoral battles, establishing the right of freeborn Englishmen to report on parliamentary debates, criticise the government in the press, and resist arrest without a warrant. However, his political success was built more on personality than principles. Wilkes reflected his age: a duel-fighting, spendthrift womaniser with a weakness for booze and a filthy sense of humour. The Georgian people loved him for it, turning him into Britain's first ever populist politician.

The centre of Wilkes's support was London, an urban colossus. By 1750, it was one of the largest cities in the world, with 750,000 inhabitants, more than fifteen times the size of its closest English rival Bristol (45,000 inhabitants). Today, it is impossible to imagine the intense bustle, and even more intense smell, of Georgian London. The full gamut of human existence could be found on London's streets: carts, carriages, delivery boys, barrow-girls, farm animals, market stalls, beggars and thieves. This seething mass of humanity contained the best and worst of human life: elegance and lewdness, kindness and cruelty, joy and despair. As a poem entitled 'A Description of London' written in 1738 suggests, Britain's capital hummed with an exuberant, threatening energy:

> Many a Beau without a Shilling;
> Many a Widow not unwilling;
> Many a Bargain, if you strike it:
> This is LONDON! How d'ye like it?

'When a man is tired of London', the writer Samuel Johnson observed in 1777, 'he is tired of life; for there is in London all that life can afford.'

As was clear walking the streets of Georgian London, life was becoming, quite literally, more colourful. For centuries, people's clothing had been a palette of browns and murky greens, but was now bursting into a riot of red, purple, yellow and indigo, as merchants traded new dyes from around the world to Britain's shores. Indian cotton and silk textiles started making their way into Britain, as did sapphires, rubies and emeralds. Unlike the plainly clothed Stuarts and the sober, frock-coated Victorians, the Georgians delighted in their frilly shirts, lace collars, silk ribbons and ludicrous wigs.

Their outfits hit peak preposterousness during the mid-eighteenth century. Georgian fashion victims covered their faces with white lead-based paint, blusher, lipstick and a scattering of fake moles made from black velvet, topped off with a mountainous wig of white-powdered hair. And that was just the men.

Meanwhile, the national palate was becoming more flavourful. Chocolate, chillies and pineapples from South

America became common in British shops, as did East Asian spices such as cinnamon, pepper and cumin. However, the most widely consumed foreign foodstuffs were tea from China, and sugar and coffee from the Americas. For many a Georgian gentleman, a day did not start until he had dunked a freshly baked bun into his steaming cup of hot coffee, while scanning a newspaper in one of the hundreds of coffee shops that lined British high streets. He would then fill his pipe and enjoy the health-bringing benefits (or so he thought) of a lungful of unfiltered Virginia tobacco.

No wonder the madcap Georgians hit our history books like a double espresso downed before breakfast. They were on one massive caffeine, tobacco and sugar buzz, like nothing experienced before in British history.

Where were all these exciting new products coming from? It is a question that can be answered with three simple words: the British Empire. Although the currant buns and sugared teas of Georgian Britain seemed so innocent and delightful, they were entirely bound up with the conquest of vast overseas territories, and the miserable suffering of enslaved workers.

During the eighteenth and nineteenth centuries, the British Empire spread across North America, the Caribbean, India and Australia. From each of these territories, merchants traded new luxuries back to Britain: American tobacco, Caribbean sugar, Indian cotton and Australian wool. These goods made British merchants astoundingly rich, 'far wealthier than many sovereign princes of Germany or Italy', according to one Swiss visitor in 1727. Take Robert Clive as an example. He played a central role in Britain's colonisation of India and amassed a personal fortune of half a million pounds, allowing him to buy a series of country estates, control over two seats in

Parliament, and a diamond necklace for his wife's pet ferret worth £2,500.

In days gone by, such Empire-builders were written about as heroes: Clive of India, Wolfe of Quebec, Nelson of the Nile, and so on. However, much recent history has tried to retell the story of the British Empire from the view of the colonised, not the colonisers. In Chapter 4, Britain's colonisation of India is told through the life of Tipu Sultan, the tiger-loving, elephant-riding ruler of Mysore, a jungle-bound kingdom in southern India. As a young man, Tipu and his father shocked the world by winning a series of spectacular victories against the British, before he was finally defeated in the Fourth (and final) Anglo-Mysore War. Today, Tipu is mostly forgotten, but by the time of his death he had become a cult figure around the world.

During its early days, the British Empire grew in a rapid and freewheeling fashion. However, towards the end of the eighteenth century, the British began to take their global impact more seriously. In particular, they began to confront their involvement in the slave trade, one of the most chilling examples in world history of humankind's capacity for cruelty. Between the sixteenth and nineteenth century, European merchants seized an estimated 13 million men, women and children from the west coast of Africa, shipped them as live cargo across the Atlantic, and forced them to work as slave labour in the Caribbean and the Americas. One such person was Olaudah Equiano, whose extraordinary story is told in Chapter 5.

The great majority of enslaved Africans were worked to an early death in the plantations of North and South America, but Equiano was lucky enough to buy his freedom in 1766. As a free man, he moved to Britain, joined the growing move-ment for the abolition of the slave trade, and published his memoirs in 1789. This first-hand account of slavery, vividly told through the voice of one of its victims, was a bestseller, forcing the people of Georgian Britain to face up to the blood being shed to build their nation's wealth. Books such as Equiano's turbocharged the abolitionist movement, and fundamentally changed the way that Georgians saw their role in the world. Writing in 1804, the artist Henry Fuseli remarked about Liverpool, a city that had grown rich through slavery, 'methinks, I everywhere smell the blood of slaves.' It is a legacy that Britain is still grappling with to this day.

Having published his memoirs, Equiano married an Englishwoman named Sally and lived out the rest of his days on a farm in Cambridgeshire, leaving a sizeable inheritance for his two mixed-race daughters. Equiano and his family were part of a growing population of black and mixed-race people living in Georgian Britain, with one estimate from 1764 putting the number at 20,000. It is easy to imagine the Georgians being as white as the grand terraces of stuccoed houses they built, but this was not the case.

In fact, reading about Georgian society, it rarely takes long for a man or woman of colour to appear. Paintings of crowd scenes from the period, particularly those with a military or urban setting, regularly include black faces. The servant who accompanied Lord Byron on his European travels was a freed slave named Benjamin Lewis. An aristocrat named Lord Camelford, who appears later in these pages, hired as his personal trainer one of Britain's best-known bareknuckle boxers: a freed slave named Bill Richmond. Equiano and Richmond both married and had children with white women, and such marriages were not unusual.

From the mid-eighteenth century, slavery was generally understood to be illegal in Britain, where there was – according to an oft-quoted legal case – 'too pure an Air for Slaves to breathe'. While many people in Georgian Britain were happy to benefit from slave labour across the seas, they preferred not to witness such cruelties at home.

Therefore, most black people living in Britain did so as free men and women, who could expect to be treated with curiosity and a certain level of cautious tolerance. Black Georgians ran businesses, had their portraits painted, inherited properties, and even voted in elections. The first black Briton to cast his ballot – a sometime actor and shopkeeper named Ignatius Sancho – did so in 1774. Of course, racism existed, and many black Georgians experienced mockery and physical attacks. However, it was not the same as the toxic prejudice, built on theories of racial superiority, which emerged during the following century.

By the 1760s, the island of Great Britain had established itself as *the* global superpower. This is all the more surprising when you consider that Great Britain was only created in 1707, through an Act of Parliament that united England and Scotland. In the decades that followed, a distinct British identity was created, based on Protestantism, trade and Empire. In the comic cartoons of the period, there emerged a new character who typified this national identity: a broad-shouldered, beer-swilling, beef-guzzling bloke named John Bull. A freedom-loving, straight-talking, comfortably well-off member of the provincial middle class, Bull was British to the bone.

Songwriters made sure that John Bull had all the best tunes. 'Rule Britannia' was first sung in 1740, and 'God Save the King' in 1744. 'Hearts of Oak' was written for the London stage in 1759 to celebrate Britain's globe-trotting victories, and remains the official marching song of the Royal Navy to this day. Its lyrics give a sense of the heady jingoism sweeping through Britain at the time:

> Hearts of oak are our ships,
> Jolly tars are our men, we always are ready;
> Steady, boys, steady!
> We'll fight and we'll conquer again and again.

Today, the Royal Navy's Surface Fleet is of interest to only a handful of anoraks. But two hundred years ago, ships were integral to Britain's national identity: the heart of Georgian Britain really was made of oak. During the eighteenth century, a state-of-the-art sailing ship was the most technologically advanced object on Earth, consisting of an infinitely complex combination of sails, rigging ropes, blocks, tackles and nautical instruments. It was on these so-called 'wooden worlds' that Britain subdued her European rivals and spread her power across the globe.

When work began on HMS *Victory* in 1759, a whopping 6,000 oak, elm, pine and fir trees were felled for its construction. Chatham, where the *Victory* was built, was said to be the largest workplace on Earth. The rope house alone was 1,140 feet long. As her empire expanded, Britain went into a shipbuilding frenzy. By 1800, it had 285 major battleships, more than the French, Spanish, Dutch and Danish fleets combined.

This was the Age of Sail, when ships symbolised imperial power but also new opportunity. In almost every one of the tales that follow, the hero or heroine will start a new life chapter by stepping on board a ship. The sound of sails filling with wind, mooring ropes being dropped, the anchor being pulled up and the wooden hull creaking into motion, was the sound of every new adventure.

No wonder that the language we use today is so bound up in the seafaring chat of Georgian Britain. We still talk of 'learning the ropes', 'keeping a wide berth' or being 'press-ganged' into service. The phrase 'chock-a-block' is thought to come from pulley blocks ramming against each other as sails were let out. 'Larking around' comes from 'skylarking', competitions where sailors would race each other to the top of their ship's mast, before sliding back down the rigging ropes.

These battle ships rarely stood idle. From 1740 until 1815, the British were almost constantly at war with France, the nation they loved to hate. As one French visitor observed of the British, 'before they learn there is a God to be worshipped, they learn there are Frenchmen to be detested.' While there were some British Francophiles who admired their neighbours' superior cooking, clothing and culture, this was the opinion of a rarefied minority. In the popular imagination, beefy John Bull could not have contrasted more sharply with the typical Frenchman: a starving, barefoot, onion-nibbling peasant, probably called something silly like Jacques or Pierre, and beaten down by centuries of oppression at the hands of devious Catholic priests and strutting aristocrats.

This fear of France was magnified by the French Revolution in 1789, an event that cast a shadow over the entire late Georgian period. It seemed to start well: the people of France rose up against their unpopular King Louis XVI, established a new national government and abolished feudalism. However, it all got a bit dark when the revolutionaries chopped off the king and queen's heads, invaded their neighbours and threatened to guillotine anyone who opposed their rule. Then, in 1799, France fell into the hands of Napoleon Bonaparte, the greatest military general Europe had seen since Alexander the Great.

These events sent Britain's fear of France into overdrive. Not only were the French threatening to invade Britain, they were planning to do so with a terrifying new ideology of liberty and equality for all mankind, and death to all aristocrats!

However, there was a small minority of radical voices in Britain who thought these ideas were not all bad. They included the writer Mary Wollstonecraft, whose tale is told in Chapter 6. Wollstonecraft was a courageous thinker who, when radicals across Europe were debating the 'Rights of Man', was one of the only people to ask, 'what about the women?' In 1792, she published *A Vindication of the Rights of Woman*, in which she argued that social convention, not biological difference, consigned women to being the weaker sex. If women were given the same rights and educational opportunities as men, she argued, they could take an equal role in public life. Bearing in mind that this was an era when women were banned from being doctors, clerics, Members of Parliament, lawyers, or just about any professional job aside from teaching, Mary's ideas were centuries ahead of their time.

Wollstonecraft's life was just as bold as her ideas. She travelled to Paris at the height of the Revolution and began a doomed relationship with an American adventurer. She had a child out of wedlock, went on a solo tour of Scandinavia, and made her living as an independent female writer. For a tiny minority of Georgian women, it was just about possible to achieve some public prominence without a man by their side.

Two more women who achieved a certain recognition were the Ladies of Llangollen, whose story is told in Chapter 7. Eleanor and Sally were both deeply unhappy members of the Anglo-Irish aristocracy, who escaped their families and built a life together in a quiet valley in north Wales. In the village of Llangollen, they spent the next fifty years living – to all intents and purposes – as a married couple. They shared a bed, spoke of each other as 'the beloved of my soul' and dressed in men's clothing. Their unusual living arrangement eventually made them famous, and Eleanor and Sally received curious visitors from all over Europe.

Among those who did get married, Georgians were often relaxed about their partners finding sexual and emotional fulfilment elsewhere. Particularly among the upper classes, marriages would be based on social advancement, so love and loyalty were not necessarily expected. Chapter 8 tells the story of Lady Hamilton who, despite her humble background, became mistress to a series of gentlemen, before finally marrying one of her lovers, Lord Hamilton, and entering the English aristocracy. On her way, she became the greatest celebrity in Europe, famed for her wit, style and dancing. Today, portraits of her still hang on the walls of museums and stately homes across Europe. Not bad for the daughter of an impoverished single mother from Cheshire. Of course, it helped that she was a certified super-babe, whose beauty the greatest painters of the age competed to capture.

Lady Hamilton lived her happiest days in Naples, where her husband was ambassador. A riotous Mediterranean port in sunny southern Italy, Naples was the undisputed party capital of Europe. It was also a popular stop on the 'Grand Tour', a voyage around Europe which was a rite of passage for wealthy young men (and occasionally women), not unlike the gap years of today. Grand Tourists would learn the history of antiquity, build their knowledge of the arts, and perfect their French and Italian. At least, that was the theory. For many a young man, it was really one long party. And a Grand Tour was not completed on the budget of today's young backpackers. You were expected to send home ancient Roman artefacts, dine with a French philosopher, and have your portrait painted by a famous Italian artist. None of this came cheap: a Grand Tour could last up to four years and cost some £5,000 (twenty times the annual income of a prosperous shopkeeper).

The next two characters in this book were great travellers, who briefly met in Athens while undertaking their own Grand Tours. As her tale in Chapter 9 will tell, Hester Stanhope was an aristocrat's wild-child daughter who played by her own rules and could not give a damn what respectable society thought. Having racked up enough inappropriate boyfriends by the age of thirty to write herself out of the marriage market, she set off on an adventure around the Mediterranean and on to the Holy Land, never to return home. Things got seriously weird when she convinced the people of Syria she was a religious prophet, and she lived out the rest of her life as a recluse and mystic on Mount Lebanon.

In the autumn of 1810, Hester sailed into the port of Athens. Lord Byron spotted the ship and leapt into the sea, swimming out to meet Hester and her companions. Following a fiery dinner fuelled by too much local Greek wine, they parted ways. Byron was not happy that this woman was his match in a debate, describing her as 'that dangerous thing, a female wit'. Hester, meanwhile, disapproved of Byron's decision to bring his newly acquired Greek boyfriend, Niccolo, to dinner.

Which brings us neatly back to that bonking bisexual Byron. His personality hangs over the entire late Georgian period, a superstar celebrity loved and loathed in equal measure. However, though his mad, bad and dangerous ways are often invoked to illustrate Georgian Britain, by 1810 he was a man out of touch with his age. As the nineteenth century dawned, a stricter moral climate was taking hold in Britain, and it was no longer so easy for an aristocratic poet to romp through life with zero regard for the consequences. As told in Chapter 10, Byron lived the last decade of his life exiled from Britain, hated by the nation that once held him aloft as their hero.

You see, by the end of the Georgian period, drinking, whoring and gambling had gone out of fashion, while politeness, respectability and godliness were making a comeback. It was during the dying decades of Georgian Britain that those famously strict 'Victorian values' were born.

The reasons for this new moral climate will be discussed in the conclusion, but some clues lie in the last two chapters. Georgian Britain's carefree atmosphere was built on an unprecedented run of political and social stability. For almost a century it remained a remarkably peaceful and law-abiding nation, despite the lack of any police force. The people were in general agreement that life was best served by a weak monarchy, a strong aristocracy, a relaxed religious life, a growing Empire and a people who knew their place. So went the popular prayer:

> God bless the squire and his relations
> And keep us in our proper stations.

On occasion, the people did rise up to show their anger. The anti-Catholic Gordon Riots of 1780, where the army shot dead over 200 rioters before restoring order to London's streets, were shockingly violent. So were the Norwich mackerel riots of 1740, which brought the city to a standstill for five whole days. But the Georgian masses never threatened to tear down the political system.

However, by 1830, this age of complacency was over. It could be argued that Mary Anning, whose story is told in

Chapter 11, played her own small part in the change. In 1812, she uncovered the entire skeleton of a Jurassic sea creature, the first of many discoveries which would revolutionise humankind's understanding of life on Earth. And Mary's life was as remarkable as her findings – the uneducated working-class daughter of a Dorset carpenter, she became one of Britain's most prolific geologists and fossil hunters.

As you can imagine, the discovery of a 200-million-year-old sea creature called the Old Testament story of creation into question, making members of the clergy feel more than a little nervous. Anning remained a Christian her entire life, but her discoveries helped fuel a culture war between reason and religion that threw Britain into an anxious spin. As the Victorian writer John Ruskin complained, 'If only the geologists would leave me alone, I could do very well, but those dreadful hammers! I hear the clink of them at the end of every cadence of the Bible verses.'

As religious figures in Britain felt more threatened, they became more assertive. Thus, the march of science to which Anning contributed helped fuel a revival in religious enthusiasm. This created one of the biggest differences between Georgian and Victorian Britain: while most Georgians were casual Christians, the Victorians preached the 'vital religion' of Evangelical revival.

An even more significant difference between the two eras was industrialisation. I have placed the story of James Watt right at the end of this book, in Chapter 12, because his invention – it is no exaggeration to say – gave birth to the modern world. In March 1776, Watt finished building the world's first efficient steam engine, able to transform fossil fuels into power. Following Watt's invention, human and animal muscle was no longer needed to power machines, drive carts, pump water or harvest wheat. The world we inhabit today, the world of cars, electricity, factories, and uncontrollable CO_2 emissions – was born that day in Tipton, a small mining town outside of Birmingham.

Watt's steam engine kickstarted the Industrial Revolution. It sent plumes of smoke into the skies, sped trains crisscrossing the countryside, and sucked thousands of men, women and children into the factories of Britain's ever-expanding cities. At the start of the Georgian period, England's three largest cities outside London were Bristol, Norwich and York – a situation largely unchanged since the Middle Ages. By the end of the period, they had been replaced by three industrial giants: Manchester, Liverpool and Birmingham. The ground beneath British society had shifted forever.

Industrialisation created a consumer society in which people could shop, travel and be entertained like never before, a world of cheap clothes, popular tourism, music halls, chocolate bars and department stores. However, it also created the miseries of urban slums and factory work, leading to a new age of radical politics and class struggle. In such a world, there was much more to riot about than mackerel and gin. As the Victorian period loomed, Britain's rapid social change, along with the now colossal size of its empire, forced its ruling class to sit up and take life more seriously. The fun and frolics of Georgian England were over. Things just got real.

While I was at university, I attended a guest lecture by a historian who specialised in the culture of Georgian society. He made an observation that has stayed with me ever since. The hedonistic culture of today's Britain, which began with the swinging sixties and emphasised fun and freedom, was not something new. Instead, it was a restoration of the social values of eighteenth-century Britain, finally making a come-back as the values set by Victorian England were overturned.

I think he had a point. The Georgians may be farther away from us than the Victorians in terms of time, but they often seem closer in terms of values. Much like today, Georgian Britain was celebrity-obsessed, money-making, socially tolerant, binge-drinking, patriotic, and helplessly amused by fart jokes. I sometimes suspect that if an emissary from twenty-first-century Britain was sent back in time to the eighteenth century, they could fit in rather well.

Of course, any generalisations about the character of a historic period are bound to be simplistic. Not all Georgians were mad, bad and dangerous to know. There were countless well-behaved, morally serious Georgians. George III was one of them. Until he went mad and started having conversations with trees, that is. His son, the disgraceful playboy Prince Regent, later George IV, conformed rather better to Georgian stereotype. As you will see in the conclusion, his shenanigans provided one last blast of Georgian debauchery before a new age dawned.

In any historical period, the behaviour of its inhabitants will span the range of human traits, from the naughty to the nice, the anxious to the carefree, the riotous to the respectable. People are people, after all. However, if the spirit of an age cannot always be seen in the behaviour its people practise, it can be seen in the behaviour they celebrate. And the Georgians loved nothing more than a rebel and a rogue.

Many of the rebels and rogues depicted in these pages – John Wilkes, Mary Wollstonecraft, Lady Hamilton, Lord Byron, Hester Stanhope – were celebrated during their day, only to be quietly put to one side by the more sober Victorians. Today, their stories demand retelling. In the pages that follow, you will be introduced to twelve of the people who I believe best represented Georgian Britain: the courageous, the quirky and the completely crazy. I hope you enjoy the ride.

CHAPTER 1

ANNE BONNY AND MARY READ

The Pirate Queens of the Caribbean

Sometime in 1718, a newly married couple arrived at Nassau, a sun-drenched port in the Bahamas. It was surrounded by palm-fringed beaches, where the white sand ran down towards a clear and turquoise sea.

Honeymooning couple in the Caribbean? I know what you are thinking. Five-star hotels, glitzy restaurants, cruise ships. But no, it was nothing like that back then.

Nassau was a dirty, danger-loving sort of town, inhabited by drunkards, murderers and thieves. They lived in tents and run-down shacks, arming themselves with pistols and cutlasses, and jealously guarding their stolen goods. The harbour was home to around forty battle-scarred ships, watched over by a small, crumbling fortress. Above the fortress flew a black flag emblazoned with a white skull. That's right, Nassau in 1718 was a pirate town. In fact, it was the rum-soaked, treasure-filled, gun-toting pirate capital of the Caribbean.

The couple who arrived that day were Anne and James Bonny. They had fallen in love while living in South Carolina, a British colony in America. Anne's father was a wealthy gentleman who disapproved of his twenty-year-old daughter's relationship with James, a penniless sailor. But Anne was a fiery-tempered young woman who could not be told what to do. She ignored her father's demands, married James without his permission, and ran away to Nassau to live with her new husband under the black flag of the pirate brotherhood.

As Anne and James sailed into Nassau harbour, the pirates swaggering up and down its shoreline would have looked, well, more or less how you would imagine a pirate to have looked. They wore short coats and baggy trousers in order to move around their boats with ease, and black tricorn hats to keep the sun out of their eyes. To their ragged clothes they would add a dash of glamour taken from the ships they plundered: a patterned waistcoat, an embroidered sash, or a silk shawl tied around their heads. They wore their most expensive loot on their bodies – pearl earrings, ruby rings, gold necklaces. In Nassau, the safest place to keep your bling was where you could see it.

The Caribbean sun and salt water turned the pirates' skin leathery and tanned, and left their long hair matted and bleached. Their enormous hands were hardened from hours spent pulling barnacle-encrusted rigging ropes, and they walked with a lopsided swagger, formed by months spent trying to stand upright as their boats rolled with the waves. Life at sea, with its battles and storms, left its marks on the pirates' bodies. Each missing arm, scarred face and peg-leg (yes, those really did exist) provided a different story of derring-do to be told in Nassau's rowdy bars and around its beachside fires.

Many of the voices telling these stories had the rural burr of England's West Country, a finger of land pointing from the south of the country into the Atlantic and towards America. Its seafaring towns – Plymouth, Poole and Bristol – were a rich source of pirates. Take a West Country accent, soak it in Caribbean rum and tobacco for a few years, and you get the pirate 'voice' of countless films and cartoons: 'Aaar! Shiver me timbers, me hearty!' etc., etc.

Pirates even developed their own language from years spent at sea. 'Avast ye! We will haul wind smartly. Belay the halyard, or I'll have you dance the hempen jig!' No idea what that means? Some pirate you'd make . . .

Anne Bonny's new home of Nassau was a long way from the small town near Cork in southwest Ireland where she was born. She learnt her habit for scandalous relationships from her father, a respectable married man and lawyer with a fatal taste for the ladies. Anne was the product of his affair with the housemaid.

As was said of Anne at the time, her childhood fulfilled the old proverb 'bastards have the best luck'. Her father became estranged from his wife, and he showered baby Anne with affection. In fact, he was so fond of her that when she grew up, he dressed her as a boy and brought her to work in his legal practice, passing her off as a young clerk. However, the arrangement did not last long. The estranged wife decided to reveal Anne's true identity to the town.

This sort of behaviour did not do in small-town Ireland and caused quite the scandal. At first, Anne's father tried to weather the disapproval, and lived openly with Anne and her mother. But the townspeople were unwilling to employ a disgraced seducer as their lawyer, and his legal practice folded. With no prospect of recovering his career in Ireland, Anne's father sold everything he owned, packed his bags, and took Anne and the housemaid to Cork, where they boarded the next ship for America. It was time for a fresh start.

Anne and her father settled in South Carolina, where he

began a new legal practice. He then became a merchant, and amassed enough money to purchase a large plantation, establishing himself as a gentleman of means. When the housemaid died, Anne – who was now grown up – looked after her father's house.

Anne's father hoped that his hot-blooded young daughter would marry well and rid their lives of the taint of scandal. So he must have been pretty pissed off when Anne ran away to Nassau with James Bonny, a man of the sea who was, apparently, 'not worth a groat'.

On arrival in Nassau, Anne and James's first task was to find somewhere to live, but their new home was little more than a shanty town, with one sun-baked dirt road running along the shoreline. There was a small wooden church, surrounded by a cluster of derelict houses. Behind the town, some scrubby fields had been cleared from the forest, where farmers grew yams and potatoes. No animals were kept, for the sea provided a limitless supply of fish and turtles.

Like most new arrivals, Anne and James probably built their own shack, with walls made out of planks scavenged from old boats, and a roof made out of canvas ripped from an old sail. James then went to sea as a pirate, leaving Anne behind. We don't know how she made a living, but there were few options in this town of good living and bad people. Perhaps she worked the bars to quench the pirates' thirst for alcohol when they came onshore, or perhaps she worked the harbourside to quench their thirst for something else.

Nassau had been a British colony, but it was attacked and burnt to the ground by the Spanish in 1703. The town was more or less abandoned, until the pirates moved in ten years later. It sits on the north shore of an island in the Bahamas and is enclosed on three sides, making it the perfect location for a pirate hideaway. Across the bay from the harbour lay Hog Island, an empty patch of sand scattered with the burnt-out, dismantled shells of stolen ships.

Between Nassau and the American mainland were the Straits of Florida. This stretch of sea linked the Atlantic Ocean to the Gulf of Mexico and the Caribbean Sea, and therefore the Old World to the New, making it one of the busiest shipping routes in the world.

Wealth from every corner of the globe poured through the Straits of Florida. All Nassau's pirates had to do was load their guns, pile into a fast-moving ship, creep out of the harbour and take their pick. From the 'treasure fleets' sailing from Mexico to Spain, they stole chests full of gold and silver. From merchant ships leaving Cuba and Jamaica, they stole rum, sugar and tobacco. Coming the other way, ships sailing from Europe to the New World provided them with guns, knives, swords, watches, and bottles of wine and brandy. The pirates also captured slave ships coming from West Africa. Some pirates offered slaves the chance to join their crew as free men, others simply sold them on to the owners of sugar and tobacco plantations.

Many of the first pirates to arrive in Nassau were runaways from the Royal Navy, who had grown tired of its low pay and fierce discipline. One such pirate was 'Black' Sam Bellamy, a farmer's son from Devon who joined the Royal Navy aged thirteen. He escaped the navy, became captain of his own pirate ship, and in March 1717 captured a British merchant vessel containing ivory, indigo dye, sugar, and chests of gold and silver valued at £30,000.

According to the pirate code, plunder was always split equally among the crew, with the captain taking only a double share. In one attack, Black Sam and his crew had made more money than they would have in a lifetime's service for the Royal Navy. Black Sam became known as the Robin Hood of the seas, and his story spread to the ports and plantations of the Americas. Before long, disgruntled sailors, escaped slaves and runaways like Anne and James Bonny were flocking to stack some cash at the Pirates' Nest of Nassau.

However, in February 1718, Nassau was at a turning point in its history. That month, a Royal Navy captain came on shore holding a white flag of truce, and gathered the town's inhabitants. He read a proclamation from King George I which put a price of £20 on the head of anyone who had 'committed Piracies and Robberies upon the High Seas'. For a pirate captain, the price was £100. However, King George offered a general pardon to any pirate willing to surrender to the British crown before that September.

The chance of a royal pardon split Nassau's pirate brotherhood in two. The pro-pardon faction wanted to bank their riches and return to a law-abiding life. But the diehard pirates wanted to amass even greater fortunes, and refused to submit to the king they hated and the Royal Navy from which many had escaped.

One such diehard was the most famous pirate of the Caribbean, Captain Blackbeard, who hailed from Bristol. Knowing that a pirate's greatest weapon was fear, he had a well-practised routine to scare the crap out of his victims. Before boarding a merchant ship, he would strap six loaded pistols to his body and tuck lit fuses into his hat, surrounding his bearded face with a halo of smoke and fire. With his fierce, wild eyes he looked – according to one source – like 'a fury from Hell'. Indeed, when Blackbeard robbed a sailor on the swampy coast of North Carolina, the man demanded to know where Blackbeard was from. Blackbeard replied that 'he came from Hell', and would take the man there if he did not hand over his money.

Blackbeard spent years marauding along the Caribbean and Atlantic coasts, robbing French, Spanish and British merchant ships, and amassing hundreds of thousands of pounds of loot. His attacks were so terrifying that no opponents ever even put up a fight.

Blackbeard's fleet docked in Nassau for the last time in May 1718, around the time Anne and James arrived from Carolina. These were heady days in the Pirates' Nest. The 700 men of Blackbeard's crew doubled the town's population overnight, and they descended on its bars and brothels for an orgy of drinking, gambling and fighting. Blackbeard probably shared a bottle of rum that month with another of Nassau's diehard pirates, Captain Charles Vane.

Blackbeard was the Caribbean's most famous pirate, but Vane was the most ruthless. He had a reputation for torturing sailors to discover where they were hiding their cargo. In one attack, he bound the hands and feet of a sailor and hung him upside down, before sticking gunpowder fuses in his eyes, threatening to burn out his eyeballs if he did not talk.

As Blackbeard and Vane's crews partied during that first week in May, they knew it might be their last visit to the Pirates' Nest. Two months later, on 24 July 1718, seven Royal Navy ships came sailing into Nassau. They carried 550 soldiers and a newly appointed Royal Governor to the Bahamas. King George I had given Governor Woodes Rogers orders to stop, once and for all, the Caribbean seas from being 'plundered and ravaged by pirates'. And Rogers was just the man for the job.

Like Blackbeard, Governor Rogers was from Bristol, and like Blackbeard, he knew what it meant to be feared. Back home in Britain he was a war hero, having spent three years sailing around the world capturing Spanish galleons. He had survived battles, plagues and mutinies, and had the scars to prove it. In 1709, he was shot in the jaw by a musket ball, splattering his teeth over the deck of his ship. In another battle four days later, his left ankle was ripped off his foot by a flying splinter of wood. Rogers was a loyal servant to the king and a devout Christian, with a violent dislike of pirates.

As Governor Rogers limped slowly from his ship onto Nassau's harbourside, determined eyes gleaming in his disfigured face, the pirates knew they had met their match. He would restore godliness and good government to the wilder shores of the Caribbean, or die trying.

As the Royal Navy's fightback against the pirates gathered pace, their rotting bodies became a familiar sight, hanging from gallows and metal cages along the American and Caribbean shorelines. In November 1717, six members of Black Sam's crew, who had been shipwrecked off the American coast, were seen swinging from the gallows in Boston.

The following December, a captain in Blackbeard's crew met the same fate in the port town of Charleston, North Carolina. Major Stede Bonnet was a wealthy plantation owner from Barbados who, having grown bored with life as a gentleman, abandoned his wife and children for a life of adventure on the high seas. The only problem was, this wannabe pirate was not cut out for the life he'd chosen. He walked around his ship in a silk dressing gown and cried whenever things went wrong. He was soon captured, and few were surprised when he swung from the gallows of Charleston harbour.

Back in Nassau, Anne Bonny would have been in the crowd that watched the first victims of Governor Rogers' crackdown swing from his gallows two days later. That December morning in 1718, nine captured pirates were taken from their prison cells, their hands tied behind their backs, and onto a stage. Having had nooses placed around their necks, they were left to stand there for forty-five minutes, waiting to hang. Some prayed, some swigged rum to dampen the fear, some cracked jokes with the crowds. Two of the pirates begged their former shipmates to rush the stage and free them, but Governor Rogers' soldiers, their muskets primed, ensured that did not happen.

At the last minute, Governor Rogers freed the youngest pirate. Apparently his parents back in Dorset had written to Rogers, promising to set their wayward son straight if his life was spared. Rogers agreed. After this show of mercy, he gave the signal. The soldiers pulled away four barrels which were holding up the stage, and the pirates fell. The nooses snapped tight around their necks, and their bodies jerked and writhed, at first violently, then slightly, then not at all.

One month later, in January 1719, an ambitious young naval officer called Lieutenant Maynard sailed into the harbour of Hampton, Virginia, with the head of Captain Blackbeard hanging from the front of his ship. Maynard had fought and killed the most famous pirate in the Caribbean, and had taken his crew prisoner. Following their trial, thirteen members of Blackbeard's crew were hanged in Hampton, their bodies left dangling in metal cages along the road out of town.

So, by the start of 1719, the cruel but cunning Captain Charles Vane was the only Nassau diehard still operating. Twice he had humiliated the Royal Navy in Nassau. The first time he stole a merchant vessel right in front of their eyes, and the second time he escaped their entrapment by sending a fireship towards two navy vessels. However, his luck would soon run out.

On any pirate ship, the captain made the big decisions, while his quartermaster took charge of the day-to-day organisation of the crew. Charles Vane's quartermaster was a charismatic pirate named Jack Rackham, known for dressing in colourful fabrics called 'calicos'. This flamboyant dress sense earned him the nickname 'Calico' Jack, and would later earn him the affections of Anne Bonny.

Their taste for robbery aside, pirates weren't complete nutcases. They lived according to a 'Pirate Code', which set out the rules for life at sea. One of the most important points of the code was that a crew could vote to replace their captain if ever they lost faith in his leadership. When Vane backed out of a fight with a French battleship in November 1718, Calico Jack accused him of cowardice. The majority of Vane's crew agreed, and voted Calico Jack to be their new captain, sending Vane out to sea in a small boat. In February 1719, Vane was caught in a storm, shipwrecked, marooned on an island, and captured by the Royal Navy. After two years spent languishing in a Jamaican prison, Captain Vane's body too could be seen swinging in a metal cage beside the main harbour in Port Royal.

You would have thought that so many dead pirates decorating the American and Caribbean shorelines would have put Anne Bonny off piracy, but not at all. It was around this time, in fact, that she first went to sea.

Calico Jack was now in charge of a seventy-five-man crew, and their loyalty to his leadership was well placed. He sailed into the harbour of Port Royal, the main base of the Royal Navy, and stole a merchant ship from right under its nose, escaping before the Navy's ships were ready to give chase. His crew had struck the jackpot: the ship's cargo was worth

£20,000, including silk stockings, laced hats and a large parcel of gold watches – just the sort of thing for strutting your stuff back in Nassau.

Having escaped with their plunder, Calico Jack and his crew spent the winter months at a popular pirate hideaway: the beautiful Isla de los Pinos, positioned just south of Cuba (and said to be the inspiration for the children's book *Treasure Island*). After a few months camping on white sand beaches, drinking rum and eating turtles, Jack and his crew were caught sleeping off their hangovers by a vengeful group of merchants from Jamaica. Jack fled into the island's forests with as much loot as he could carry, and the merchants took back their ship.

What was Calico Jack to do? Simple. He sailed back to Nassau on a smaller boat, met with Governor Rogers, and asked to take the King's pardon. He claimed that Charles Vane had forced him and his men into piracy, and Rogers – who despised Vane – was only too happy to believe him. So Calico Jack became a free man, and passed a year spending his ill-gotten gains partying in Nassau.

As a sharply dressed former pirate captain, famed for his wealth and bravery, Calico Jack could have had the pick of Nassau's women, so whom did he choose? Anne Bonny, of course. Before long, she gave birth to his child. However, Anne was still married to James. Calico Jack asked Governor Rogers whether James and Anne's marriage could be annulled. Rogers – who let's not forget was on a mission to bring respectable Christian values to Nassau – refused. Were Anne and Calico Jack to continue their sordid relationship, he responded, he would throw Anne in jail and have her whipped by her own husband.

Governor Rogers was not a man to cross. Over the past

two years, he had steadily established his control over Nassau. The fortress had been rebuilt, with fifty cannons guarding the entrance to the harbour, while a battleship provided thirty-six more cannons. On land, he had 100 soldiers, along with another 500 volunteer militiamen (many former pirates), at his command. The Pirates' Nest was now Rogers' town.

To continue his relationship with Anne Bonny, Calico Jack had only one option: return to the high seas as a pirate, taking her with him. They hastily assembled a crew of half a dozen pirates, and late one night stole a sloop – a small, speedy sailboat. In fact, they stole the speediest sloop in Nassau, belonging to a certain John 'catch-him-if-you-can' Ham.

Back at sea, Calico Jack spent the summer of 1720 doing what he did best: relieving merchants of their cargo. The pirates' most common tactic was to disguise their boat as an innocent merchant vessel. Their unsuspecting victim would be happy to see another merchant ship approaching, until that ship raised its pirate flag, and the crew – who had been hiding in the hold – assembled on deck, waving their grue-some array of pistols, cutlasses and homemade grenades. This moment was designed to be as soil-your-trousers-scary as possible for those on board the merchant ship. Most gave up straight away, ensuring no blood was shed.

Anne Bonny, armed with a machete in one hand and a pistol in the other, became the most fearsome member of Calico Jack's crew. In fact, there was only one crew member who could equal Anne for cursing, swearing and general nastiness. That was her pal, Mary Read.

Anne met Mary in Nassau, and they bonded over their similar pasts. Like Anne, Mary was an illegitimate child, and had also been brought up as a boy to hide her identity. She continued to live as a man into adulthood, and joined the

British army. Having been sent to fight the Spanish in Flanders (modern-day Belgium), she was billeted in a tent with a handsome young Flemish soldier. One night, the soldier discovered Mary's secret, and was pretty damn happy to find out he was sharing his tent with a woman. Love blossomed in that little tent, so when the campaign against Spain ended, Mary and her Flemish soldier left the army, married, and became the proprietors of a little pub outside the city of Breda named the Three Horse-Shoes.

But it was not to last. Sometime around 1714, Mary's husband died, the Three Horse-Shoes went out of business, and her happy life in Flanders collapsed. So she set sail for the New World to start her life over. However, the ship carrying Mary across the Atlantic was captured by pirates. They took a liking to Mary and invited her to travel with them to Nassau. She said yes. And there, in the Pirates' Nest, Mary joined Calico Jack's crew.

On board Calico Jack's ship, Mary and Anne dressed like their male crewmates, wearing jackets and trousers, with silk bandanas wrapped around their heads. The only means of recognising their true sex, according to one terrified fisherwoman they robbed on the coast of Jamaica, 'was by the largeness of their breasts'. In fact, it is claimed that Anne initially believed Mary to be a handsome young man and took a liking to her. It was only to stop Anne's flirtatious advances that Mary let her into her secret. When Calico Jack flew into a jealous rage and threatened to cut Mary's throat for stealing Anne's affections, Anne let Jack into the secret of Mary's sex as well.

However, Mary, Anne and Jack's life at sea would not last long. Governor Rogers was furious that he had been tricked by Calico Jack into trusting his promise to take the King's pardon. On 5 September 1720, he proclaimed that Jack and his crew were 'Pirates and Enemies to the Crown of Great Britain'. Sailors across the Caribbean armed their ships and set out to sea to hunt them down. Jack, who had buckets of bravery but very little sense, carried on robbing ships regardless.

In late October, his boat was spotted off the northern shore of Jamaica, and a pirate hunter named Captain Barnet followed it through the night. As usual, Calico Jack and his crew stayed up late drinking rum, and rose at ten o'clock the next morning nursing their sore heads. They were met by the muskets, cannon and swivel gun of Captain Barnet's well-armed sloop. Not what you want with a hangover.

Calico Jack and his crew fled below deck, leaving only the two bravest members facing the enemy. Who were they? Anne Bonny and Mary Read. Mary shouted through the hatch, demanding her crewmates fight like men, but they stayed cowering in the hold. She then fired her pistol, killing one and wounding another. But it was no use – the pirates were outnumbered and outgunned. Barnet's men fired their swivel gun, destroying the pirate ship's mainsail and making escape impossible. Jack and his crew were arrested, and taken back to stand trial in Jamaica. Anne and Mary's pirate careers were over.

Eighteenth-century Jamaica was awash with money due to its trade in sugar and rum. However, Port Royal, its major city, had a reputation for low living every bit as squalid as Nassau. One visitor in 1697 called it the 'dunghill of the Universe', and gave a memorable description of a town 'as sickly as a hospital, as dangerous as the plague, as hot as hell, and as wicked as the devil'. There were few places in Port Royal as sickly, dangerous, hot and wicked as its jail.

Calico Jack was tried for piracy on 16 November and sentenced to death the next day. On the morning of his execution, Anne Bonny was taken to his cell to say goodbye to her lover captain. 'I am sorry to see you here,' she consoled him, 'but if you had fought like a man, you need not have hanged like a dog.'

Along with five of his crewmates, Calico Jack was taken to Gallows Point, a windswept spit of land pointing out of Port Royal, and hanged. His body was then placed in an iron cage, which swung from a gibbet on Dead Man's Cay, a small rock in the middle of the harbour. Anyone sailing into the Jamaican capital had to pass Calico Jack's body, rotting in the Caribbean sun and pecked apart by gulls. To all those tempted by a pirate's life, Dead Man's Cay was a chilling warning of their fate.

As for Mary and Anne, they were tried ten days later. Those watching the trial were amazed when the two women refused to defend themselves, staying silent for the entire proceedings. The judge, Sir Nicholas Lawes, had no other option but to read out the doom-laden verdict: 'You Mary Read, and Anne Bonny, are to go from hence to the place from where you came, and from thence to the place of execution; where you shall be hanged by the neck till you are dead. And God be merciful to both your souls.'

But there was one more twist left in this tale. Having been sentenced to death, Anne and Mary finally spoke, informing the courthouse that they were both pregnant. Judge Lawes ordered an inspection of the women, which confirmed they were telling the truth. Pregnant women could not be hanged, as it would kill their unborn children. So Mary and Anne lived to see another day.

Mary Read's adventure, which had taken her from England

to Flanders, and on to Nassau, ended in her Jamaican prison cell. Five months after the trial, she caught a fever and died.

Anne's fate is less clear. Evidence has been found of a woman named Anne who married a local man in South Carolina a year after Anne Bonny's trial. Some believe that Anne's father secured his daughter's release from jail and brought her home. If that is true, then Anne went on to have eight more children, before dying at the age of eighty-four in 1782. However, such behaviour does not seem in keeping with Anne's buccaneering ways. I prefer to believe she returned to piracy, and died at the bottom of the deep blue sea. But we will never know for sure.

What became of Nassau? Governor Rogers finally had his way, and brought law and order to the town. Its motto became 'Piracy expelled, commerce restored'. Today it is the capital city of the Bahamas, and a tourism hotspot. Where the fortress once stood, there is a hotel. Hog Island is now Paradise Island, and the burnt-out ships have been replaced by a luxury resort and water park.

Around 1723, Governor Rogers was approached by a writer, researching a book about Caribbean pirates. Rogers recounted to the author all of the tales you have been reading about here: Captain Blackbeard, Calico Jack, Anne Bonny and Mary Read. Published in 1725, the book – *A General History of the Pyrates* – kickstarted the world's fascination with these outlaws of the sea. Had Governor Rogers never told their stories, the pirates of the Caribbean may well have been lost to history.

Since *A General History of the Pyrates* was published, our fascination with these nautical outlaws has never gone away. Thanks to that book, and works it inspired such as Robert Louis Stevenson's *Treasure Island,* every young child still learns about peg-legs and parrots, flying the Jolly Roger and chests of stolen gold, yo ho ho and a bottle of rum. Some myths have been added to pirate lore over the centuries – they did not bury treasure or force traitors and cowards to walk the plank. But much of what we think we know about pirates is true.

Today, the main street alongside Nassau's harbourside is called Woodes Rogers Walk. However, three hundred years later, visitors to Nassau rarely want to hear about its former governor. It is the pirates who entrance us, with their lawless lives and daring adventures. None more so than the infamous Anne Bonny and Mary Read, who stood like men when the rest of their crew fled like dogs.

CHAPTER 2
BONNIE PRINCE CHARLIE

The Stuart Prince Who Came to Take Back His Throne

In Georgian Britain, people saw the Scottish Highlands as belonging not just to another country, but to another century. And they had a point. In some ways, life in the far northern mountains and the islands to the west had remained unchanged since the Middle Ages. Most of the population were poor cattle farmers who dressed in tartan and wore bonnets over manes of uncombed hair. They lived in huts and hovels, spoke an ancient language called Gaelic, and ate oats soaked in cows' blood.

Highland society was governed by a system of clans, large families each ruled by a chief. When not standing on a remote mountainside watching over their cows, clansmen liked to beat the crap out of each other in long-running, and seemingly pointless, feuds. Armed with enormous swords called claymores, and dressed in long tartan shawls called plaid, they were a rough, tough, warrior people.

The Highland scenery is breathtaking: its mountains are divided by narrow lochs and deep glens, and give way to a scattering of windswept isles. Highland weather, however, can be grim. And it was particularly grim one August evening in

1745, when a French warship came limping towards Eriskay, an island off Scotland's west coast.

On board the ship was a young student returning from Paris, where he was studying to be a priest. His chin was unshaven from two weeks at sea, and he wore a suit of plain black cloth and a cheap wig. As the ship neared Eriskay, one of the student's companions spotted an eagle hovering above them. He turned to the student and remarked, 'Sir, I hope this is an excellent omen. The king of birds is come to welcome Your Royal Highness upon your arrival in Scotland.'

As the men disembarked the warship, night was falling and the weather was filthy. Rain soaked through their clothes, and wind ripped across the island's scrubland. They searched for shelter, but little could be found until they met a poor farmer named Angus MacDonald who showed them to his home. Actually, it was more of a hovel than a home. A tiny, windowless room, filled with smoke from an open fire. There was not a piece of bread or grain to quell the men's hunger, so they roasted fish over the flames.

The student was restless, and kept walking outside to escape the smoke. MacDonald became increasingly annoyed with this pampered young brat, and remarked, 'What a plague is the matter with that fellow, that he can neither sit nor stand still, and neither keep within nor without doors?' When his host showed the student his bed for the night, he did not look impressed. MacDonald replied that the bed and its sheets were good enough for a prince!

At that comment, the young man must have smiled, for he was not, in fact, a student priest returning home from Paris. He was Charles Edward Stuart, the grandson of the last Stuart king of England and Scotland. And he had landed in Scotland that evening to reclaim his ancestors' throne.

Since the day he was born, Prince Charles (as he liked to call himself) had been taught that the kingdoms of England and Scotland were his by right. In 1688, the overwhelmingly Protestant people of England and Scotland had kicked his Catholic grandfather, King James II, off the throne, leading the Stuart family to settle in Rome and establish a royal court in exile. Prince Charles had been brought up in Rome dreaming of his lost kingdoms, an exiled prince with a super-sized sense of entitlement. That evening on the windswept isle of Eriskay, Prince Charles was – for the first time in his life – standing on the land his family had once ruled. His adventure had begun.

At twenty-four years of age, Charles looked every bit the young prince. He was tall, athletic, and had the confident swagger of a man raised in the royal courts of Europe. He had pouting lips, deep brown eyes and tousled red hair. 'Bonnie' is the term used in Scotland to describe such a handsome young man, and so the name stuck: Bonnie Prince Charlie.

Ever since Prince Charlie's grandfather was deposed, there had been people across Britain who remained secretly loyal to the Stuarts. They were furious that Britain was now ruled by a bad-tempered, boggle-eyed German named George II, whose claim to the throne was minuscule. Supporters of the Stuart claim were called Jacobites, after the Latin for James, the name of Prince Charlie's exiled grandfather. The Jacobites were a bit like a cult, with secret signals and signs that they used to identify each other in a crowd. Jacobites would visit Prince Charlie and his father in Rome, pledging their support for that fateful day when a Stuart monarch would return to Britain and reclaim the crown.

Support for the Jacobite cause was particularly strong in the rugged Highlands of Scotland, where Prince Charlie's ship landed that August evening. Many Highland clans were Catholic and remained deeply loyal to the Stuart family, who had once ruled Scotland as an independent kingdom many centuries ago.

Prince Charlie was a born optimist, and his plan was simple: he would raise an army of Highland clans, take Scotland, then march on to England and glory. However, when he met with the chief of a local MacDonald clan the following morning, the chief stated that he and the other clan chiefs could not support the Prince. 'Go home,' the MacDonald chief advised. 'I am come home,' replied the Prince.

The problem was that Bonnie Prince Charlie had arrived to conquer Britain without an army. The English and Scottish Jacobites knew they could not take on the might of the British army alone. They all expected Prince Charlie to bring with him a foreign invasion force, most likely provided by King Louis XV of France. Prince Charlie had spent the previous year in France planning his invasion with Louis XV, but he had infuriated Louis by behaving like an arrogant little twerp, so the king withdrew his support.

By that point, Prince Charlie was so drunk on the prospect of seizing back his ancestors' throne, he stuck to his invasion plan regardless. He arrived at Eriskay that August evening on board a small ship, with just seven supporters. Most of them were old men, and only two had military experience. Things did not look good.

In a letter he sent his father before leaving for Scotland, Prince Charlie wrote, 'Let what will happen. I have taken a firm resolution to conquer or to die, and stand my ground as long as I shall have a man remaining with me.'

'Conquer or die.' Those were the inspiring words he now used to win round the Highland clans.

The first clans to rally to Prince Charlie's cause were the MacDonalds. As the largest of Scotland's families, different MacDonald clans spread across the Western Isles, Skye and the Scottish mainland. And they despised the British government. Before long, the MacDonald clans of Clanranald, Glencoe, Keppoch and Glengarry had joined Prince Charlie. However, other MacDonald clans stayed away, as did the McLeod clan of Skye.

For his invasion to succeed, Prince Charlie desperately needed to win the support of the Cameron clan, who were famed for their large, well-trained army and ruthlessness in battle. Their chief, Lochiel, had grown up with the legend of his famous warrior grandfather Ewan Cameron. So the story goes, Ewan was once pinned down by an English soldier, and escaped the only way a brave Highlander could. By ripping out the soldier's throat. With his teeth.

When Lochiel came to visit Prince Charlie on the Isle of Skye, he repeated that without French support, Charlie's invasion was doomed. Prince Charlie countered that the French would only send support once a Jacobite army had proved themselves in battle. They had to strike first, Charlie insisted, and their support would grow with every victory.

Was Prince Charlie a deluded fool, or was he the real deal? Lochiel could not decide. But he could not help but be impressed by the young prince's charisma and determination, and finally agreed to fight.

Prince Charlie now had the makings of an army. One week later, he launched his campaign by raising his royal standard among a gathering of the clans at Glenfinnan. An open green space overlooking a beautiful loch, flanked on either side by mountains, there are few more dramatic locations that Prince Charlie could have chosen. He arrived on time at 1 p.m., dressed in scarlet, with a bodyguard of MacDonald men. However, one hour later, Lochiel and the Cameron clan were nowhere to be seen. Two hours later, still no sign. Had Lochiel lost his nerve?

Then, over the mountaintops, Prince Charlie heard the drone of bagpipes and the beating of drums. One thousand Cameron warriors poured into the valley, zig-zagging down the mountainside with their guns, claymores, plaid and bonnets. They even brought with them eighty British prisoners, captured a few days earlier in a Highland ambush.

Here at Glenfinnan, Prince Charlie was declared Prince Regent, with the power to rule over England and Scotland on behalf of his father, the true King James III (who was still alive, but too old and weary to join in his son's adventure). The MacDonald and Cameron clansmen whooped in support and threw their bonnets in the air. Casks of brandy were cracked open so toasts could be drunk, and Gaelic cries of 'deoch slàinte an Righ' ('a drink to the King's health') floated across the loch and echoed off the mountainsides. The Stuart comeback had begun.

From Glenfinnan, the Jacobite army marched south to Edinburgh. At long last, Prince Charlie was fulfilling the mission that had been instilled in him since birth. He marched at the head of his army, crossing mountain paths, wading through rivers, and sleeping rough in the glens and moors. You had to give it to him: he was a man on a mission. Even his Highland troops complained that the pace he set was too fast.

News about the return of a Stuart prince spread across Scotland and Prince Charlie's army swelled as excited Highlanders flocked to his cause, each wearing the distinctive tartan of their clan: the Stewarts of Appin, the Grants of Glenmoriston, the MacGregors of Glencairn and Glengyle.

At sunrise on Monday 17 September, the Jacobite army arrived outside Edinburgh. The city's tiny garrison of British soldiers did not even put up a fight, so the Jacobites walked straight through the city gates. Edinburgh was a modern city, whose lowland population had little respect for their barbaric Highland neighbours. They must have had quite a shock when they woke up that Monday morning to find their city under the rule of this band of hairy, smelly mountain-men.

It was now time for Prince Charlie to make his grand entrance, and he wanted everyone to know he was a big deal. The returning Stuart prince rode into Edinburgh to the sound of trumpets, wearing a tartan coat, a blue sash over his shoulder, and red velvet breeches. On his head he wore a blue bonnet laced with gold and adorned with the Jacobite emblem: a white silk cockade. Few people in Edinburgh were Jacobite supporters, but they cheered him on regardless, unable to resist the romance and charisma of this remarkable young prince.

News of Prince Charlie taking Edinburgh quickly reached England, and King George II put a price of £30,000 on his head. But who was going to stop him? The British army was busy fighting the French in Flanders. Only a small force of 4,000 second-rate British soldiers remained in Scotland, led by a second-rate general named Sir John Cope.

Three days after taking Edinburgh, Prince Charlie received news that General Cope's army was closing in. The Jacobite army marched out of the city and found the British forces nine miles to the east, camping beside a village called Prestonpans. It was an excellent defensive position: a flat field guarded to the north by the sea, to the west by a ten-foot wall, and to the east by a large marsh.

By this point, Prince Charlie had chosen a veteran Jacobite soldier named Lord George Murray to command his army.

Murray was a skilled military tactician and a brave warrior, but also stubborn and short-tempered. From the moment they met, Charlie and Murray clashed. Murray soon realised Charlie could be reckless and stupid, while Charlie treated Murray like an annoying dad. When Charlie asked to lead his army into the battle, Murray told him his life was too valuable for such a risk. When Charlie began making orders to advance without Murray's approval, Murray threw his gun on the floor and vowed never to draw his sword for the Prince unless they drew back.

Having asserted his control over Prince Charlie, Murray ordered that the army wait until morning for a dawn attack. With two equally sized forces, he knew victory would be hard won. Then at midnight, the Jacobite army gained a crucial advantage. A local laddie who knew the surrounding terrain came to Murray and told him of a narrow track that led through the marsh, towards the British army.

Murray immediately changed plans, and at 4 a.m. the Jacobite army began creeping through the marshes. They positioned themselves 1,000 yards from the British camp and waited for sunrise, their hearts pounding. As Cope's soldiers woke up that misty morning on the field of Prestonpans, they were met with the fearsome sight of a Highland charge. Two thousand Highlanders fell upon the camp, screaming their bloodcurdling battle cries and waving their barbaric array of weapons in the air: muskets, claymores, daggers, scythes and clubs. Not what you want to see first thing in the morning.

The British soldiers hardly had time to arm themselves, and – trapped on each side by the sea and the high walls – were unable to retreat. The Highlanders cut the British to pieces. As defeat quickly turned to slaughter, ten British soldiers were killed for every one Highlander. By the end of the battle, the bloody field of Prestonpans was littered with torsos, limbs and severed heads. One brave young laddie was presented to Prince Charlie for his heroism: he alone had brought fourteen of Cope's soldiers to the ground with his sword.

The next day, Bonnie Prince Charlie returned to Edinburgh a conquering hero, his rule over Scotland secured. He could not have asked for a better start to his campaign. Two months after landing in Eriskay with just seven men, he had built an army, defeated the British, and made himself Prince of Scotland. It seemed the arrogant little twerp was coming good.

Prince Charlie spent the next month enjoying life in his new kingdom, attending balls and having his portrait painted. New clans joined the Jacobite army, as the MacPhersons, Gordons, Maclachlans and the men of Atholl swelled their ranks to over 5,000 soldiers. More good news arrived on 14 October, when a French ship sailed into Edinburgh's docks loaded with 4,000 guineas, 1,300 guns, six cannons and ten French artillery experts. A gift from King Louis XV.

However, Prince Charlie had no intention of sticking around in Edinburgh. Everything he had achieved so far had been the result of speedy action, carried out with daring and courage. His Jacobite army had to continue this momentum by marching on London.

Lord George Murray disagreed. He told Charlie it would be madness to launch an invasion of England as the winter was closing in, when they could spend Christmas in Edinburgh and wait to fight the British army in the spring. But Prince Charlie did not want to listen to boring old Captain Cautious, and insisted on invasion. Murray finally backed down, and the Jacobite army marched out of Edinburgh on 31 October.

As the Jacobite army crossed the border into northwest England, Prince Charlie's enthusiasm grew even greater. He rose at 3 a.m. each day, leading his army from the front for thirty miles of marching through wind, sleet and snow. After a two-day siege, the Jacobites took Carlisle, then marched south through Cumberland and Lancashire, where people lined the roads to cheer the Stuart prince. When he rode into Manchester on 28 November, he received a hero's welcome. The city turned out in force to drink, dance and sing Jacobite songs, shouting 'God bless his Royal Highness Prince Charles!'

However, something was wrong. While the people of England enjoyed cheering Prince Charlie on, very few were prepared to join his army. They were glory fans, willing to join in with the fun, but not prepared to shed blood. Prince Charlie had promised the Scottish clansmen that as they marched south, a flood of English Jacobites would join their cause. But that flood turned out to be a trickle. By the time they left Manchester, Prince Charlie's army contained barely 300 Englishmen.

As they moved deeper south into English territory, the Jacobite soldiers were beginning to feel vulnerable. Rumours were circulating of three British armies, each numbering 10,000 troops, closing in on them. Worst of all, Bonnie Prince Charlie's long-promised French reinforcements were still nowhere to be seen. As the cold winter weather set in, and memories of their summer triumphs began to fade, morale among the men of the Jacobite army plummeted. By the time they reached Derby on 4 December, the Highland soldiers were cold, exhausted and afraid. Charlie's army of 5,000 pissed-off Scotsmen was ready to turn home.

Prince Charlie assembled his council of war the next day, and pleaded with them to carry on. They were just 100 miles from London, and it was now or never, no surrender! But while

Prince Charlie had once seemed courageous, he now seemed reckless. A vote was taken, and not a single council member voted to continue the march. The spurned prince raged against this cowardice, scolding his council, 'You ruin, abandon, and betray me if you don't march on!' But Prince Charlie had ridden his luck for too long, and now it was running out. The Jacobite army began their retreat the following day.

That fateful day in Derby would forever be remembered among the Jacobites as 'Black Friday'. The day their dream died. Prince Charlie, who had been an inspiring leader on the march south, became a stubborn, sulky child as they retraced their steps north. He stayed up late drinking, often slowing his army's retreat by sleeping in the following day. As the Jacobite troops traipsed back through the towns that they had passed with giddy excitement just a month before – Manchester, Preston, Carlisle – they were beaten, pelted with stones, and shot at by snipers. On Prince Charlie's twenty-fifth birthday, his army crossed the River Esk and were back in Scotland.

As they retreated, the Jacobites were shadowed by a crack force of British redcoats, who had been recalled from Europe to destroy Prince Charlie's campaign. The troops were led by George II's very own son, the Duke of Cumberland. Tall and heavy, with a mean, flabby face, Cumberland's name sounds like a sausage, and he looked like one too. But he was also an accomplished soldier, feared for his ruthlessness. The Jacobite army marched in fear, knowing Cumberland and his men were never more than a few days' march behind them.

In Glasgow, the Jacobite army received a cool reception: most of its lowland population remained loyal to King George II. So the Jacobites continued north to Stirling, where they attempted a half-hearted siege of its castle. The decisive, gung-ho Prince Charlie of old was a distant memory. While his army laid siege to the castle, he lay in bed with the flu.

At the end of January 1746, Lord George Murray came to visit Prince Charlie. The strained relationship between the prince and his general had now turned into outright hatred. When Murray suggested they call off the siege and retreat farther north into the safety of the Highlands, Prince Charlie exploded like a petulant child. More retreat? More surrender? He smashed his head on the wall, and screamed and swore at Murray. But Prince Charlie knew he had lost his men's support, telling his general, 'I take God to witness . . . that I wash my hands of the fatal consequences which I foresee but cannot help.'

From Stirling, the Jacobite army began trudging their way back to the Highlands, where the whole sorry saga had begun five months before. The weather was worse than ever, with a bitter wind blowing snow, sleet and hail into the soldiers' faces. Icicles hung from their eyebrows and beards, and their horses dropped dead from exhaustion. The soldiers wrapped themselves in their plaid and lumbered on, the false warmth of whisky their only relief.

On 19 February they arrived at the ancient city of Inverness, capital of the Highlands. But there was little comfort waiting for them. Prince Charlie, exhausted from the march north, took to his bed with pneumonia. The only food for his army was oats, and having run out of money, he could offer no pay. Many Highland soldiers simply put down their guns and walked home to their farms.

For those Jacobite troops that remained, all they could do was wait for Cumberland's arrival. Prince Charlie was still promising that their saviours – the French – were coming to reinforce them, but he was deluded. In early April a message arrived from the court of King Louis XV. All plans to provide French assistance to the Jacobite cause had been postponed. Prince Charlie and his army were on their own.

The Jacobite army's day of reckoning came in April at Culloden Moor. By now, Prince Charlie had taken control of the army from Lord George Murray. However, the character traits which had once made the prince such an inspiring leader had curdled into a destructive cocktail. His bravery had become stupidity, his confidence stubbornness, his optimism self-delusion. Having never lost a battle, Prince Charlie believed his Highland army was invincible. It turned out to be anything but.

On 15 April, Prince Charlie marched his army to a large open moor near the village of Culloden. That day was the Duke of Cumberland's birthday, and the Prince was convinced Cumberland was going to attack. Who wouldn't want to seize victory against their enemy on their birthday? The Jacobite army spent the whole day waiting in the cold on Culloden Moor, each soldier having a ration of just one biscuit to stay fed. However, by the time the sun went down, Cumberland and his army were nowhere to be seen.

So Prince Charlie devised a cunning plan. The Jacobite army would march through the night and carry out a surprise attack on the British army's camp some ten miles to the east. Some local lads from the Mackintosh clan volunteered to guide the Jacobite army through the moors, assuring Prince Charlie they would make the British camp by 1 a.m. Then they could slay the British soldiers in their tents as they slept. Prince Charlie was trying to recreate the miracle of Prestonpans from the previous summer. But would the same trick work twice? In a word, no.

The Jacobite army got off to a bad start, leaving two hours

later than planned. Progress was painfully slow as its soldiers trudged through boggy moors on empty stomachs and in the dark. By sunrise, they were still four miles away from the British camp, and without the cover of darkness, a surprise attack was impossible. The Jacobite army had no other option but to turn around and walk all the way back. The exhausted troops returned to Culloden Moor at 6 a.m. and collapsed into the surrounding heather bushes for few hours' sleep. Prince Charlie's cunning plan had been a colossal error.

Three hours later, news reached Prince Charlie that Cumberland's army was now approaching. In a mass of confusion, the Jacobite soldiers scrabbled to prepare for battle. Having only eaten a biscuit in the past twenty-four hours, and having been up all night completing a totally pointless march and retreat, they were in no fit state to fight. Prince Charlie's advisors begged him to call off the battle. One even threw himself at Charlie's feet, but it was no use. Instead, Charlie rode his grey horse up and down the Jacobite battle line, waving his sword in the air and promising it would 'cut off some heads and arms today . . . go on my lads, the day will be ours!'

It was an impressive display of bravery, but the Jacobite soldiers could see the manic look in Prince Charlie's eyes. Beneath all the bluster, even the Prince knew that 5,000 sleepless and starving Jacobite rebels would be mincemeat when faced with 9,000 highly trained British troops.

At 11 a.m., Cumberland's army came into view. They moved with mechanical precision to the beat of their drums, identical with their red coats, muskets and tricorn hats. While the Jacobite rabble whooped and jeered at the enemy, the British marched towards them in menacing silence. A panicked Jacobite officer asked Lord George Murray whether they stood a chance. He replied solemnly, 'We are putting an end to a bad affair.'

The two armies lined up facing each other across the moor. At 1 a.m., the British cannons began firing. Prince Charlie, who had once been able to do no wrong, could now do no right. His choice to fight the British at Culloden Moor was disastrous; it was a wide-open space where his troops were a sitting target. No amount of Highland courage could withstand cannonballs hurtling towards them with merciless precision. Prince Charlie was very nearly hit, and retreated behind the front line. When he sent a message back to Murray ordering the Jacobite army to advance, the messenger's head was blown straight off his shoulders by a cannonball.

The British cannons then switched to firing exploding canisters of nails, bullets and scrap metal called 'grapeshot', which tore into the Jacobite line. Everything was going against them, even the wind, which blew smoke from the cannons into their eyes. By now, the Jacobite soldiers on the right flank had lost patience, and decided to do what they knew best – a Highland charge. But while this tactic had been so successful in the past, it was suicidal at Culloden Moor.

As the charging Highlanders passed through the black cannon smoke, they were confronted with ranks of British soldiers, who met them with repeated volleys of musket fire. The Highlanders were mown down, in some places the dead lying five deep. Those who made it past the musket fire were impaled on a wall of British bayonets.

On the left flank of the Jacobite army stood the MacDonald clan. As the greatest of the Scottish clans, the MacDonalds had been given the honoured right flank of the Scottish army since the days of the medieval king Robert the Bruce. But Prince Charlie had insisted on placing them on the left. In protest, the MacDonald clansmen refused to fight. All was confusion and chaos, until Lord George Murray ordered the Jacobite army to retreat, leaving over 1,000 clansmen dead and dying on Culloden Moor.

All in all, it took just forty minutes for Cumberland to annihilate the Jacobite army and destroy once and for all the Stuart claim to the British throne. To this day, Culloden remains the last battle ever fought on British soil.

'Conquer or die.' That had been Prince Charlie's promise to his father the previous year. In the end, he did neither. Prince Charlie escaped the battlefield and went into hiding, abandoning his army to their fate.

The Duke of Cumberland saw every Jacobite soldier as a traitor to his father King George II, and offered no mercy. He ordered his cavalry to cut down the retreating Jacobites with their sabres. Wooden huts containing wounded men were burnt with their inhabitants still inside. Exhausted soldiers who had slept through the battle were murdered where they lay. When the British army reached Inverness, little distinction was made between citizen and soldier – all were rebel scum in Cumberland's eyes. Not for nothing was he given the nickname 'the Butcher'.

Prince Charlie spent the next two and a half months on the run, a fugitive with £30,000 on his head. Along with a band of his closest supporters, he lived off the land, taking shelter wherever he could find it in the caves, mountains and moors of the Scottish Highlands.

The Butcher's troops were everywhere in the Highlands that summer, rounding up 3,500 suspected rebels, packing them into prison boats and sailing them to London for trial. The British government saw the Jacobite uprising as an opportunity to destroy the Highland way of life. Their troops swept through the Highlands in an orgy of burning, looting and rape. The clansmen's homes were destroyed, and their cattle were driven south to be sold, or fed to British troops. Thousands of destitute Highlanders had little option but to starve, migrate to the lowlands or emigrate to the Americas. Clan chiefs had their ancient legal rights removed, and the wearing of clan tartan and the playing of bagpipes were outlawed.

Bonnie Prince Charlie was never caught, and in late September he was picked up by a French ship off the east coast of Scotland and returned to France. His great adventure over, he lived out the rest of his life in Italy, filled with bitterness and regret. From time to time, he made plans to reclaim his throne, but as he realised his dream was drifting away, he succumbed to alcoholism and depression. The Stuart Prince died in Rome at the age of sixty-seven, a sad, sorry man.

But isn't this supposed to be the story of a hero's adventure? Bonnie Prince Charlie's life doesn't sound all that heroic. But that is the funny thing about him. As the failure of his adventure faded from memory, his legend grew and grew. His valiant bid to take back his ancestors' throne became part of modern Scottish folklore, inspiring one of the greatest Scottish folk songs of all time:

> Speed bonnie boat like a bird on the wing
> Onward the sailors cry.
> Carry the lad that's born to be king
> Over the sea to Skye

The deluded Charles Stuart of reality was replaced with the Bonnie Prince Charlie of legend. He became a symbol of bravery, reckless adventure and the romance of loyalty to a lost cause. Today, his story is one of the great 'what ifs' of British history. What if Prince Charlie hadn't turned back at Derby? What if he hadn't lost at Culloden Moor? What if Britain's history had been completely transformed by a rebel army of Highland soldiers, led by the man who would be king?

CHAPTER 3
JOHN WILKES

The Badly Behaved Icon of English Liberty

At the height of his career, John Wilkes was the most famous politician in Britain, a tireless campaigner for the rights of freeborn Englishmen. However, for the first thirty years of his life he was a badly behaved womaniser, famous only for his filthy sense of humour. How did this sleazy playboy transform himself into a courageous radical, who moved power from Parliament to the people on the street? It is one of the great untold stories of English politics.

Like many a Georgian gentleman with too much cash and too little to do, Wilkes dedicated his early life to the satisfaction of Pego, the nickname he gave to his you-know-what. Having married at the age of twenty for no other reason than money, he liked to joke that his aim in life was to sleep with every woman he knew, aside from his wife.

It was a surprising aim for Wilkes to set himself, seeing that he was astonishingly ugly. Wilkes was so ugly, in fact, that children would cry and run to their parents at the mere sight of his face. Cross-eyed and short-sighted, his large, over-hanging nose and forward-jutting jaw caused his mouth to purse and the bottom row of teeth to stick out. But Wilkes made up for his ugliness with bucketloads of charm. When asked about his success with women, he would explain that it took him just 'half an hour to talk away my face'.

Wilkes belonged to a tribe of fun-loving Georgian gentlemen who called themselves 'libertines'. Mixing high education with low morals, they were the sort of men who were at their happiest debating the works of Ancient Greek poets in a brothel. As members of the wealthy elite, libertines disliked organised religion, loved freedom, and valued wit above all else.

Born in 1725, Wilkes did not start life among the wealthy elite. His mother and father were from London's wealthy working class: she was the daughter of a leather tanner, and he owned a gin distillery. They lived in the London suburb of Clerkenwell, in a red-brick house newly built for people just like them – straightforward, hard-working cockneys.

However, Wilkes's father wanted his son to move up in the world. He sent him to boarding school, where young John blossomed and became a talented scholar of Greek and Latin. From there, Wilkes went to university in Holland, where he pursued two of his great loves – books and women. As he later described his university days, 'My father gave me as much money as I pleased, so I had three or four whores and got drunk every night. I woke up with a sore head in the morning, and then I read.'

On returning from Holland, Wilkes was convinced by his father to marry the daughter of a wealthy family friend. Her name was Mary Mead, and it would be hard to imagine a worse match for the young Wilkes. Mary was ten years his senior, very religious, very proper, and so crippled by nerves she could barely leave home. Now she had reached the age of thirty, her family desperately wanted Mary to marry, and

Wilkes was the only man they could find who would say yes. What was in it for him? Mary's family was wealthy, and marriage to her brought with it Prebendal House, a swanky pad in the county of Buckinghamshire.

So, following their wedding in 1747, Wilkes and his wife took up residence in their fancy new manor. Marriage to Mary also brought him acres of farmland across the south and east of England, with enough annual income to mean he never again had to work for a living. Very chilled. Wilkes's transition from son of a London gin-distiller to respectable member of the rural gentry was complete.

The only problem was that Wilkes could not stand married life – he later described himself as a 'schoolboy dragged to the altar'. Following their wedding, John and Mary Wilkes were never seen together in public until they met in a court of law to agree their separation. Before long, Wilkes was spending much of his time back in London, partying with his fellow libertines.

As a wealthy young man with a devilish sense of humour, Wilkes was a hit on the London social scene, and he became a regular at the Beefsteak Club. This was an all-male group of actors, artists and men of leisure who met every Saturday for riotous dinners celebrating two great British institutions – Beef and Liberty. Conversation consisted mostly of piss-taking, something they called 'chaffing'. Any member of the club too sensitive to take a joke was escorted from the dining room, stripped to his underclothes, wrapped in a tablecloth and returned for more humiliation. Banter! Dinner consisted only of beefsteaks and wine.

Back in Buckinghamshire, Wilkes became friends with Thomas Potter, the Member of Parliament for Aylesbury. The son of an archbishop, Potter had rebelled against his religious upbringing by living a life of wild debauchery. More than any other individual, he led Wilkes astray, and was later described as his 'evil genius'. Together, they enjoyed epic drinking sessions, chasing women and writing dirty poems. Fat, gout-ridden and constantly drunk, Potter was totally depraved. He once told Wilkes how sad he was that, when he died, all anyone would still be talking about was that time he was caught having sex. In a meadow. With a cow.

Potter introduced Wilkes to the Hellfire Club, a group of aristocratic libertines who held secretive parties in an abandoned monastery beside the River Thames. Guests entered the premises dressed as monks, through a doorway on which was carved the club motto, 'Fay ce que voudras' ('do whatever you want'). They built a Temple of Venus, with an oval entrance shaped to resemble a vagina. What took place during these gatherings was shrouded in secrecy, but talk of orgies and devil worship was probably not too far wide of the mark.

All this hell-raising had its cost, and despite the income from his estates, Wilkes was permanently in debt. However, until he turned thirty, Wilkes refused to take anything – his marriage, his finances, or even himself – seriously.

So, what turned this reckless scallywag into a radical political campaigner? It all started in 1757, when Thomas Potter stood down as MP for Aylesbury and suggested his drinking buddy Wilkes take his place. At first, Wilkes made little impact on Parliament. His misshapen jaw gave him a speech impediment, and he struggled to get his voice heard during debates.

However, three years later, George III was crowned king of Great Britain. A stubborn and dim-witted young monarch, George was devoted to a Scottish nobleman named the Earl of Bute. George loved Bute, but everyone else hated him, particularly Wilkes. When the king chose the Earl of Bute to be his prime minister, dismissing the highly popular William Pitt the Elder, Wilkes was outraged. He believed that George was becoming a tyrant, with no respect for the views of Parliament and the people.

Wilkes turned to journalism, and discovered that his political power lay not in Parliament, but in the pen. In 1762, he established a weekly newspaper called *The North Briton* (the title was a dig at Bute's Scottish heritage). Savage and sarcastic, nothing like it had ever before been seen in the British press. Freedom of the press had technically existed in England since the lapsing of state censorship laws in 1694, and Wilkes intended to take full advantage of this newfound freedom with his paper. Its articles tore into government policies and lifted the lid on government corruption. These attacks were as brutal as they were hilarious, but always written in puns and metaphors to avoid prosecution for libel. Bute, for example, was 'the boot'. Get it?

The common people loved *The North Briton*, and loved its editor, the cross-eyed cockney rebel who was sticking it to the King. Needless to say, George III wanted to destroy the newspaper, but Wilkes was careful never to print anything libellous enough to be arrested. When visiting France, Wilkes was asked how far freedom of the press really extended in England. 'I cannot tell,' he replied, 'but I am trying to find out.'

He found out, sure enough. By April 1763, Wilkes was sitting in a prison cell in the Tower of London, while government agents trashed his home, smashed the locks and doors of his cabinets, and took whatever papers they pleased.

Wilkes had overstepped the mark in issue 45 of *The North Briton*, where he attacked the 'odious measures' outlined in the King's Speech. The sentence that landed him in the Tower suggested that, from the angered people of England, 'a spirit of liberty ought then to arise'. The government interpreted this as a call for insurrection, and issued a general warrant to arrest all authors, publishers and printers associated with *The North Briton* for treason.

In May, Wilkes was taken to court, where he appealed against his arrest. Standing in the dock, he delivered a stirring speech on his right to criticise the King's government, as a crowd of supporters cheered him on from the gallery. The judge demanded silence, insisting he would not be swayed by a rabble. 'This is not the clamour of a rabble, my Lord,' Wilkes responded, 'but the voice of Liberty, which must and shall be heard!'

Wilkes won the case, and was free to go home. As he left the court, thousands more supporters lined the streets to applaud him. Looking at their cheering faces, Wilkes realised that he had done something quite remarkable: by taking on the King and his government, he had unlocked the power of popular politics.

At this time, only the wealthiest members of British society had the vote. The common people of England – its tailors, butchers, dockers and carpenters – were locked out of politics. In Wilkes, they saw a radical politician who was prepared to speak for their concerns, giving a voice to the voiceless.

For Wilkes's supporters, the number 45 – associated with the issue of *The North Briton* which had landed him in jail – took on an almost spiritual significance. Up and down the country, they painted the number 45 on their front doors and the sides of their carriages. They hung leather boots from gallows, symbolically executing the Earl of Bute. Shopkeepers sold Wilkes-themed merchandise: tobacco papers, dishes, teapots, badges and miniature statues, all displaying Wilkes's unmistakably ugly face. He was even drawn by the greatest cartoonist of the age, William Hogarth: Wilkes's scurrilous form of liberty was symbolised by a cap of liberty above his head, drawn to resemble an upturned chamberpot. Wilkes had become a cult figure.

Having failed to try him in a normal court, George III decided that Wilkes should instead face trial before his fellow MPs in Parliament. The first day of the trial was 15 November 1763. The House of Commons was packed that afternoon, its members looking particularly portly and pompous in their wigs and fine clothes. That day in Parliament was an almighty brouhaha. MPs voted Wilkes guilty of 'scandalous and seditious libel', and approved a motion for the hangman to burn all remaining copies of *The North Briton*.

Little did Wilkes know that, while he was being tried in the House of Commons for libel, he was also being tried that very same day in the House of Lords for blasphemy. The case concerned a poem that Wilkes had composed many years before with his partner in crime, the farmyard-loving Thomas Potter. Entitled 'An Essay on Women', it was said to be the filthiest poem ever written in the English language.

The poem was read by Lord Sandwich, whose greatest contribution to mankind was placing a slice of beef between two slices of bread and naming the creation after himself (true story). As Sandwich read out the offending words, some of the Lords roared with laughter, others shrieked in horror, and others left the room, unable to listen any further.

Wilkes had taken 'An Essay on Man', a poetic rumination on God's moral order by the revered English poet Alexander Pope, and turned it into a salacious ode to sexual pleasure. Take, for example, Pope's pious couplet: 'since life can little more supply / Than just to look about us and to die.' Wilkes had rewritten this as – 'since life can little more supply / Than just a few good fucks and then we die.'

Sandwich then passed around the House of Lords the poem's front page, on which was illustrated a ten-inch penis. The Latin motto across the bottom of the page read, 'In recto decus', which could be translated 'In uprightness is beauty', but could also be translated along the lines of 'Beauty in a bumhole'. The poem was clearly obscene. However, it was not illegal. Wilkes had written it for the private amusement of Potter and his pals at the Hellfire Club. It was never meant for publication. But, by producing it as evidence for his trial in the House of Lords, the government achieved its aim. Wilkes's reputation was in tatters.

Back in the House of Commons, the MPs carried on braying and harrumphing until two o'clock in the morning. Wilkes weathered the attacks with characteristic good humour, but as he walked home in the early hours, one MP had really got under his skin.

Samuel Martin was just the type of snivelling, unprincipled suck-up that Wilkes despised. Wilkes saw Martin as a man with no loyalty who cared only about furthering his own political career. Having been made a government minister at the Treasury, Martin oversaw a plot to supply the British army in Germany with rotten oats at a reduced price and pocket the money that was saved. Wilkes broke the story in *The North Briton*, where he described Martin as 'the most treacherous, base, selfish, mean, abject, low-lived and dirty fellow that ever *wriggled* himself into a secretaryship'. Ouch.

During the first day of his trial, Martin accused Wilkes of being a coward for insulting him anonymously in *The North Briton*. The following morning, he sent Wilkes a letter stating, 'I desire that you may meet me in Hyde Park immediately, with a brace of pistols each, to determine our difference.' Martin had challenged Wilkes to a duel, and having had his honour questioned on the floor of the House of Commons, Wilkes had no option but to accept.

Wilkes met Martin in Hyde Park that afternoon, his two pistols primed and ready. The duellists then walked to the middle of the park and found a patch of grass hidden from public view. They stood back to back, held their pistols in the air, walked six paces, and turned. Then they lowered their pistols towards each other, one eye closed to take aim.

'Now, sir!' yelled Martin. Both fired. Both missed.

Throwing their first pistols to the floor, Martin and Wilkes took out their second pistols. They lowered the guns again, and fired. This time Wilkes's pistol failed to fire, but Martin's pistol let off its shot. Wilkes crumpled to the ground.

Martin ran towards Wilkes and told him, 'I have killed you, I am afraid.' But Wilkes shook his head and insisted Martin should skedaddle to avoid arrest. Then, somehow, Wilkes stood up, pressed his hands against his stomach to stop the flow of blood, and staggered out of the park towards Pall Mall, where his trusty servant was waiting for him.

Wilkes's life had been saved by the brass button on the front of his overcoat. The bullet was deflected as it hit the button, and entered his body with a downwards trajectory, ending up lodged somewhere in his right groin. A doctor was called to Wilkes's house. There were no painkillers in those days, so Wilkes simply bit down on a leather strap as the doctor cut open his groin with a sharp scalpel and removed the bullet, along with a patch of his overcoat.

As Wilkes lay in bed recovering he was, conveniently, too weak to return to the House of Commons and finish his trial. In reality, he had no intention of doing so. One month later, during the dead of night, he loaded a carriage with his personal belongings and escaped London. For two miserable days, his carriage jolted along the uneven winter roads, each bump sending a burst of pain through his unhealed gunshot wound, until he reached Dover on Christmas Eve. The following morning he boarded a boat to France. On Christmas Day 1763, Wilkes became an outlaw and an exile.

As 1764 dawned, Wilkes was in Paris, his career in ruins, his reputation disgraced and his finances a mess. To pay off his debts, he was forced to sell Prebendal House and his library of 1,700 books. Wilkes could have let misery get the better of him, but he was an eternal optimist. When a grand Parisian lady teased him for having no money, stating that 'a person without a shirt should have no pride', Wilkes responded that on the contrary, a man without a shirt must have pride, because then at least he has something.

Wilkes's silver-tongued charm worked as well in French as it did in English. The great and the good of Paris society flooded him with invitations to their parties, eager to meet this outlaw journalist who had taken on the King. He even found a new mistress, a feisty Italian ballerina, who amazed Wilkes with her Mediterranean custom of undressing before joining him in bed (the English still went about such business fully clothed).

Most importantly for Wilkes, he was able to spend time with his one true love, his thirteen-year-old daughter Polly. She was the only child of Wilkes's failed marriage, and he adored her. Seeing no reason why she should not be educated like a son, he had sent her to Paris to live with a private tutor. Wilkes's parting letter told Polly, 'you have an excellent genius, given you from heaven . . . Read the best books, and they will be your pleasure through life.'

Wilkes lived with Polly for much of his exile, and they remained inseparable for the rest of their lives. However, after four years in France, Wilkes once again felt London calling. A general election was due to take place in early 1768, and he was planning an audacious political comeback.

Wilkes knew that the moment he set foot on English soil, he could be arrested. However, he also knew that if he whipped up enough public support, the government might be too afraid to touch him. And what better way to whip up public support, he realised, than to run for Parliament? As Wilkes wrote to his brother, 'In politics, as in war, great and bold actions succeed, when more cautious fail.'

So Wilkes returned to England, and announced that he would run as Member of Parliament for Middlesex. Including all of London and its surrounding towns and villages, Middlesex had the largest numbers of voters for any parliamentary seat in England. And as it turned out, Londoners were still wild about Wilkes. Four years in exile had only strengthened the legend of this duel-fighting, king-bullying icon of Liberty. They welcomed him back with open arms.

To vote in the Middlesex election, Londoners had to travel thirteen miles along the Great West Road to the county town of Brentford. London printers produced 40,000 pro-Wilkes leaflets, and London cab drivers (horse-drawn cabs, not taxis) offered free lifts to Brentford for anyone promising to vote for Wilkes. Along the Great West Road, the doorway of every house, whether the owner liked it or not, was painted with the number 45.

Late in the evening on 29 March, Wilkes and his supporters were in Brentford, waiting for the vote to be counted. The result? Wilkes had only gone and won, gaining 1,292 votes, compared to 827 for his nearest rival. Wilkes leapt onto the stage and told his supporters: 'The eyes of the whole kingdom, of the whole world, are upon you, as the first and firmest defenders of public liberty!'

Wilkes then led a riotous torchlit procession back into London, as his supporters – the joiners, carpenters, soap-boilers and distillers of London town – chanted 'Wilkes and Liberty!' and 'Forty-five forever!' They drank the pubs dry, and as they passed the homes of Wilkes's enemies among the political elites, including the Earl of Bute, they smashed their windows. They even stopped the carriage of the Austrian ambassador and demanded he give a cheer for Wilkes. The ambassador refused. So they lifted him out of his carriage, held him upside down, and painted a '4' on the sole of one shoe and a '5' on the sole of the other.

Wilkes had unleashed the power of 'the mob', and George III had no idea what to do next. Even the King's six-year-old son, the Prince of Wales, was caught up in the excitement. Whenever he wanted to annoy his father, the Prince would burst into the King's dressing room at Windsor Palace, shout 'Wilkes and Liberty!' and run away.

Wilkes openly dared the government to arrest him, but its members were now so terrified of the mob it seemed they were unwilling to do so. After his election victory, Wilkes twice submitted himself to the King's Court and asked to be imprisoned, before a judge finally sent him to the King's Bench, a prison in south London.

However, as Wilkes headed towards the River Thames, his supporters unhitched the horses and took control of his carriage, pulling it all the way to Spitalfields to the east of the city. Here, Wilkes enjoyed one last piss-up in the Three Tuns tavern. In the early hours of the morning, he escaped his loving supporters through the back of the pub and walked to the King's Bench, finally taking his place in jail.

Wilkes's trial resumed in May, and a large crowd of supporters gathered outside the King's Bench to process with him to Westminster. The King sent a magistrate, along with a regiment of red-coated soldiers, to keep order. Wilkes's supporters greeted the soldiers with a hail of mud and stones, shouting 'Damn the king, damn the Parliament, damn the justices.' When the magistrate was hit on the head with a stone, he shouted 'Fire!'

A crackle of musket shot rang out across the field, and Wilkes's supporters ran in panic. As the smoke drifted away from the soldiers' guns, six men lay dead on the ground, another fifteen wounded. News of the St George's Fields massacre spread around London, and the city descended into violent riots. For over a week, Wilkes's supporters tore through the streets, vandalising the homes of anyone suspected of opposing their hero. Paralysed by fear and unsure what to do next, King George III came close to abdicating.

Once the trial was over, Wilkes was sentenced to two years in jail. Stuck in prison, he was now a martyr, sacrificing his own freedom for the cause of English Liberty, and Wilkes-mania hit new heights.

Across the country, Wilkes-themed dinners and parties were held in honour of the brave freedom fighter. In Newcastle, a company of forty-five gentlemen met at forty-five minutes past one, sat at tables with the number 45 inlaid in mother-of-pearl, and shared 45 lb of sirloin beef, eaten from plates painted with the number 45. In Hampshire, a wig maker designed a new wig with forty-five curls of hair. From the American city of Boston, Wilkes received a letter of support signed by forty-five men calling themselves the Sons of Liberty.

One signatory was John Adams. Three decades later, he would become the second President of the United States of America.

The captain of an English merchant ship even claimed to have met a Chinese man in Beijing who owned a miniature statue of Wilkes. As he told the English captain, 'Your king fooly king. Do so here, cutty head. Inglis no love your king.' The icon of Liberty had gone global.

Wilkes rather enjoyed his two years in prison. In Georgian England, you paid for your prison cell, and Wilkes's supporters paid for him to be held in a spacious ground-floor suite, where he kept a servant and could have as many guests as he liked. His daughter Polly was a regular visitor, bringing her father two canaries to keep him company.

His loving supporters sent gifts to Wilkes's prison cell: oysters, Cheshire cheese, ducks, turkeys, geese, fowls, smoked tongues, fish, and gallons of wine, madeira and beer. The prosperous people of Guildford gave him grapes, melons and a pineapple. The people of Newcastle sent him a whole salmon. He even started a new relationship with the wife of one of his supporters, a certain Mrs Barnard, who would sneak away from her husband at night to join Wilkes in his cell.

As Wilkes was in prison, the Middlesex election had to be re-run in February 1769. Wilkes submitted himself as a candidate, ran a successful campaign from his prison cell, and won the election. But the government refused to recognise his victory. So, one month later, a third election was held. Again, Wilkes ran. Again, Wilkes won. Again, the government called for a re-run. And again, Wilkes won. After four separate Middlesex elections, each won by Wilkes, the government was exasperated. They excluded Wilkes from Parliament and declared his opponent the winner.

For Wilkes, this was the greatest outrage yet. He wrote a

series of articles from his prison cell arguing that, by refusing to recognise his election victory, the government was essentially telling the people of England who they could and could not vote for. Wilkes's articles were read across the country and cut to the heart of the most important question in English politics. Where should power ultimately lie? With the politicians, or the people?

The people of England knew what they thought, and 60,000 voters wrote letters to King George III demanding that Wilkes be given his seat. As the issue was debated in Parliament, the MP for Newport asked whether 'base-born people' such as 'mechanics and booksellers' had the right to question the King's government. Increasingly, it was believed, they did. Shockwaves went through Parliament when members of the King's own government began siding with Wilkes. No longer able to hold together his cabinet, the prime minister resigned in January 1770. From his prison cell in south London, Wilkes had brought down the government.

One month later, Wilkes was released from prison, and the nation erupted in celebration. Parties were thrown, cannons were fired, fireworks were lit, and a new dance was invented: the 'Wilkes's wriggle'. In Greenwich, an inn lit up the words 'Wilkes and Liberty' with 300 candles.

Something had changed in British politics during Wilkes's Middlesex election campaign. The common people realised that government should be based on their support, and not their obedience. Nobody, not the king, not the government, not the army, could decide who the people could and could not vote for, even if they chose a disgraced outlaw with a dirty sense of humour sitting in a south London prison cell. Some historians claim that the seeds of British democracy were first planted by Wilkes during the Middlesex elections of 1769.

Following his release from jail, Wilkes spent another thirty years in politics campaigning to bring power to the people. In 1774, he was elected Lord Mayor of London. The same year he finally returned, in triumph, as Member of Parliament for Middlesex.

Back in Parliament, Wilkes was as energetic as ever. He led a campaign to allow journalists to report from inside Parliament, opening up the previously secretive world of parliamentary debates to the public. In 1776, he became the first MP in British history to suggest that all men, even 'the poorest peasant', should be given the right to vote (something that would not be achieved until almost two centuries later). In 1782, Wilkes won his sweetest victory, when Parliament retrospectively reversed the exclusion they had imposed in 1769. From that day onwards, Parliament has never been allowed to exclude any member who has been elected, fair and square, by the British people.

However, as Wilkes grew older, his radicalism began to fade. He even became friends with George III. Many English radicals felt betrayed, angry that their one-time leader was fraternising with the elites he had once fought. As an old man, it was Wilkes's turn to have his windows smashed by the London mob. But after his house was attacked, Wilkes refused to press charges, observing 'they are only some of my pupils, now set up for themselves'.

However, the old libertinism never entirely left Wilkes. One friend remembered seeing an ageing Wilkes hurrying through the West End of London, and stopping the old man for a catch-up. Wilkes was looking for a lady friend, and rushed on, shouting, 'Don't stop me. I have an erection now. Did it go down, I don't know when I shall have another!'

In the winter of 1797, the 72-year-old Wilkes was dying,

Polly at his bedside. His last act was to ask Polly for a glass of wine and drink a toast to 'my beloved and excellent daughter'. Then he handed her the glass, closed his eyes, and passed away.

Historians have always found it hard to decide how Wilkes should be remembered. Some think he was a genuine campaigner for people power, others a publicity-addicted self-promoter. Wilkes clearly had an enormous ego, but he also had enormous bravery. So many of the rights we take for granted today – the right to criticise the government in the press; the right to vote for whoever we want in elections; the right to know what is debated in Parliament – were won by Wilkes, and he risked his own life and freedom in the process.

And for some reason, the people of Georgian England simply adored Wilkes. Ultimately, I think this was due to his resilience. Whatever tricky card life dealt him, be it imprisonment, exile, bankruptcy, social disgrace or a pistol shot to the stomach, he bounced back with more energy than before. In 1763, Wilkes wrote to Polly during his first spell in prison, telling her, 'As an Englishman, I must lament that my liberty is thus wickedly taken away, yet I am not unhappy, for my honour is clear, and my health good, and my spirit unshaken, I believe indeed, invincible.'

An invincible spirit. Though he said so himself, nobody could deny it.

CHAPTER 4
TIPU SULTAN

The Indian Ruler Who Kept the British Empire at Bay

From 1760 to 1800, British armies swept through India, establishing a rule over the country that would last for 200 years. This land of extraordinary natural riches, of sugar, silks, spices, diamonds and rubies, would become known as the 'jewel in the crown of the British Empire'.

The British had first visited India during the 1600s as merchants. They never dreamt that India – at the time the wealthiest nation in the world – could become theirs. India was ruled by the magnificent Mughal emperor, who sat upon a gold and gem-encrusted 'peacock throne' in his capital city of Delhi. British merchants spoke of the marvels of the Mughal world: vast cities, exquisite palaces, and treasuries full of gold and precious stones. To visualise the peak of Mughal culture, picture the Taj Mahal, completed in 1653 by the emperor Shah Jahan (meaning 'King of the World') as a mausoleum for his favourite wife.

However, by the early 1700s the mighty Mughals were losing their grip on power, and their empire broke apart into a patchwork of dozens of smaller, warring kingdoms. Watching this descent into chaos were the British merchants of the East

India Company, a trading corporation which had spent the past century quietly doing business out of its two ports on India's eastern coast, Calcutta and Madras. However, as the company watched the Mughal Empire disintegrate and war sweep the country, it turned its ports into fortresses, and built up its own army.

Before long, the Company Army was sucked into the power struggles of rival Indian kingdoms. The main battle tactic of Indian armies was the cavalry charge, but this stood little chance against British cannons, which scattered deadly grape-shot and British infantrymen, who were trained to shoot rapid volleys of musket fire. Grapeshot and musket volleys could mow down any Indian cavalry charge, no matter how fero-cious, and the Company Army began defeating Indian armies five, even ten times its size. This led to a startling realisation: from the rubble of the Mughal Empire, Britain could build her own empire in India.

Across the north and east of India, kingdoms fell like dom-inoes to the Company Army. The refined Mughal rulers looked on in horror as these rough-mannered merchants from across the seas took over their palaces and looted their treasures. 'What honour is left to us,' asked one Mughal nobleman, 'when we have to take orders from a handful of traders who have not yet learned to wash their bottoms?' But little could be done to stop the relentless rise of the East India Company. By 1815, the British ruled over some 40 million Indian people.

There was, however, one Indian ruler the British could not defeat. When their two armies met outside Madras beside a village called Pollilur in September 1780, the Indian army outnumbered the Company Army twenty to one, and 'covered the plains', in the words of one Indian historian, 'like waves of an angry sea'. Even more frightening for the British, this

Indian army had fifty cannons, every bit as effective as their own.

As the battle began, Indian cannons and rockets pulverised the tightly packed British troops, hitting two carriages full of gunpowder and causing a tremendous explosion. This opened up a hole in the British defences, into which 25,000 Indian cavalrymen charged. Seeing that a massacre was about to take place, the British commander tied a white handkerchief to his sword and waved a flag of surrender.

When the fighting stopped, corpses from the Company Army littered the battlefield. Dying soldiers were trampled by elephants, stripped of their clothes and left naked in the glaring sun, to be picked apart by wild animals. Indian soldiers hacked off the heads of their dead enemies and took them to their ruler, who rewarded them in proportion to the number they could bring. Some 7,000 soldiers from the Company Army were eventually taken prisoner during the campaign, around one-fifth of the British forces in India. The Battle of Pollilur was, in the words of one British officer, 'the severest blow that the English ever suffered in India'.

Who was this Indian ruler? During the battle, he could be seen leading his army to victory from on top of his elephant. Riding alongside him was his son, a skilled military general. It would take the British thirty years and four separate wars to defeat this fearsome father-and-son team. His name was Haidar Ali, and his son was Tipu.

Haidar Ali ruled a richly fertile land in southern India called the Kingdom of Mysore. In its heartlands, farmers grew all manner of wonderful foods: cashews, almonds, mangoes, sugar cane, chillies and cardamom. Surrounding these farms were forests full of tigers and elephants, which Haidar and his son never tired of hunting. West of the heartlands rose a great mountain range called the Ghats, which guarded the route to the Arabian Sea. And below the Ghats lay the rainforest-fringed beaches of the Malabar coast, where farmers grew coconuts and black pepper, fishermen filled their nets with kingfish and prawns, and merchants traded with Africa and the Middle East. These tropical lands were – and remain today – not far from paradise.

Haidar's ancestors were soldiers of fortune, originally from the Mughal power centre in northern India, who had moved south to fight for various kings during the break-up of the Mughal Empire. Despite being Muslim, Haidar Ali entered the service of the Hindu king of Mysore, rising to become commander-in-chief of his army. He clearly did not think much of his employer, however, and removed the king from power in 1761, making himself the *de facto* ruler of Mysore.

Haidar Ali was a ruthless fighting man who remained illiterate his entire life, but he was remarkably shrewd. As a young officer he fought against the British and alongside the French, and saw at first hand the superiority of European tactics.

Once he became ruler of Mysore, Haidar employed French soldiers to train his army, French ironworkers to build him cannons, and French sailors to create a Mysore navy. On an island in the middle of a fast-moving river he built a new capital city named Patan, and hired French engineers to surround his island city with European-style defences. Huge walls rose out of the river beds, bristling with cannons.

However, inside Patan's fearsome walls lay a sumptuous royal palace. The gardens had avenues of cypress trees and borders of rose and jasmine, while the orchards teemed with pomegranates, apples and peaches.

Haidar gave the British their first bloody nose during the First Anglo-Mysore War in 1767. The British had taken

Mangalore, Haidar's favourite port on the Malabar coast. Haidar marched west, but realised he had too few troops to launch a successful siege. So he recruited 20,000 peasants and armed them with replica muskets fashioned from ebony wood. As soon as the British commander saw this enormous army marching towards him, he surrendered Mangalore and sailed away, allowing Haidar and his fake army to walk into the port unopposed.

The siege of Mysore demonstrated Haidar's cunning, but also his brutality. Left behind in Mangalore were over one 1,000 Indian troops who had been fighting for the East India Company (it is worth knowing that at any one time, around 80 per cent of the British army in India was made up of Indian soldiers called 'sepoys'). The vengeful Haidar cut off each of the sepoys' noses and upper lips and sent them marching out of the city, an army of hideously disfigured men. Perhaps they were lucky. Haidar's other punishment was to chain his enemies' hands and feet behind their backs, attach that chain to an elephant's foot, then send the elephant on a stampede, dragging the victim to his death as his face scraped along the ground.

Haidar knew he would always be seen as a cruel dictator. However, he wanted his son Tipu to become a civilised and sophisticated prince. At the royal palace in Patan, Tipu's tutors taught him to read and write in Hindi, Urdu, Persian and Arabic. Religious tutors taught him to read the Qur'an and understand Islamic law, while French tutors taught him mathematics and science. Tipu, by all accounts, was a fine young student. Haidar did not neglect Tipu's military education. He chose his top general, Ghazi Khan, to train Tipu in the art of war, and aged just fifteen, Tipu was given his first command on the battlefield.

When Haidar died in 1782, Tipu was well prepared to inherit the throne of Mysore. At the age of thirty-two, he was a celebrated military general. He was not tall, around five feet seven inches, but he was stocky and muscular. He had a long fine nose, arched eyebrow, and a large, curled moustache. His manner was cool and detached, but his darting black eyes showed that his mind was never at rest.

It was Tipu's duty, as Haidar's eldest son, to prepare his father's body for the funeral. As he unwound Haidar's turban, a letter fluttered to the floor. Tipu unfolded the paper and read his father's final instructions: 'I have gained nothing by war with the English, but am now alas no longer alive. If you, through fear of disturbances in your own kingdom, repair thither without having concluded peace with the English, they will certainly follow you and carry the war into your country. On this account, therefore, it is better to make peace on whatever terms you can procure . . .'

However, before Tipu could make peace with the British, he had to make his mark as a leader. Tipu suspected that the governor of Mangalore was planning to betray him to the British, and sent one of his top generals – Muhammad Ali – to investigate. However, Muhammad Ali was friends with the governor, and pleaded with Tipu to spare the governor's life. Tipu responded, 'In order to confirm or establish your government, you must give the sword no rest.'

Unwilling to surrender his friend, Muhammad Ali tried to escape along with the governor. They were captured and brought back to Tipu. The governor was killed, Muhammad's soldiers had their noses and hands sliced off, and Muhammad himself was imprisoned. Fearing what gruesome punishment Tipu was dreaming up next, Muhammad committed suicide by swallowing diamond powder.

Meanwhile, back in Patan, Tipu discovered that a group of noblemen was attempting to place the Hindu royal family back on the Mysore throne. According to one source, Tipu had the conspirators flogged, and chillies and red pepper rubbed into their open wounds. Another source claims he kept them in iron cages until they nearly starved, and then fed them to his pet tigers.

Having shown himself to be as ruthless as his father, Tipu was ready to make peace with the British. The Second Anglo-Mysore War, which ended in 1784, was a thumping triumph for the kingdom of Mysore. Tipu demanded that the peace negotiations take place 400 miles from Madras in Mangalore, forcing the British Commissioners to trek from one side of India to another. Clearly, Tipu had no intention of meeting the British halfway. As the commissioners neared Mangalore, they woke up one morning to see gibbets erected outside their camp: a bit of friendly intimidation from their host. When the Treaty of Mangalore was signed, the British handed all of their conquests on the Malabar coast back to the Kingdom of Mysore.

In return, Tipu returned his British prisoners. They included some forty officers who had been chained up inside a rat-infested prison in Patan for the past four years. Some had died of disease, some had gone mad. Others had kept themselves sane by playing with dice fashioned out of animal bones, and a backgammon set made from bamboo.

Prisoners who required extra punishment had been chained to the wall of an ingenious riverside dungeon. As the river rose and fell, so too did the water level in the dungeon, giving the prisoners a constant fear of drowning. Those in the lower ranks of the Company Army, most of whom were Indian sepoys, were circumcised, forcibly converted to Islam and made to serve as slave-soldiers in Haidar's army. Captured British drummer boys were dressed in saris, so they could entertain Haidar and Tipu's court as dancing girls.

One of the British officers in the Patan prison was Colonel David 'Davie' Baird, a battle-hardened Scottish veteran of the Indian Wars. Six foot tall and tough as old boots, Baird was captured at the Battle of Pollilur, having been shot in the leg, stabbed in the arm and slashed across the head with a sword. However, when his mother back home in Edinburgh heard her son was in prison, her response said it all: 'I pity the man who was chained to oor Davie.'

Somehow, Baird recovered from his wounds and walked free in March 1784. As he dined on fried plantain and sherbet that evening in a village outside Patan, his first proper meal in four years, he had little idea that fifteen years later, he would once again set foot on the island city.

The British used stories such as the Patan jail to depict Tipu as a brutal Indian tyrant. However, there is little evidence that Tipu enjoyed torturing and killing his enemies. What really drove him was a passionate desire to make the Kingdom of Mysore the richest, best-governed and most advanced state in India. For fifteen years, he worked with that tireless energy seen in all great leaders to achieve his aim.

Tipu rose each morning at dawn, had a massage, washed, and did a spot of weight lifting. He then ate his first breakfast, a light meal of sparrow brains, before inspecting the state of his treasury. This was followed by a meeting with his doctors, who checked his health, and his astrologers, who checked his fortune. Servants then presented Tipu with flowers, fruits and vegetables from his gardens, before he sat down to a second, more substantial breakfast of fruit and nuts at around 9 a.m.

Tipu's morning routine over, he was ready for business.

He sat on his throne in Patan's Great Hall wearing simple but elegant clothing: a robe of fine white cloth fastened with one diamond button, a long pearl necklace, and a turban in the 'Arab style', with one end of gold-embroidered silk hanging over his shoulder. Two slaves stood by his side, waving fans to keep away the flies. Mysore's civil servants processed through the hall to update Tipu on their work. The postmaster then delivered Tipu's letters, which he read before dictating any necessary responses. Finally, a selection of Mysore's governors reported on events in their regions. The business of the day over, Tipu and his entourage processed out of the hall as heralds cried out: 'May thy sight be clear! His Justice is unparalleled! Health to the Refuge of the World!'

Tipu spent his afternoons touring Patan, inspecting its defences, meeting new army recruits and enjoying the scents of his sumptuous gardens. During the warmer months, he would sit in his summer house, where he had painted a huge mural of the Battle of Pollilur. You can still see it today, depicting in exquisite detail the British soldiers being hacked to death by Haidar and Tipu's rampaging cavalry.

Evenings were spent having dinner with his family. Tipu had twelve sons and eight daughters, and – like his father before him – was a stickler for hard work and good manners. Retiring to his room at night, he read himself to sleep, choosing from a library of 2,000 books, covering law, theology, history and science. He awoke early the next morning ready for another day working for the prosperity of Mysore.

There was no stone in his kingdom that Tipu left unturned. One set of instructions he sent to a regional governor survives today, and contains 127 different demands. Tipu orders cash advances for peasants unable to afford ploughs during the harvest, tax concessions for sugar cane and coconut farmers, and – perhaps less popularly – a doubling of the tax on alcohol and a ban on *bhang* (cannabis).

Tipu learnt about European ideas of science and rationality through his French allies, and used them to reform his kingdom. He created a new system of measurement, where the standard unit of length was a *dekk*, equivalent to 24 thumbs, and the standard width of a thumb was set at 12 grains of rice. Distance was measured by the *cos*, around 2¾ miles. If a Mysore state postman was unable to cover a *cos* in exactly 33¾ minutes, he would be flogged. In a burst of rationalisation, Tipu reorganised the structure of his army, created a new currency and devised a new system of local government. He had a thing for measurement: one of his prized possessions was a thermometer imported from France.

Tipu's Mysore soldiers became world leaders in the use of artillery rockets. Tipu refined their design with long firing tubes attached to bamboo sticks, and blades like the feathers on an arrow, which allowed them to fire at an advancing army from up to two kilometres away. Tipu's rockets were not very accurate, but they would terrify enemy troops and horses. Tipu also encouraged international trade. Having spotted the growing demand for silk textiles, he sent trade envoys to China who brought silkworms back to his kingdom. To this day, Mysore remains India's leading producer of silk.

Legend has it that while hunting in the Mysore jungle as a younger man, Tipu came face to face with a tiger. His gun failed and the tiger leapt on the young prince, so Tipu reached for his dagger and killed it. True or not, there is no doubting that Tipu was obsessed with tigers. As his fame spread across the world, he became known as the 'Tiger of Mysore'. With good reason . . .

Tipu dressed his troops in tiger-striped uniforms, had the

handles of his pistols and swords shaped as tiger heads, and designed cannons which fired missiles out of the mouths of roaring tigers. On the veranda of his Patan palace he kept six pet tigers. Inside his palace, he sat on a magnificent tiger throne, topped with a snarling tiger's head made of gold, its teeth and eyes fashioned from rock crystal. Tipu's favourite toy was a large mechanical tiger mauling a British soldier. Inside was an organ, which could simulate the tiger's roar and the screams of its helpless victim.

As the Tiger of Mysore's fame grew, so too did his confidence. Tipu's father had always taught him the importance of forming alliances with other Indian states. But Tipu believed he was now strong enough to go it alone. To the north of his kingdom lay a powerful collection of Hindu rulers known as the Maratha Confederacy. Haidar had always kept the Marathas as allies, but in 1785, Tipu declared war on his Hindu neighbours. He then offended his Muslim allies by refusing to recognise the authority of the Mughal emperor, something all Muslim rulers in India were expected to do, despite the emperor's weakness. Not Tipu. He declared himself the *Padshah*, or 'Great King' of Mysore, and ordered his Muslim subjects to praise him, not the emperor, during their Friday prayers.

The Tiger of Mysore was, it seems, getting a bit too big for his boots. This meant that when he declared war on the East India Company in December 1789, starting the Third Anglo-Mysore War, he had to fight on his own.

The war was a complete disaster for Tipu. By May 1791, the Company Army had chased the Tiger of Mysore all the way back to his Patan lair. Some 20,000 British troops surrounded its great defensive walls, ready to lay siege. However, Tipu was saved by the early arrival of the monsoon that year. As the British set up camp, a colossal thunderstorm broke, soaking the Company Army and filling the rivers that surrounded the island city. The siege was called off and the British army marched back to their base in their captured Mysorean city of Bangalore.

Here, the Company Army was met by 12,000 reinforcements bringing fresh supplies of oxen, sheep, hens and rice. But these were not British troops. They were from Britain's newest allies, the Marathas. In January 1792, the Company Army marched out of Bangalore once more, with allies from the Marathas and the Kingdom of Hyderabad swelling their ranks to some 50,000 troops. Two weeks later, they arrived outside Patan. This well-fed, well-drilled army of three nations – their drums beating, their elephants trumpeting and their newly polished armour glinting in the sun – must have been a terrifying sight. No wonder Tipu's own troops began to desert him. Knowing he stood no chance, Tipu asked for peace negotiations to begin.

The ensuing treaty was a devastating blow to Tipu's power. He handed over half of the Kingdom of Mysore to his enemies, with the territories equally shared by the Marathas, the Kingdom of Hyderabad and the East India Company. He also had to pay war reparations of 30,000 rupees (some £390 million today), and was given just two years in which to do so. To make sure the money came through, the British took two of Tipu's sons back to Madras as hostages.

Many leaders would have crumbled in the face of such a loss, but Tipu fought on. He despised the British, referring to them as 'hogs' due to their pink skin and foul manners. If he was to go down, he would go down fighting. Tipu looked abroad for help. He sent ambassadors around the Muslim world, to the Ottoman emperor, the Sultan of Oman and the

Shah of Afghanistan, hoping that their common religion could be the basis for a military alliance. But none would help.

Next, Tipu tried to resurrect the Kingdom of Mysore's old alliance with the French. By the late 1790s, France's top general was a man surprisingly similar to Tipu: a short, tireless and immensely ambitious military and political leader called Napoleon Bonaparte.

In 1798, Napoleon was attempting an audacious invasion of Egypt. His ultimate aim was to travel through Egypt, sail across the Arabian Sea and fight the British Empire in India. In February 1799, he sat down at his headquarters in Cairo and wrote a letter addressed to 'the Magnificent SULTAN, our greatest friend, TIPU SAIB'. He informed Tipu of his masterplan and asked him 'eagerly' to send an ambassador to Cairo. The letter ended, 'May the Almighty increase your Power and destroy your enemies. BUONAPARTE.' This was the salvation Tipu had been waiting for.

Unfortunately, the letter never reached Tipu. Napoleon's invasion of Egypt failed, and his letter was intercepted by British spies in the Arabian port of Jeddah. From there, the letter was sent to the East India Company headquarters in Madras, providing final evidence that Tipu was negotiating with Britain's enemy. This could mean only one thing: a fourth, and final, Anglo-Mysore War.

By this date, it was absurd that the East India Company was still being called a 'Company'. In reality, it had become an empire, and its governor-general held all the powers of an emperor. In January 1798, an ambitious new governor-general named Richard Wellesley arrived in Madras. Aggressive, acquisitive and deeply ambitious, Wellesley would be, more than any other individual, responsible for building British power in India.

Back in Patan, Tipu kept a book beside his bed in which he recorded his dreams. In one dream, 10,000 'well-built, stout and young' French troops come to his aid. In another, the Kingdom of Hyderabad sends 4,000 horsemen to help him. But in reality, nobody was coming to help Tipu. In one of his final dreams, Tipu sees an invading army marching towards his city. When they are stopped by the river, they create a bridge of elephants to cross. Tipu, it seems, knew his days were numbered.

The Company Army left Madras for Patan on 3 February 1799. It had around 40,000 Company soldiers, 6,000 elite cavalry from Hyderabad, and 100,000 bullocks used to carry their equipment and provisions. Governor Wellesley called it the 'finest army which ever took the field in India'. They arrived outside Tipu's walls on 5 April and began their siege two days later. Tipu fought off his attackers the best he could, firing a barrage of cannons and rockets, but it was little use.

After a month of blasting away at the northern wall of Patan, the British had opened up a breach 100 feet wide, and the first assault on the island city was set for 4 May. As the British officers discussed who should lead the attack, a tall, grizzled Scot insisted that the job was his. It was General Davie Baird, desperate to be the first British soldier to enter the city in which he had been held prisoner all those years ago.

On the morning of the siege, Tipu consulted his astrologers. They recommended that he make a sacrifice of three elephants, two buffaloes, a bullock and a goat. Tipu duly did so, and then inspected his reflection in an iron pot full of oil, hoping it would show his destiny. But regardless of what he saw, his fate was sealed. At 1.30 p.m., General Baird and 4,000 British infantrymen charged across the river, scrambled through the breach and ran into the city.

Tipu was there at the breach ready to oppose them, surrounded by his elite Lion of God battalion. As the red-coated soldiers surged through the breach, Tipu's own servant urged him to surrender. Tipu flung back, 'Are you mad? Be silent!' Instead, he mounted the ramparts and started firing at the British troops, his servant reloading his hunting rifles and passing them to him as if he were on an elephant shoot.

Tipu was soon surrounded by British troops. He received two bayonet wounds to the leg and a bullet to the left breast. A British soldier noticed the gold buckle on his belt and reached to steal it. With a dying swing, Tipu slashed the thief with his sword. Then another British soldier calmly lifted his gun and shot Tipu through the head. The Tiger of Mysore let out his last roar, and fell into a heap of dying men.

It took just an hour for the Company Army to seize control of Patan. That evening, General Baird was taken to the rampart where the great sultan had fallen. By the light of a lantern, he searched through the dead bodies, finally locating Tipu. It was just 300 yards from the prison where Baird had once been held. Baird's companion, Major Alexander Allan, inspected Tipu's corpse and recorded, 'His eyes were open and the body was so warm that for a few moments [we] were doubtful whether he was not alive; on feeling his pulse and heart, that doubt was removed.'

As night fell, the British army rampaged through Patan, and the sultan's palace was stripped of its riches. It was estimated that gold, diamonds, pearls, emeralds and rubies worth some £2 million were looted that night and shared between the Company troops. Governor Wellesley's younger brother

Arthur was given the job of bringing order the next day, which – as he recounted in a letter to his older brother – he did in the usual fashion: 'hanging, flogging, etc. etc.' As for Tipu's pet tigers, Arthur Wellesley had them shot.

The officers of the East India Company would eventually return to Britain with their loot. Today, Tipu's treasures – his clothing, jewellery, weapons and books – are scattered through the country houses and museums of England, Scotland and Wales. At the Victoria and Albert Museum in London, you can see Tipu's mechanical tiger, at Powis Castle in Wales his tiger-shaped cannon, and the golden tiger head of Tipu's throne is now part of the Crown Jewels. When Tipu's body was laid out for his funeral procession, one soldier whipped out a penknife and snipped off the sultan's moustache. The whereabouts of that particular souvenir, however, remains unknown.

Back in Madras, Governor Wellesley wrote to the Minister of War in London: 'The death of the Sultan will probably enable me to gratify your voracious appetite for lands and fortresses . . . Perhaps I may be able to give you a supper of Oudh and the Carnatic [two more independent Indian states], if you should still be hungry.'

After thirty years of defiance and four separate wars, it took just a couple of days for the British to liquidate the glorious riches of the Kingdom of Mysore. Patan was abandoned. Today, it has reverted to its Hindu name, Seringapatam. The enormous fortifications still rise out of the river bed, but where that great island city once stood, there is now just a dusty little town. Cows and goats roam where royal gardens once flowered, and Tipu's palace lies in ruins.

There is, however, one small memorial where Tipu made his last stand. According to legend, as the British pounded away at Patan's walls, the Sultan's advisors suggested that he escape the city via a secret passageway. Tipu refused, choosing to die in the city that he and his father had built. 'One day of life as a Tiger', Tipu is said to have replied, 'is far better than one thousand years of living as a sheep.'

CHAPTER 5
OLAUDAH EQUIANO

The Former Slave Whose Story Shocked the World

There could be few more terrifying prospects for a child than being kidnapped from their home and sent to a strange country, never to see their family again. But this is what happened to Olaudah Equiano at the age of eleven.

Equiano was brought up in a village in what is today southern Nigeria. It sat in a beautiful and fertile valley, where he and his family lived simple but happy lives. Like everyone else in the village, Equiano's parents farmed cows, goats and hens, and grew vegetables. They lived in a hut made of mud, red like the earth on which it stood. Children were bred to be warriors, learning from a young age how to throw a spear or draw a bow so they could defend their village from outsiders.

As the youngest child in a family of seven, Equiano was adored by his mother, who liked to dress him in carved pendants and jewellery. His father was a village chieftain, and Equiano hoped that he might grow up to be a similarly powerful figure. But this was not to be. One day while Equanio's family were working in the fields, he and his sister stayed at home. Three strangers crept into their house, captured them, bound their hands, and stuffed their mouths to prevent them from screaming. From this day onwards, Equiano later wrote, 'an end was put to my happiness'.

Equiano and his sister were marched through the woods. With each corner they turned, they hoped to be turning back to their village. But they were in fact being marched farther and farther away from their family and the life they knew. That night, Equiano and his sister cried themselves to sleep, holding each other in their arms. In the morning, they were separated.

For the next few months, the sun would rise over Equiano's left shoulder as he was marched south. At one point, he was forced into a house full of other captives in which, to his amazement, he saw his sister. Equiano ran into her arms, and they were unable to speak, such was their joy at being reunited. But the reunion was brief. The next day, Equiano and his sister were separated. Equiano would never see a member of his own family again.

After six months of travel, Equiano reached the coast. Having only ever seen water in rivers and lakes, he stared out over the Atlantic Ocean in amazement. Near the shore was a wooden ship, and no sooner had Equiano appreciated the awesome size of this object than he was dragged on board. Here, he saw white men for the first time in his life. With their pale faces and long hair which hung loose to their shoulders, he assumed they were evil spirits. What did they plan to do? Eat him? This was Equiano's fear, until some other captives told him of his fate: he was to be taken to the white man's country, to work as a slave.

That day in 1756, Olaudah Equiano became one of the estimated 13 million Africans transported across the Atlantic to work as slaves in the 'New World' of North and South

America. Slavery has existed throughout human history, but never on such a scale. At this time, European nations such as France, Spain, Portugal and Britain were busy building empires in the Americas. The hot and humid conditions offered the perfect environment for growing tobacco, sugar and coffee. But an endless supply of workers was required to till the fields and harvest the crops. The answer? Capture African people and ship them over the Atlantic to the Americas, by the million.

Equiano's two-month journey across the Atlantic was as close as anyone can imagine to a living hell. The slaves were kept chained below deck on wooden floors, packed so closely they hardly had space to turn. Disease was everywhere. Slaves were left lying in their own waste and vomit, with open wounds and sores forming where their skin rubbed against the bare wood. So repulsive was the stench of these ships, sailors claimed that while at sea you could smell a slave ship before you saw it.

Below deck, Equiano saw young children drown after falling into the tubs of human waste. When he was taken above board to be cleaned and exercised, he saw fellow captives leap overboard in desperation, preferring to sink to the bottom of the Atlantic rather than continue life on board the ship. At night, Equiano's sleep was tormented by the human cargo crying for home and groaning as they died. His only hope was for death to save him from this horror.

But Equiano survived the voyage and arrived at the Caribbean island of Barbados. Here, the slaves were taken off the ship and placed in pens, like sheep in a field. A group of merchants assembled outside the pens. On the beat of a drum, they rushed towards the slaves, manically bidding against each other for the healthiest, strongest and best-looking specimens.

Slaves were forced to jump up and down, were poked and prodded and had their teeth inspected like farmyard animals. But still being a small boy, no merchants bid for Equiano. So he was loaded into another boat and taken to North America, and the British colony of Virginia.

Almost everyone in Virginia was involved in the same trade: growing tobacco to feed the pipes of men and women back in Europe. It was a tobacco plantation owner named Mr Campbell who finally purchased Equiano.

Planting, harvesting and drying tobacco was tough work. At Mr Campbell's plantation, Equiano saw African men, women and children labouring in fields under a ferocious sun. Many had scars across their backs, wounds from the whips that were used to punish those who did not work hard enough, or who showed disobedience. While Mr Campbell and his family lived in a large, English-style mansion on the edge of the plantation, the slaves lived in wooden huts beside the fields.

From sunrise to sunset the slaves laboured, six days a week, every week of the year, with no hope of freedom, until an early death brought on by exhaustion or abuse. All over the Caribbean, North and South America, millions of African slaves were condemned to such an existence: given life imprisonment for no other crime than the colour of their skin and the place of their birth.

However, in Virginia Equiano enjoyed his first turn of good fortune. After a few weeks labouring in the tobacco fields, he was given a job working directly for Mr Campbell inside his mansion. There must have been something special about Equiano, as throughout his life, those who met him were instantly drawn to him. Perhaps it was his character, his intelligence, his sense of humour? Whatever it was, it worked on

Mr Campbell, and it worked on Mr Campbell's friend who came to visit the plantation a short time after Equiano's arrival.

Michael Pascal, a lieutenant in the Royal Navy, offered Mr Campbell £40 to purchase Equiano. Campbell agreed, and soon Equiano was sailing back across the Atlantic Ocean, this time bound for England. The next adventure in his remarkable life was about to begin.

Equiano and his new master arrived in England in the winter of 1754, and war fever was sweeping the nation: Britain was soon to be at war with its old enemy, France. Lieutenant Pascal had originally purchased Equiano as a gift for some of his friends back in England, but when the Seven Years War began in 1756, he decided to take this bright young slave-boy with him to sea. Britain and France both ruled global empires, and as the war travelled around the world, so too did Equiano. Wherever his master's ship was sent, Equiano would be on board.

Life on board a battleship suited Equiano. Sharp as ever, he quickly learnt to speak English, and was a popular figure among the crew who became Equiano's first white friends. African sailors serving in the Royal Navy were a common sight, and Equiano's shipmates treated him as an equal. They taught him how to shave and dress, how to play marbles, and how to read and write.

Equiano was present at some of the major battles of the Seven Years War, fighting the French in Canada in 1758, and off the coast of Portugal the following year. During these battles he worked below deck as a 'powder boy', carrying gunpowder to the cannons as they fired volley after volley at the enemy ships. It was perilous work. If a spark caught Equiano as he carried gunpowder across the ship, he would be blown apart. Enemy cannonballs ripped through the wooden vessel, and Equiano saw many of his friends killed by the splinters, shrapnel and hot metal. But Equiano survived and in 1762, at the age of seventeen, he was promoted to the rank of able seaman.

Lieutenant Pascal could see that Equiano was intelligent. During a break in their fighting in 1759, Pascal sent Equiano to live with cousins in London, who sent him to school, read him the Bible and had him baptised. The care that Pascal provided for Equiano made his betrayal in the winter of 1762 all the more shocking.

The Seven Years War was coming to an end, and Equiano was dreaming of freedom. While the British enslaved millions of African people in their Caribbean and American colonies, slavery was generally understood to be illegal in Britain. When Equiano landed at a naval base outside London called Deptford, he assumed that he had earned his freedom fighting for Britain against France. He was ready to collect his pay and prize money from the Admiralty, pack up his small collection of books and clothing, and start a new life. But when Lieutenant Pascal got wind of Equiano's plans, he stole his pay and prize money from the Admiralty, and forced him back onto a boat on the River Thames.

Equiano screamed at his master that he was a free man and the law protected him from this capture. Equiano's crewmates protested against Pascal's decision, but Pascal carried on regardless. He sailed Equiano down the Thames to Gravesend, where he found a ship bound for the Caribbean. Pascal, who for five years had nurtured Equiano like a son, sold him back into slavery. For the second time in his life, Equiano was crossing the Atlantic in chains. As he later wrote, 'My heart was ready to burst with sorrow and anguish.'

Equiano arrived on the Caribbean island of Montserrat six

weeks later. Lieutenant Pascal had asked the ship's captain to find Equiano a slave master who would treat him well – not much of a parting gift to the friend he had betrayed. True to his word, the captain sold Equiano to Robert King, a businessman from Philadelphia. King owned a fleet of ships that sailed all through the Caribbean and to North America, trading goods from colony to colony. Like many of Philadelphia's inhabitants, King was a Quaker. Quakers belonged to a religious sect which preached the equal moral worth of all human beings, and many were opposed to slavery. As slave owners went, King was decent and humane. He quickly realised that Equiano was literate, educated and keen to learn, as well as being a capable seaman. King assigned Equiano to work for a ship's captain named Thomas Farmer, who would train him as a 'clerk', a sort of secretary carrying out King's business dealings across North America.

Captain Farmer was amazed by Equiano's hard work, and would remark that he was worth more than any three of his white employees put together. Meanwhile, Equiano learnt from Farmer about navigation, mathematics and business. Before long, they were close friends.

Now it must be stressed at this point how unusual Equiano's experience of slavery had become. As a clerk, his work allowed him to travel across the Americas, and when he arrived at a port, Captain Farmer granted him freedom to do as he wished. Equiano was given an education, and even allowed to work for money during his spare time. But he was never able to forget the pain and suffering of his fellow Africans still working in the fields, in particular the brutal sugar plantations that he visited in the Caribbean.

Known as 'white gold', Caribbean sugar was the British Empire's most precious commodity, making five times as much money as tobacco. It was grown on an industrial scale at plantations whose British owners – known as 'Sugar Kings' – amassed extraordinary fortunes. Processing sugar was exhausting work. Slaves toiled beneath the blistering Caribbean sun, cutting the tough, ten-foot-high cane and transporting it to the mill, where it was crushed to release its juice. This juice was then boiled to leave a solid residue of refined sugar, in vats whose fires reached an infernal heat for the slaves who fed them.

Competition amongst plantation owners was fierce, and their profit margins depended upon squeezing the most labour possible out of their enslaved workers. This job was given to white slave drivers known as 'overseers', men described as 'human butchers' by Equiano. Armed with a long whip made of cowhide, they employed every form of cruelty imaginable to ensure slaves worked hard and did not rebel. Overseers burnt onto slaves' skin their owners' initials with red-hot irons, leaving a scar which allowed them to be identified if they ran away. Equiano saw overseers punish runaway slaves by dropping burning wax onto their skin, locking them in a small box for days on end, or even cutting off their limbs.

Equiano saw rebellious slaves punished with an iron muzzle placed around their mouth to prevent talking or eating, and screws wound tight on their thumbs to create excruciating pain. He saw overseers sexually abuse their female slaves, some as young as ten years of age. He witnessed one slave who had attempted to poison his overseer being hanged to within an inch of his life, and then burnt alive.

Such torture was unimaginable, but the petty cruelties of slave life also disgusted Equiano. Slaves would sometimes be permitted to work at jobs in their spare time to make some money, only for the money to be stolen by their overseer. Equiano observed how male slaves often took wives in plantations many miles away from their own. Why? Because if a woman broke the plantation rules and was to be whipped, her own husband could be forced to carry out the punishment.

But what could Equiano do about the suffering he saw? Nothing. All he could do was plan his own freedom.

Travelling across North America and the Caribbean, Equiano soon understood how goods varied in price between the different islands and colonies. During each voyage, Captain Farmer gave Equiano some cargo space on the ship for his own trade, and Equiano – it turned out – was a natural businessman. He bought barrels of pork and live turkeys on the American mainland, and sold them on Caribbean islands where meat was scarce, for three times the price. He bought sugar and rum where it was produced in the Caribbean, and sold it in America. He bought fruits such as lemons and limes on islands where they were plentiful, and sold them on islands where they were scarce. In this way, Equiano gradually turned his pennies into shillings, and shillings into pounds.

Every penny he made, Equiano saved, with the hope that one day he could buy his freedom. It had cost Mr King £40 to buy Equiano in 1763, and King promised Equiano that if he saved the same sum of money, he could effectively buy himself back and become a freedman. In July 1766, Equiano sailed to Philadelphia with his friend Captain Farmer and £47 in his pocket. Equiano arrived at King's office in the bustling port city, praying the businessman would stay true to his word. At first, King did not. 'What! Give you your freedom?' he exclaimed. 'Why, where did you get the money?' Equiano had only been in his employment for three years, he continued, and had he known he would save this money so quickly, he would never have made such a promise!

But Captain Farmer came to the rescue of his friend,

pleading with King: 'Come, come. I think you must let him have his freedom . . . I know Gustavus [Equiano's slave name] has earned you more than a hundred-a-year, and he will save you money, as he will not leave you. Come, Robert, take the money.' And with those words, King agreed. Equiano was overcome with a rush of blissful happiness, recalling that 'these words of my master were like a voice from heaven.'

King sent Equiano to the Philadelphia Register Office, where for the price of one guinea he received his papers declaring that from 11 July 1766 he was a freedman. He later wrote, 'I who had been a slave in the morning, trembling at the will of another, was become my own master, and completely free.'

Free, perhaps, but not equal. While Equiano carried on working for King, he soon realised that life in Britain's colonies could be as dangerous for a freed African as an enslaved African. White colonists still felt they had the right to abuse and torment Equiano, and as a freedman, he did not have an owner who might defend him. The situation was made worse when Equiano's dear friend Captain Farmer, 'mild, affable, generous, faithful, benevolent, and just', fell sick and died on board his ship as it sailed from America to the Caribbean.

In the slave town of Savannah, Georgia, Equiano twice had to talk his way out of being flogged by men who wanted to put this well-dressed, wealthy black man, with ideas above his station, in his place. The final straw was when he was stopped on the road outside Savannah by two white men. They accused him of being a runaway slave, and attempted to kidnap him to sell him back into slavery. Equiano, as he so often could, talked his way out of the situation. But he knew he might not be so lucky the next time.

Equiano realised his only hope for safety was to return to

England, where as a young seaman he would have seen former slaves living as free men and women. On 26 July 1767, he set sail for London, and said goodbye to the slave society he had inhabited for the past decade. 'I bade adieu to the sound of the cruel whip', he later recalled, 'and all other dreadful instruments of torture; adieu to the offensive sight of violated chastity of the sable females, which too often had accosted my eyes; adieu to the oppressions (although to me less severe than most of my countrymen); and adieu to the angry howling.'

After seven weeks at sea, Equiano arrived in London. He began training as a barber, hoping to make an honest living cutting hair. But he craved the adventure of a life at sea. Experienced seamen such as he were always in demand among ship's captains, who would pay handsomely for his skills while paying little attention to the colour of his skin. So, for the next fifteen years, Equiano travelled the world as an able seaman.

Equiano's adventures at sea could be the subject of a whole other story. He crisscrossed the Mediterranean, visiting the great port cities of Nice, Cadiz, Naples, and Smyrna in Turkey, which he admired for its delicious grapes and pomegranates. He sailed back to the Caribbean and Philadelphia, and saw the fine city of New York. He was even involved in a project to establish a new British colony on the shores of Honduras.

There is one of Equiano's adventures from this period which has to be retold. In 1773, he lent his services to an expedition, sponsored by King George III, to find a 'Northern Passage' to India via the Arctic. On 21 May Equiano set sail on board HMS *Racehorse*, along with a crack team of experienced sailors. The *Racehorse* was accompanied by another smaller ship, which included a fourteen-year-old future admiral named Horatio Nelson.

As the *Racehorse* and her crew sailed north, the cold cut through to their bones. Equiano and his shipmates were issued with a pint of brandy a day to keep warm. When they arrived at the Arctic, Equiano marvelled at the beauty of this land where the sun did not set, and where a plain of smooth unbroken ice stretched to the horizon. He saw whales, walruses, seals and polar bears. But the Arctic's beauty soon gave way to danger. Trying to find a passage north through the ice, the *Racehorse* became locked into the ice sheets, unable to move. Stuck in the ice for three days, Equiano was certain that he would die there, frozen and starved to death beside the North Pole. But eventually the ice parted and the *Racehorse* sailed free.

This near-death experience prompted in Equiano a spiritual awakening. Back in London, he became a Methodist, and vowed to lead a better life. Two years later, while moored in the sun-drenched Spanish city of Cadiz, he woke up from his sleep and felt the beams of God's heavenly light break through to his soul. He realised that from the day he was taken from his family in Africa, to that morning in Spain, the invisible hand of God had guided and protected him. In return, Equiano decided that he must abandon his adventures and dedicate his life to helping his fellow man.

By the 1780s, there was a growing campaign in Britain to abolish the slave trade, and ultimately slavery itself. Many of the campaigners, known as abolitionists, were Christians who saw slavery as opposed to Jesus' teaching that all humans are of equal worth in the eyes of God.

Equiano was one of an estimated 20,000 people of African descent in Britain at this time, the great majority living as free men and women. Clearly, the British people were willing to enjoy the benefits of slavery provided they did not have to witness its cruelties first hand. They ate their sugared sweets, sipped their warm coffee and smoked their Virginia tobacco without having to consider the African blood across the ocean that had been shed to produce such luxuries.

Equiano now realised his calling in life: to confront the people of Britain with the truth about slavery, so they could ignore the issue no longer. In London, he led a small group of freed slaves who campaigned for abolition, calling themselves the 'Sons of Africa'. By writing letters and articles for newspapers, Equiano and the Sons of Africa gained national attention. Equiano soon achieved fame as an energetic and fearless campaigner. He wrote in defence of marriage between black and white couples, an idea which was out of the question for many – abolitionists included – during this period. In March 1788, he even presented a petition to Queen Charlotte, the wife of King George III, calling on her 'benevolence and bounty' to add her support to the abolition of slavery in the West Indies.

Encouraged by his successes, Equiano decided what the abolitionist campaign needed was a genuine African voice revealing, through first-hand testimony, the true horror of slavery. So, from his house at 53 Baldwin's Gardens in Holborn, London, Equiano set about writing his memoirs.

All the events of Equiano's life about which you have been reading – his capture in West Africa, his twice being sold into slavery, his work in the Caribbean, his return to England as a freedman – were set down on paper. And running through his whole life story was an urgent moral message: 'Tortures, murder, and every other imaginable barbarity and iniquity, are practised upon the poor slaves with impunity. I hope the slave trade will be abolished. I pray it may be an event at hand.'

The Interesting Narrative of the Life of Olaudah Equiano, The African was published in April 1789. On the front page was a portrait of Equiano, dressed in the fine clothes of an English gentleman. His eyes looked out at the reader with intelligence and humanity, and his hand held a Bible open at Acts 4:12: 'Salvation is found in no one else, for there is no other name under heaven given to mankind by which we must be saved.'

The book was a sensation. Reviewers marvelled at the accomplishment of Equiano's writing, and this was a great part of its power. A year previously, Equiano had entered into an argument with a writer for the *Morning Chronicle* who defended slavery on the basis that Africans were mentally inferior to Europeans, claiming that as a people they sat somewhere 'between the Monkeys and the Whites'. But here, with Equiano's memoirs, was a son of Africa whose abilities as an author equalled those of any European.

The first run of 500 copies sold out within a year, and over the following five years nine more editions were published, each printed in their thousands. As was common for new authors during this period, Equiano paid for the first print run himself. To raise the money required, he asked potential readers to pay for the book in advance. The list of subscribers survives today, and includes many famous politicians, inventors, businessmen, the Bishop of London, and none other than the Prince of Wales. Editions were printed in Scotland, Ireland, Holland, Germany and America. Equiano's life story was an international sensation.

For the next three years, Equiano toured the British Isles, selling his book from town to town, city to city. A shrewd businessman, he offered a discount for any customer buying six copies or more, and had a deluxe edition printed 'on fine paper, at a moderate advance of price'. In every place he visited – from Derby to Dundee, Bristol to Belfast – he was met with ready customers for his books and halls full of listeners, eager to hear the great man himself talk. During this time Equiano found fame, but he also found love, in the form of Susan Cullen from the picturesque Cambridgeshire village of Soham.

Equiano was famous enough for his marriage to Susan to be announced in the national press. On 19 April 1792, the *General Evening Post* reported: 'Olaudah Equiano, the African, well known in England as the champion and advocate for procuring a suppression of the Slave Trade, was married at Soham, in Cambridgeshire, to Miss Cullen, daughter of Mr. Cullen of Ely, in the same County, in the presence of a vast number of people.' The following year Susan and Olaudah had their first child, Ann Mary, and two years later their second, Joanna.

Equiano's entire life had become living proof that those who defended slavery on the basis of African people's inferiority were wrong. Here was a former African slave, now bestselling author, living the life of a wealthy gentleman with his English wife and two mixed-race daughters. And even though many critics attacked Equiano's marriage and dismissed his book as lies, Equiano embraced his role as a public figure without fear.

But did his book achieve its goal? Did Equiano live to see the slave trade – which had ripped him and millions of others away from their families to be taken over the Atlantic Ocean – abolished? No. He died on 31 March 1797, aged fifty-one. Had he lived ten more years, Equiano would have seen Parliament abolish the Atlantic slave trade in 1807. Slavery itself was only abolished in the British Empire in 1833.

In his will Equiano left his surviving daughter, Joanna, an inheritance of £950 and a silver watch, probably given to him as a reward for his role in the North Pole expedition. At the time of his death Equiano was, it is thought, the wealthiest man of African descent in Europe.

Sadly, Equiano's fame did not outlast his death. His work was forgotten over the next century, only to be rediscovered by historians in the past fifty years. However, one historian researching Equiano's life has cast doubt on whether Equiano was really, as he claimed, born in Africa. In the records of St Margaret's Church where Equiano was baptised in 1759, his birthplace was recorded as Carolina (the tobacco-producing colony in America). In 1773, when he set sail for the North Pole on HMS *Racehorse*, he recorded his place of birth as 'South Carolina'.

Does this mean that Equiano's account of his upbringing and capture in West Africa, and his subsequent voyage across the Atlantic, was made up? Perhaps. It is possible that he invented this part of his life so that his memoirs would have more impact, revealing the horrors of the Atlantic passage to his readers.

However, if this was the case, Equiano would still have based his account on the countless true stories he heard from fellow slaves of the hell they suffered on that journey. And even if Equiano did not experience it himself, some 13 million African people did. Through his writing, Equiano allowed that experience to be known.

The transatlantic slave trade was one of the most horrific assaults on human dignity the world has ever seen. Whatever the truth behind Equiano's upbringing, nobody can deny the significance of his life. His memoir was the first to reveal to British readers the true misery of the trade in human cargo on which the wealth of their empire was based. Today, it remains a definitive statement of the yearning of all humans to be free.

As Equiano wrote while remembering his treatment in the American colonies, 'I would sooner die like a free man, than suffer myself to be scourged by the hands of ruffians, and my blood drawn like a slave.'

CHAPTER 6

MARY
WOLLSTONECRAFT

The Free-spirit Feminist
Who Invented Women's Rights

In 1784, Newington Green was one of the most popular gathering places in England for social misfits and political radicals. A village on the northeastern edge of London, it had a small chapel beside a pretty green, surrounded by handsome family homes. Within these houses flourished a remarkable community of freethinkers, none more so than a fiery young teacher and writer named Mary Wollstonecraft.

Like many residents of Newington Green, Mary was committed to leading an alternative lifestyle. She did not eat meat, and was opposed to the time and money Georgian women spent on their appearance. Refusing the tyranny of whalebone corsets and white face powder, Mary wore a plain dress, black woollen socks and a beaver hat, with her hair hanging loose over her shoulders. A passing visitor to Newington Green may well have mistaken her for the local milkmaid, until they engaged her in conversation, at which point they would have discovered a woman of extraordinary intelligence and learning.

Mary ran a small girls' school from a townhouse on the edge of the Green, where she lived alongside her best friend

Fanny and her two younger sisters. It was an unusual experiment in communal female living, which suited Mary well. She knew married life was not for her. As she wrote to a friend a few years earlier, she did not want 'a husband and half a hundred children at hand to tease and control a poor woman who wishes to be free'.

It is little surprise that Mary had reached such a conclusion, for the men who had populated her life so far were a miserable succession of bullies, brutes and scumbags. First there was Mary's father, a violent drunk named Edward. He inherited a considerable fortune of £10,000 from his father, who had made his money in the silk-weaving trade of London's East End. However, Edward aspired to leave the mucky world of London workshops and become a gentleman farmer, so he moved the Wollstonecraft family to live in the Essex village of Epping.

Unfortunately, Edward was a bad businessman and an even worse farmer. Each time he moved to a new farm, his business would fail, forcing him to move his family to a yet smaller farm, farther from London, to start over. First to Epping, then to Barking, then to Yorkshire and finally to Wales. Mary had the lonely childhood of a girl on the road. While other children played with their friends, she spent days alone in her garden or nearby woods, talking with imaginary angels.

Perhaps it was Edward's failure to succeed as a member of the rural gentry that led him to take out his anger on his wife. As a child, Mary would sleep on the landing to prevent her father from reaching her mother when he arrived home late at night, blind drunk, full of rage, fists clenched.

Even though she sought to protect her, Mary had little respect for her mother, a petite Irishwoman named Elizabeth.

While Mary was outspoken and rebellious, Elizabeth was meek, turned into a shadow of herself by years of violent abuse. What is more, she showered love and attention on her eldest son, Ned, leaving Mary feeling neglected.

Mary could not stand the differing values her parents applied to her brother simply because he had been born a boy, as she later recalled: 'What was called spirit and wit in him, was cruelly repressed as forwardness in me.' To make matters worse, Ned was a bullying older brother, who took pleasure in tormenting and humbling his outspoken younger sister.

The only happiness Mary found within her family were her two younger sisters, Eliza and Everina, to whom she became something of a second mother. In October 1782, Mary's nineteen-year-old sister Eliza married Meredith Bishop, a boat-builder from the Thameside village of Bermondsey. At first, Mary was happy for Eliza, describing Meredith as 'a worthy man' from a 'truly eligible situation'. However, ten months after the wedding, having given birth to a baby girl, Eliza began to have violent, uncontrollable panic attacks.

Meredith was unable to deal with his young wife and asked Mary for help. When Mary arrived at the family home in Bermondsey, she wasted no time in concluding that Meredith was a rotten piece of work, who was making violent demands for sexual gratification from her sister. Mary took charge of the situation and began planning Eliza's escape. One day in January 1784, when Meredith was away from home, Mary and Eliza caught a coach to central London, and then east to the village of Hackney, where they took lodgings under false names.

The only problem was that Eliza had left her baby girl in Bermondsey. Perhaps Mary convinced Eliza that they would win her daughter back at a later date, but this was not to be. Eight months after Eliza's escape, her baby girl died, just short of her first birthday. Eliza was never able to say goodbye, and was highly unlikely ever to remarry. Mary's father and brother, who were always suspicious of their wild-child daughter and sister, never forgave Mary for – in their eyes – destroying Eliza's family and ruining her chances of a happy life.

But Mary was unfazed. Her growing resentment against men and marriage only gained further confirmation a few years later from the experiences of her best friend Fanny. Mary and Fanny had met as teenagers and developed an intense friendship. Like Mary, Fanny was the product of an abusive father and a browbeaten mother. But while Mary was spikey and argumentative, Fanny was elegant and charming, and a talented artist. From the moment they met, Mary wanted to spend her life with Fanny. As she wrote to a friend, 'The roses will bloom when there's peace in the breast, and the prospect of living with my Fanny gladdens my heart: You know not how I love her.'

However, there was one major obstacle to Mary's plans: an Irish businessman named Hugh Skeys, who had proposed to Fanny when she was a teenager. Luckily for Mary, Skeys was a feckless fiancé, and kept Fanny waiting for almost ten years before they married, as he tried to make his fortune living abroad in Lisbon.

Thus, in 1784, Mary and her companions found themselves living in their Newington Green townhouse: the formerly married, the yet-to-be-married and the never-to-be-married (or so she liked to claim). However, it was not to last.

Things began to fall apart when Skeys summoned Fanny to Portugal in January 1785, so that they could finally marry. However, Fanny was unwell from the moment she arrived in

Lisbon. By that November, Fanny's health was still in decline, and now she was due to give birth, so Mary travelled to Portugal to be by her best friend's side. Her arrival was not enough to spur a recovery. Fanny gave birth that December, but within days both she and the baby were dead.

A distraught Mary had to mourn the love of her life on a perilous sea voyage from Lisbon back to London, through raging February storms. When she reached London, she was faced with yet another spectacle of female suffering: the notorious prostitutes of London's docklands falling upon the travellers and sailors in a desperate attempt to turn a few pennies. In her later writing, Mary described the 'vulgarity, dirt, and vice' of the London docks as a 'complicated misery' which 'sickened' her soul.

Back in Newington Green, Mary's school had fallen apart, and the venture was quickly wound up. For the next year, Mary worked as a governess for Lord and Lady Kingsborough, one of the wealthiest families in Ireland. She lived with them in their magnificent home of Mitchelstown Castle, near Cork, teaching and supervising their large brood of children.

However, Mary's Irish sojourn did not last long, ending with a spectacular falling out between her and Lady Kingsborough, who (wrongly) accused Mary of trying to seduce her husband. Mary returned to London in the summer of 1787 with a fresh hatred of the aristocracy but a new love for Ireland, even though 'the men', according to one of her later letters, 'are dreadful flirts'.

Twenty-eight, unmarried and penniless, Mary had few prospects. However, before leaving for Ireland, she had penned a modestly successful book on female education, entitled *Thoughts on the Education of Daughters*. It was published by Joseph Johnson, London's leading radical bookseller. When she returned to London, Mary headed immediately to Johnson's shop in St Paul's Yard, hoping to find help. It would prove to be one of the best decisions she ever made.

Johnson, a gentle soul, was the first decent man to enter Mary's life. As a short, shy, asthmatic bachelor of forty-nine, he was surprisingly unassuming for a man of such radical convictions. His books backed the boldest ideas of the day: female emancipation, religious toleration, the abolition of slavery, the reform of Parliament.

In Mary's fierce intelligence and hatred of injustice, Johnson saw something he could nurture. He set her up in a house south of the River Thames at 45 George Street where she could live rent free, lent her a modest sum of money to rebuild her life, and arranged for her bills and housework to be taken care of – even offering his own cousin as a maid. In return, Mary dedicated her prolific pen to Johnson's publishing business, contributing to the growing demand for books and journals aimed at children and female readers.

The arrangement was a perfect basis for Mary's growing ambition to carve out a career as a female author, something almost unheard of in eighteenth-century England. As she declared in a letter to her sister Everina, 'I am going to be the first of a new genus.' Her letter continued, 'You know I am not born to tread in the beaten track: the peculiar bent of my nature pushes me on.'

These were some of Mary's most productive years. She even embarked on her first love affair, with one of the most notable members of bohemian London: a bisexual Swiss writer, artist and creator of pornographic paintings named Henry Fuseli. Eighteen years her senior, Fuseli was married, a bit of a rogue and entirely (but wrongly) convinced of his own genius. However, he was great company, and his outrageous conversation, fired out in a heavy Germanic accent, must have entertained Mary.

Thankfully, Mary did not let her love affair with Fuseli distract her too much from her work. She wrote intensely, churning out children's books, a novel, and translations of foreign works (having taught herself French, Italian and German). Mary had only ever received a few years' education in a village school in Yorkshire, but she was a committed self-educator, always reading, always learning.

However, in every historic life, hard work alone is not enough: a large dose of luck is also required to achieve greatness. It was Mary's good fortune to embark on a career as a radical writer just two years before the biggest rupture in the history of modern Europe: the French Revolution.

In the summer of 1789, the people of France rose up on the streets of Paris, seized power from their hopeless monarch Louis XVI, and began demanding social and political reform. British radicals such as Mary and her Newington Green set were exhilarated by these events. As the Romantic poet William Wordsworth wrote, 'Bliss was it in that dawn to be alive. But to be young was very heaven!'

One of the great heroes of British radicalism at the time was Dr Richard Price, the minister at Newington Green Chapel. Price was a dreamer who believed it was possible to remake politics and society based on reason and justice instead of tradition and hierarchy. He wanted to see humankind build heaven on Earth, and his ideas had an enormous impact on the young Mary.

On 4 November 1789, Price delivered a sermon in central London, claiming that the British people, instead of fearing the French Revolution, should embrace its ideas. 'I see the ardour for liberty catching and spreading,' he proclaimed.

'The dominion of kings changed for the dominion of laws, and the dominion of priests giving way to the dominion of reason and conscience.'

Price's sermon sparked a war of words with a Member of Parliament named Edmund Burke, who saw radicalism and revolution as a catastrophic threat to the stability of Great Britain. The French Revolution, Burke wrote, was trying to change too much too fast, and could only end in bloodshed. A fierce national debate had begun, and the radical publisher of St Paul's Yard, Joseph Johnson, wanted in on the action. Who could he employ to smash out a response to Burke? Why, his young protégée Mary Wollstonecraft, of course!

Nobody in London could write with Mary's speed and passion. In less than a month, she had finished her book. It was entitled *A Vindication of the Rights of Men*.

Mary's defence of her hero Dr Richard Price sold well, but was overshadowed a few months later when Thomas Paine, the most famous radical writer in the English-speaking world, published his almost identically titled book, *Rights of Man*. In response, Joseph Johnson suggested that Mary should write a second book, with the same title as her previous work, save for one small change: *A Vindication of the Rights of Woman*. It was a book that only Mary could write, and would prove to be her masterpiece.

Again, Mary wrote in a frenzy, pouring thirty years of anger, hurt and frustration at the hands of male domination into 300 pages of pure, unfiltered Wollstonecraft. She delivered her manuscript to Johnson in just six weeks. The book was a sensation.

It is worth remembering just how limited women's lives were at the time that *Rights of Woman* was published. Women were not allowed to vote, attend university, or pursue any professional career aside from teaching. Married women had no legal status: from her wedding day onwards, everything a wife owned or earned was the property of her husband. Divorce was almost impossible, particularly if the wife wanted to separate. Among the lower classes, it was not uncommon to see men selling unwanted wives at the local market.

In opposition to such a society, *Rights of Woman* set out a new vision. Mary argued that women are not naturally subordinate to men – the 'weaker sex', to use a term that would later become popular – but are made so by society. She imagined a society where women could pursue careers, choose marriage partners and own property on the same basis as men. And for this revolution to be achieved, Mary believed that education was the key. Drawing on her own experience as a teacher, she claimed that if women's subordination to men was created by society, it could be undone by schooling.

Like her hero Dr Price, Mary dreamt of a perfect society. The unhappy marriages she witnessed growing up – her abused mother, her traumatised sister, her neglected best friend – would no longer occur, she claimed, if men and women could marry as equal partners in a relationship. While wives remained dependent upon their husbands for financial support, marriage would remain, in one of Mary's most famous phrases, 'legal prostitution'.

To those critics who claimed Mary was trying to replace male domination with female, she answered, 'I do not wish [women] to have power over men; but over themselves.'

A Vindication of the Rights of Woman was well received for such a radical book. Of course, Mary had her critics. The politician and writer Horace Walpole described her as a 'hyena in petticoats'. But others were more favourable. Women, in particular, found Mary's words electrifying. In a letter to her husband, the aristocratic Lady Palmerston teased: 'I have been reading *The Rights of Woman*, so you must in future expect me to be very tenacious of my rights and privileges.'

Mary was now the talk of the town, and success suited her. Many commented on how her appearance, often described as plain during her twenties, now blossomed in her thirties. She even had her portrait painted, and – putting aside her objections to female beautification – had her hair powdered and her face made up.

However, Mary's heyday was short-lived. As a writer, she had pinned her reputation on the success of the French Revolution. But during the summer of 1792, events across the Channel darkened. Extreme revolutionaries were taking control in Paris, and unleashing chaos. King Louis XVI was arrested; the monarchy was abolished; Catholic churches were ransacked for gold and silver; and those suspected of opposing the revolution – clergymen, aristocrats, foreign nationals – were massacred by the thousand. The infamous era of the guillotine, the Revolution's neck-slicing execution machine, had begun.

Public opinion in Britain turned almost overnight. Radicals who had supported the Revolution, including many of Mary's friends, were attacked in the streets, their homes burnt to the ground. Effigies of Thomas Paine were burnt, and there was talk that Mary Wollstonecraft would be next.

However, Mary was not the type to admit she had been wrong. Instead, she doubled down on her support for the Revolution, declaring that she would travel to Paris and take part in its events herself. This was a remarkably bold decision. At a time when most foreign nationals were trying to escape Paris, here was someone, a single woman no less, planning to go the other way.

Mary arrived in Paris on 11 December 1792, the same day

that Louis XVI was put on trial for treason. From the window of the apartment where she was staying, she watched Louis being taken to his trial along the street outside, empty apart from patrolling soldiers.

Revolutionary France scared Mary much more than she expected, and during her first month she hardly left her rooms. From her writing desk, she hallucinated bloody hands shaking at her, and eyes glaring through the glass door. For the first time in her life, she slept with a candle lit beside her bed.

Thankfully, matters improved for Mary at the start of 1793, as she began socialising with other English radicals living in Paris and some of the Revolution's leading politicians. It was through this social circle that Mary met the man who would change her life for ever.

Gilbert Imlay was a tall, handsome American with an easy-going charm. He had fought in the American Revolution, written an atrocious novel, and was now trying to make his fortune as a businessman. Thirty-nine years old and unmarried, he was a lifelong chancer. Despite all that she knew about the cruelty of men such as Imlay, Mary was about to make a dreadful mistake. Sometime in the spring of 1793, she fell in love.

That February, the French government had declared war on Britain and banned British nationals from leaving the country. This left Mary trapped in France, and treated with increasing suspicion by the revolutionary government. She needed emotional support, and that was what Imlay offered. He told her of his dream to return to America having made his fortune, and build a farm on the nation's enormous, untamed frontier. Mary fooled herself into thinking she might play a part in this future.

Sometime that summer, they made love. Though Mary had

enjoyed many flirtations, she was probably still a virgin at the age of thirty-four. In her delirious letters to Imlay, she thanks him for the 'sensations that are almost too sacred to be alluded to'. Mary adored her American man, telling him 'my heart whispers that you are one of the best creatures in the world.' In reality, he was a cad.

That August, Mary realised she was pregnant. Right on cue, Imlay lost all interest in her. They lived together in Paris for a few weeks before Imlay moved to Le Havre on the Normandy coast 'on business', leaving Mary pregnant and alone. The letters she wrote to her absent lover that autumn tell the tragic story of a great woman brought low by love for a man so inferior to her in both intellect and character. They turn from breathless declarations of love to desperate cries for attention.

Mary spent Christmas without Imlay, writing to him in January 1794, 'I am hurt by the person most dear to me.' That month, she finally gave in, and turned up uninvited in Le Havre. No sooner had she arrived, however, than Imlay claimed to have business back in Paris, leaving Mary alone once again.

Imlay did return to Le Havre for the birth of his child in May. Mary had an easy labour, and named her daughter Fanny, in honour of her best friend who had died nine years before. However, her hope that fatherhood would bring Imlay back to her side were dashed when he announced, in August, that he was moving to London.

Proud Mary held out for another year in France. Then, in the spring of 1795, she returned to London. The French Revolution, once so full of promise, had ended in chaos. What was more, Mary's personal life seemed to be living proof of the faults in her theories. How painfully ironic to find herself,

Europe's most outspoken critic of male domination and marriage, in love with a man who refused to make her his wife. Both Mary's life and her ideas lay in tatters. Sometime that May, it all proved too much to bear. She wrote to Imlay telling him 'I am nothing', took an overdose of laudanum and fell unconscious.

Thankfully, Mary was found before it was too late, and recovered. Her suicide attempt was a cry for help, which Imlay did – in his own selfish way – decide to answer. A Norwegian captain had recently stolen the cargo from one of Imlay's ships, and he needed someone to visit Sweden and Norway to gain compensation. Only a scoundrel like Imlay could ask a new mother, recovering from a suicide attempt, to investigate his overseas business venture. But Mary, still loyal to the man who spurned her, was only too keen to help.

Mary packed her bags and left for Scandinavia that summer. She proved to be a natural traveller: friendly to strangers, curious about other cultures, and able to put up with hardships on the road (even with a one-year-old child in tow). As well as pursuing Imlay's compensation, she explored Scandinavia's culture and natural beauty, writing Imlay long letters about its woods and waterfalls, its political situation and strange local customs.

Mary hoped her trip to Scandinavia was a test, which if completed successfully would finally win back Imlay's heart. However, when she returned to London that October and visited his house, she discovered he was now living with another woman, a young actress no less. Overcome with grief, Mary returned home and wrote to Imlay in what she claimed would be her last ever letter. 'Soon, very soon shall I be at peace. When you receive this, my burning head will be cold.'

She handed the letter to a servant, left her daughter with a nurse, and walked out into the rainy night.

As she set off down the Thames, Mary allowed her dress to soak through to her skin. When she reached Putney Bridge, she walked halfway along, clambered over its rickety wooden railing and looked down at the cold, dark Thames below. Her clothing heavy with rain and clinging to her skin, she jumped. Gasping and choking in the winter water, Mary pushed the air out of her layers of clothing so that she might sink to the river bed more quickly.

However, two watermen had seen Mary jump, and their boat reached her before she sank. They heaved her out of the water and took her to a nearby pub, where a doctor was called. Proud to a fault, Mary was disappointed at being saved. In a letter to Imlay, she regretted returning to the 'living death' that was her life, and defended her suicide attempt as 'one of the calmest acts of reason'.

Thank God her act failed. Mary would live for two more years, enough time for a final cycle of joy and despair. At the beginning of 1796, she wrote to Imlay asking him to return all the letters she had sent him from Scandinavia. He obliged, and Mary packaged them up into a new book, *Letters Written During a Short Residence in Sweden, Norway, and Denmark*. These letters told an intensely emotional story, that of a solitary woman on a doomed mission to regain her wayward lover's heart, amongst the foreboding beauty of Scandinavia's wilderness. In its windswept coast and thundering waterfalls she found a reflection of her own disordered mind, whilst in its fishing villages and hillsides of tinkering cowbells, she found repose.

This was the age of literary Romanticism, and Mary's willingness to lay bare her soul, coupled with her evocations of Scandinavia's natural beauty, was bang on trend. Though not

so famous today, in her lifetime Mary's Scandinavian travelogue was by far her most popular work. One of the book's
admirers was a famous philosopher and political radical named
William Godwin, who wrote, 'If ever there was a book calculated to make a man in love with its author, this appears to
me to be the book.'

Godwin had not always felt this way about Mary. They had
met some years before at a dinner party thrown by Joseph
Johnson at St Paul's Yard, and had spent the whole evening
arguing about the existence of God. Godwin was a committed
atheist, Mary a strong Christian. By the end of the dinner,
their hatred was mutual.

However, four years later, Godwin was ready to reconsider
his opinion. With typical forwardness, Mary turned up at his
house in the bohemian enclave of Somers Town, north of
London, one April morning, saying she wanted to lend him
a copy of Rousseau's most recent novel. Of course, she had
other intentions.

The door was answered by a bald, bookish man, forty years
of age, who had spent most of his life too immersed in philosophy to think about women. However, as two of the greatest
minds of their generation, Mary and Godwin found an immediate connection. After their first night together, he wrote to
her, 'I see nothing in you but what I respect and adore.' In
another letter, he instructed her: 'Be happy. Resolve to be
happy. You deserve to be so.'

Compared to dashing, handsome Imlay, Godwin was a bit
of a geek. But the relationship was not without passion. In
November, Mary wrote to thank him for the previous night,
adding 'I have seldom seen so much live fire running about
my features as this morning.' A month later, she realised that
she was pregnant.

Godwin was in a tricky position. As one of Britain's most famous social critics, he was well known for his opposition to marriage. But Mary, about to become a mother for the second time, now craved the reassurance of marriage vows. Godwin put his theoretical principles to one side, and on 29 March 1797 they married. So began the last few months of Mary's life, a brief period of domestic tranquillity, as she and Godwin readied themselves for the arrival of their first child.

Having given birth so easily to Fanny, Mary was confident that all would go well next time round. However, her second birth was a slow and painful process, followed by a panicked realisation that the placenta had not been delivered. This was a potential death sentence, as a retained placenta would prevent a new mother's womb from contracting, causing her to bleed to death. Godwin called for a doctor, who worked through the night, trying to remove all remaining traces of the placenta from Mary's womb.

At first, Mary seemed to recover. She and Godwin spent a happy few days getting to know their new daughter, named Mary after her mother. However, when Godwin went for a walk with friends a week later, he returned home to find Mary as white as a sheet, her teeth chattering, and her body convulsing so violently that the bed shook beneath her. In removing her placenta, the doctor had introduced a blood infection. Over the next few days, her condition worsened. She was dying.

True to her character, Mary told anyone who would listen that she was going to overcome her fever through sheer force of will, but her condition only got worse. How cruel that Mary, who had twice tried to take her own life, was now fighting with such desperation to hang on. As Mary was dying, she and Godwin at least found time to share one last joke about their longstanding disagreement on religion. 'Oh Godwin, I am in heaven,' she claimed from her bed. 'You mean, my dear, that your symptoms are a little easier,' he replied.

Mary held on for a week, as Godwin looked on in helpless agony. On Sunday morning, he rose at six o'clock and sat by her bed. At twenty to eight, she died. Godwin was an emotional wreck, unable even to attend her funeral.

To overcome his grief, Godwin set about writing a memoir of Mary's life. He naively believed that if he told her life as honestly as he could, including all her foreign adventures, suicide attempts and love affairs, the public would realise what an extraordinary woman she was. In a tragedy of good intentions, his book had exactly the opposite effect.

By the late 1790s, social attitudes in Britain were hardening. War with France, and the disastrous course of the French Revolution, had led to a resurgence in conservative ideas about social issues such as equality between the sexes. In this context, Godwin's memoirs of Mary secured her reputation not as a visionary, but as an irresponsible and deeply misguided firebrand.

As for Mary's daughters, their two lives demonstrated the two sides of her troubled existence. Fanny Imlay was adopted by Godwin, but remained a lost soul, dying alone in an inn in Swansea at the age of twenty-two having taken a fatal overdose of laudanum. However, Mary Godwin became a celebrated novelist. In fact, she features later in this book under the name Mary Shelley, holidaying with Lord Byron in northern Italy, where she helped to create the gothic genre of literature with her novel *Frankenstein*.

It would take another century before Mary Wollstonecraft's reputation was rescued by a new generation of feminist writers. From today's perspective, we see a woman of extraordinary courage and convictions, able to articulate a world of equality between the sexes that most of her contemporaries could not even imagine. Mary began a campaign to empower one half of the human race that, up to that point in human history, had been largely silent. That the battles she began are still being fought so fiercely today only goes to show how far-sighted her vision really was.

CHAPTER 7
LADIES OF LLANGOLLEN

Two Lovers Who Built Paradise
in a Welsh Valley

Sarah Ponsonby and Eleanor Butler were born into the cream of Irish society, so-called – according to one Irish wit – because it was 'rich and thick'. However, unlike the families into which they were born, Sally (as Sarah was known) and Eleanor were clever, free-spirited and unconventional. They were also, some historians have suggested, one of Britain's first openly lesbian couples.

Sally came from a powerful clan of Irish aristocrats called the Ponsonbys, but never really knew her parents. She was orphaned at the age of seven and left in the care of her step-mother and a half-brother, who cared more for each other than for her. These lonely years, Sally later recalled, were ones of gloom and despair. When Sally was thirteen, her stepmother died, leaving her entirely alone.

A distant cousin named Lady Betty Fownes agreed to take Sally into her home in southern Ireland, a beautiful mansion called Woodstock nestled in a valley beside the River Nore. At first, Sally enjoyed her new life. She was sent to school twelve miles away in Kilkenny and was a good student. Lady Betty was a loving carer. Her own daughter, also called Sally, had recently married and moved away, so Lady Betty trans-ferred her motherly affection fo this sad, lonely orphan.

Unfortunately, Lady Betty was unwell, and not long for this world. Sometime around 1776, her husband, a powerful poli-tician named Sir William Fownes, began casting around for a replacement wife once Lady Betty died. Having only recently turned fifty, he still fancied himself as a bit of a looker, and his eye landed on the pretty young orphan who had shared his house for the past seven years. Sally Ponsonby had just turned twenty-one.

Needless to say, Sally was disgusted by Sir William's advances. Trapped under the same roof as this creep, she became desperate to escape, and turned to her closest friend and soulmate, Eleanor Butler, for help.

Eleanor was sixteen years older than Sally, and a very different character. Where Sally was mild and well-mannered, Eleanor was sarcastic and prickly. As a young girl, she had received a first-class education at a Catholic convent in northern France, where the nuns introduced her to the world of literature, history and philosophy. This gave her a passion for learning, and a love of all things French.

Having become something of an intellectual, Eleanor received a rude shock when she returned to rural Ireland. An outspoken and well-educated young woman with a masculine appearance (though Sally thought her 'uncommonly hand-some'), Eleanor struggled on the marriage market. By the age of thirty-seven, she was a confirmed spinster, and generally seen by her parents as a dead weight on the family fortune.

It was a fortune that Eleanor's family, the Butlers, were desperate to rebuild. They lived in Kilkenny Castle, a grey and gloomy Norman structure which loomed over the town. Its interior had been unchanged for centuries, the ancient portraits, moth-eaten tapestries and wall-mounted weapons speaking of the family's former glory.

The Butlers had once been one of the most powerful aristocratic families in Ireland, descended from – it was said – the butler who accompanied King Henry I of England on his invasion of Ireland during the twelfth century. However, unusually for Irish aristocrats, the Butlers had remained Catholic after the English monarchy turned Protestant. As a punishment, they had their titles and privileges removed, and their fortune went into decline.

Eleanor's father was plain old Mr Butler, having been stripped of his title as Earl of Ormonde. He was a brutish sort of a man whose interests included hunting, whoring and playing cards, so he was generally baffled by his bookworm daughter, with her fancy ideas and French turns of phrase. Having failed to marry her off to a rich husband, Butler declared that Eleanor should return to France, enter a convent and live out the rest of her days as a nun. Eleanor could not bear this idea, and began to suffer from migraines, nightmares and panic attacks which continued for the rest of her life.

Looking with horror at the futures their families planned for them, both Eleanor and Sally began to work out an escape. They had met when Sally was at school in Kilkenny and Lady Betty asked Mrs Butler whether Eleanor could keep an eye on her adopted child. Despite the age gap, Sally and Eleanor bonded, particularly over their shared love of books. Their relationship grew stronger with every passing year, and they came to realise that their only chance of living happy lives was to live together.

On Tuesday 30 March 1778, Lady Betty and Sir William awoke to find that Sally had disappeared from Woodstock. In the dead of night, she had dressed in men's clothes, armed herself with a pistol, scooped up her pet dog Frisk, and climbed out of the parlour window. From there, she made her way to a barn on the edge of the estate. Waiting in the barn was Eleanor, who earlier that night had sneaked out of Kilkenny Castle, also dressed in men's clothes, stolen a horse, and ridden to Woodstock.

After their rendezvous, Eleanor and Sally rode twenty-three miles to the port of Waterford, where they planned to catch the next ship to England and there start a new life. However, they missed the boat, and spent the following night hiding in a barn on the edge of town.

Sir William of Woodstock and Mr Butler of Kilkenny Castle both mobilised search parties to find their runaway girls. Sir William's men got there first, discovering the couple in a carriage just outside Waterford, given away – it was claimed – by the yapping of Sally's dog. Lady Betty was sent for and arrived in a coach later that day, ready to bring Sally home to Woodstock. Having caught a dreadful cold during her night in the barn, Sally was willing to follow Lady Betty's command, providing that Eleanor could come with her.

Lady Betty agreed, only for the Butler search party – led by Eleanor's brother-in-law – to arrive just in time to reclaim her. Eleanor begged and pleaded not to be separated from Sally, but her captors would not listen. Half fainting with emotion, Eleanor was bundled into a carriage and taken to her brother-in-law's estate to be kept under his watchful eye, while her furious family worked out what to do next.

Both families were relieved by the fact that no men were involved in the escape, but also confused. Did Sally and Eleanor plan to escape together? If so, what exactly was their relationship? Were they just very good friends? Or was there something more *physical* going on? It was a question that would freak out their families, fascinate Georgian society, and be debated by historians for centuries to come. Were Sally Ponsonby and Eleanor Butler one of the first lesbian couples documented in British history?

Slowly, Sir William and Lady Betty started to realise the depths of Eleanor and Sally's friendship and listened to their wishes. However, the brutish Butlers were unwilling to risk the horrendous embarrassment this could cause their family: for a spinster daughter to elope was bad enough, but with another woman? Gadzooks! They commanded Eleanor to remain at her brother-in-law's house until she saw sense and agreed to her future as a nun.

However, Eleanor was far too headstrong to be held captive. She escaped from her brother-in-law's house, travelling to Woodstock once more. This time, she hid in a cupboard in Sally's room, while the housemaid, a tall, forceful Irishwoman named Mary Carryll, smuggled food into the bedroom. Eleanor was discovered after a couple of days, and joined Sally's negotiations with Sir William and Lady Betty.

Like heart-struck lovers through the ages, Eleanor and Sally pleaded that their only chance of happiness was with each other. Desperately trying to change her mind, Sir William kneeled at Sally's feet and promised to give her anything she desired, if only she would remain at Woodstock. Sally replied that even if the whole world knelt at her feet, it would not change her wish to live and die with Eleanor. Anyway, her bags were already packed. The meek little orphan had been emboldened by love. Her mind would not be changed.

Ten days later, a letter arrived from Kilkenny Castle. Mr Butler had finally given in, and gave his permission for Eleanor to leave Ireland with Sally. Victory! In the face of two bitterly opposed families, and the entire social convention of Georgian society, Eleanor and Sally had won the right to follow their dream of a life together.

In April 1778, they caught a coach from Woodstock to Waterford, and from there they sailed to Wales, never to see their Irish homeland again. Travelling with them was Mary Carryll, the Woodstock housemaid who had become doggedly loyal to Sally and Eleanor during their struggle, and remained in their employment for the rest of her life.

Six weeks later, Sir William woke in the early hours of the morning with a stomach ache. After two weeks of agonising pain, he died. Many in the family suggested it was God's punishment for his behaviour towards Sally. Lady Betty died three weeks later. Blissfully unaware of the chaos they had left in their wake, Sally and Eleanor spent the summer planning the rest of their lives together. They had dreamt of this moment for years, and now their time had finally come.

Sally and Eleanor did not know where they wanted to live, but they knew how they wanted to live. They wanted to retire, not from work (they were members of the aristocracy, they did not work) but from society: the dances and dinners, the stately homes stuffed with portraits, the gossiping relatives who did not understand them. They wanted to escape all this and hide away in a place of rural beauty, where they could focus only on those things they loved the most: reading, gardening, cooking, and each other.

Having landed at Milford Haven in south Wales, Eleanor and Sally spent the summer of 1778 enjoying their new-found freedom. They travelled the length of Wales, through the beautiful, historic towns of Pembroke, Carmarthen and Aberystwyth, and over the border into England. However, one location captured their hearts beyond all others.

In the gentle hills of north Wales, the village of Llangollen sits in a lush, green valley beside the River Dee. It was a poor, sombre sort of place, enlivened only by groups of Irish travellers stopping by on their way to the English border.

However, the situation of Llangollen is stunning. To the north is a steep hill, on top of which the haunting medieval ruins of Crow Castle loom over the village. To the south, the view stretches towards the rugged Berwyn Mountains. The surrounding hills contain forests, streams and the crumbling remains of a medieval abbey. On their first visit to Llangollen, Sally climbed up to Crow Castle and looked over the Dee Valley, describing it in her journal as 'the Beautifullest Country in the World'.

It was in Llangollen that Eleanor and Sally decided to settle. Before leaving Ireland, they had convinced their reluctant families to provide them with a small income: £200 a year from Eleanor's father, and £80 a year from Sally's adopted sister Mrs Tighe. It was no fortune, but enough money to live at the lowest end of the rural gentry. And that was all they desired.

Eleanor and Sally found a plain, square house on the southern edge of Llangollen village with stone walls, a slate roof and five rooms. It sat on four acres of land beside a hillside stream which rushed over fern- and moss-covered rocks towards the River Dee. They named their property Plas Newydd, meaning 'The New House'.

Eleanor and Sally set about transforming Plas Newydd into another Eden, a demi-paradise where they could perfect the art of living. Alone at last, they planned to derive the largest enjoyment they could from life's simplest pleasures. The property would provide for most of their daily needs: milk and butter from their cow, eggs from their hens, vegetable beds, fruit trees and a beautifully landscaped garden.

Of course, Eleanor and Sally knew this would require discipline to maintain, so they developed a daily routine called 'The System'. A typical day might start at six in the morning with a walk around the grounds, checking on their vegetables, admiring their flowers, and saying hello to their livestock. To guide this walk, Eleanor and Sally laid out a neatly raked gravel path and called it the 'Home Circuit'.

With the Home Circuit complete, a light breakfast would follow, usually featuring newly laid eggs. Then, a morning spent on some improving activity: gardening in the summer, or painting, knitting and language learning in the winter. Mary Carryll would prepare lunch using as many ingredients as possible from the kitchen garden: asparagus and new potatoes in the spring; wild strawberries and peas in the summer; mushrooms and apples in the autumn. If guests were visiting, her speciality was an exemplary salmon pie.

Afternoons were spent in their library, corresponding with friends and reading. Always reading. Having first bonded over books, Eleanor and Sally saw the improvement of their minds as life's highest calling. They taught themselves Italian, and employed the local vicar to teach them Latin, so that they could tick off another of their geeky life goals – translating the *Aeneid*.

Their reading was deep and wide-ranging, as they built up a famously well-stocked library: classical mythology, French philosophy, English novels, Italian poetry, Welsh history. A wealthy patron of the arts called Mrs Piozzi became a frequent visitor to Plas Newydd and wrote that these two eccentric women had an 'unaccountable knowledge . . . of all living books and people and things'. Conversation with them was, she claimed, 'like magic'.

At the end of a warm summer's day, evenings were spent in

the garden. In the winter, they snuggled in the library beside a fire with Tatters the cat. Sally might knit a purse to send to a friend as a gift, while Eleanor would read aloud from a favourite book. Then to the bedroom, where they shared a bed for all their happy retirement. Thus The System was completed for that day, ready for more or less the same the next.

Eleanor and Sally recorded these idyllic days in their journals, always describing them as 'heavenly', 'celestial', 'glorious', as if constantly remembering to acknowledge their good fortune. One 1788 entry for a spring day spent planting carnations and reading in the garden ends: 'A day of such exquisite such enjoyed retirement. So still. So silent.'

In a curious way, they lived rather like nuns. Plas Newydd was their secular convent, a refuge from the vice and viciousness of contemporary society. As Sally wrote in her journal in 1788, adapting Andrew Marvell's poem 'The Garden':

> Society is all but rude
> To this delicious Solitude
> Where all the flowers and Trees do close
> To weave the Garland of Repose

However, even in a poor corner of rural Wales, a garland of repose cost money. Plas Newydd may have felt humble to two daughters of the aristocracy, but it still required four staff – a gardener, a footman, Mary the housekeeper and a kitchen maid. In the early years, making ends meet was an ongoing headache for Eleanor and Sally.

Their first financial shock came in June 1783, when Eleanor's father died. Mr Butler did not include a single reference to his runaway daughter in his will, leaving Eleanor's family with no obligation to provide support. Her brother had converted to Protestantism, won back the family title as the 17th Earl Ormonde and was restoring the family's fortunes. But he had hated Eleanor ever since their childhood, and she hated him. He was not going to show any charity to his sister, and their income was now short by £200 per year.

It would take four years of loans, gifts and graft before Eleanor and Sally found themselves back on a stable footing. Georgian Britain did not hand out pensions for the poor, but they did for the rich. Through the 'Civil List', the King's government approved annual payments of varying amounts for any great person or family who had fallen on hard times: an 'aristocratic dole', in the words of one historian.

In 1787, having written countless letters and called in whatever favours she could, Sally was added to the Civil List. The pension was awarded in recognition of her heroic grandfather, General Henry Ponsonby, who famously had his head blown off his shoulders whilst pausing to take snuff fighting the French at the Battle of Fontenay in 1745. The government agreed to provide Sally with £100 a year, and Plas Newydd would live to see another day.

Lean years returned in the 1790s, when Britain entered a cripplingly expensive war with France and Civil List pensions frequently went unpaid. Eleanor's migraines and panic attacks became worse than ever, as she was consumed with fear that their perfect idyll would be destroyed and they would be forced back to Ireland, or worse still, debtors' jail.

In 1794, Eleanor held her nose and wrote to her sister-in-law Lady Ormonde. Her brother had done well, marrying one of the wealthiest heiresses in Ireland, with a private income of £1,600 a year. But still no spare money could be found for the estranged Eleanor. In her letter to Lady Ormonde, she railed at 'the unmerited cruelty of this treatment' and asked whether, from her vast fortune, she could spare just £100 a year. This trifling figure would, Eleanor continued, 'fulfil my utmost ambition and secure yourself my liveliest gratitude'.

Lady Ormonde wrote a terse response requesting no future correspondence, but adding in the final sentence, 'Your Brother desires I may inform you that your Legacy is lodged at Mr Le Touches and that you may draw for it when you choose.' Again, Plas Newydd was brought back from the brink.

Eleanor and Sally used the money they did receive to transform their boxy little cottage into a miniature mansion. Even in their retreat, they wanted to keep up with the latest trend, which was for Gothic architecture, and the three windows at the back of the house were adorned with pointed, mock-medieval arches.

It was not always easy for two women to deal with the local tradesmen. Eleanor's journal from 1788 records her view of the local thatcher, a 'snuffy, sauntering, lazy creature'. It continues, 'Think the Thatcher horrible. Told him so. Fought him.' Neither did Eleanor have much luck with their gardeners, who often had a taste for the booze. She discharged Moses Jones for 'outrageous Drunkenness'; according to her journal entry, 'This morning he began to mow. He cut three Swards of Grass, laid Down his Scythe, ran to the Ale House. Returned, began to Mow. Then went again.' The local doctor, meanwhile, was a 'Dirty Village Quack'. But their relationship with the townspeople did gradually improve, as they went from being seen as curious outsiders to the much-loved 'guardian angels' of Llangollen.

As the years ticked by, the house filled with curious objects. One of their first big purchases, for the library window, was an Aeolian harp which was played by the wind. By the time of their deaths, it had been joined by telescopes, kaleidoscopes, tigers' feet, walrus, whale and seal teeth, elephants' hair, pistols, and a monkey made out of sponge.

However, their main focus was not the house. Georgian Britain, not unlike today, was obsessed with gardening. Eleanor and Sally's library contained all the latest books by England's most fashionable landscapers, who were promoting a more naturalistic, less formal approach to garden design. Following this 'picturesque' style of landscaping, they put their modest four acres at Plas Newydd at the cutting edge of English garden design.

At the front of the house were four separate enclosures linked by the weaving gravel paths of the Home Circuit. The garden was approached through a Gothic arch, whose bell was used to summon their gardener – a useful tool, seeing that the likes of Moses Jones were so fond of spending their afternoons sleeping off a pub visit.

The path wound its way from the dairy, to the hen run, to the neat flower beds, where they planted forty-four different types of rose, including Maiden's Blush, Rose d'Amour, and the beautifully scented Provence roses. In a quirky touch, the ladies nailed wooden boards to various trees, on which they painted their favourite life mottos in French and Latin.

The path then led to the kitchen garden, so central to life at Plas Newydd. In a letter to a friend who planned to visit, Eleanor boasted of its produce: 'For breakfast you shall have a couple of new laid eggs from our jersey hens . . . Your dinner shall be boil'd chickens from our own coop. Asparagus out of our garden. Ham of our own saving and mutton from our own village. Your supper shall consist of gooseberry fool, cranberry tarts, roast fowl and salad. Don't this tempt you?'

At the back of the house, beneath the ruins of Crow Castle,

was Eleanor and Sally's favourite spot: a secluded lawn sloping down the hill from the library windows towards a shrubbery full of lilacs, laburnums and white broom. It was here that they spent those summer evenings without end, hidden from the world. A well-known poet named Anna Seward, who visited Plas Newydd on many occasions, celebrated its owners for converting 'two and a half acres of turnip ground' into 'a fairy palace amid the bowers of Calypso'.

The story of Eleanor and Sally's relationship was so remarkable, and their lifestyle so seductive, that word of the Ladies of Llangollen, as they became known, quickly spread. In trying to escape from Georgian society, they ended up finding that Georgian society came to them. At first, it was a trickle of friends and acquaintances. But by the end of their lives, it was a continual stream of statesmen, celebrities and royalty.

One early visitor was the potter, scientist and inventor Josiah Wedgwood, who treated them to a lesson on the surrounding rock formations. The same year, the brilliant, but often drunk, Irish playwright Richard Sheridan visited, though the Ladies thought he was 'a very ill looking fellow'. In 1790, the famous botanist Mr Sneyde visited, and advised them on how to avoid die-back in their apricot tree and leaf curl in their nectarines.

The Romantic poets were big fans of the Ladies of Llangollen. Anne Seward rhapsodised about their gardens, and she was followed by Robert Southey and William Wordsworth, the greatest poet of the age. Following his stay in 1821, Wordsworth wrote an ode to Plas Newydd, which ended:

> Sisters in love, a love allowed to climb.
> Ev'n on this earth, above the reach of time.

Members of the Anglo-Irish aristocracy liked to drop in to Plas Newydd on their way from London to Dublin. The Irish aristocrat and future Foreign Secretary Viscount Castlereagh declared the Ladies to be 'a model of perfect friendship'. He was perhaps more interested in their friendship than most, as he was a secret homosexual. Fifteen years later, Castlereagh slit his own throat when political enemies threatened to expose his love life. Same-sex relationships were not always easy in Georgian Britain.

Another Anglo-Irish visitor was Sir Arthur Wellesley, the future Duke of Wellington. In 1806, the Ladies presented him with a small prayer book in Spanish that had once belonged to the library at Kilkenny Castle. When he left to fight Napoleon's army in Spain two years later, Wellington took the Ladies' prayer book with him and – so it was claimed – used it to learn enough of the language to communicate with his Spanish allies.

By the start of the nineteenth century, the cream of English society was descending on Plas Newydd in droves: King George III's son the Duke of Gloucester one day, a Russian ambassador the next, an Austrian prince another. Even the Romantic poet Lord Byron, the greatest celebrity of the age, sent a complimentary copy of his bestselling poem *The Corsair* to the famous Ladies when it was published in 1814.

Wearing black riding jackets and top hats, Eleanor and Sally always appeared – from the waist upwards – to be dressed as English gentlemen going on a morning canter. They adopted the 'Titus' hairstyle fashionable among young men at the time – short-cropped hair, brushed forward – and kept this style right until the end of their lives. When he first met the Ladies, one visitor claimed he could have mistaken them for 'a couple of hazy or crazy old sailors'. A potter in Swansea even designed a tea service on which he painted the Ladies in their eccentric, cross-dressing gear. The mark of true celebrity: fans could now buy Ladies of Llangollen merchandise.

Of course, Georgian gossips loved speculating about the Ladies' relationship. Today, we can see that their letters and journals were full of the language of love, referring to each other as 'the beloved of my soul', 'the delight of my heart' or 'the joy of my life'. But was this love sexual? In June 1822, a visitor arrived at Plas Newydd with the express intention of finding out. Her name was Anne Lister, but she is better remembered today as 'Gentleman Jack'.

In her Yorkshire home of Halifax, Gentleman Jack was well known for living, to all intents and purposes, as a man. She wore men's clothes, carried pistols and spoke in a deep voice. Having inherited her uncle's country estate, she became a successful businesswoman, making a series of shrewd investments in coal mines and stone quarries. According to her private diaries, she was also a prolific seducer of women. These diaries have been described as the Dead Sea Scrolls of lesbian history.

Gentleman Jack arrived in Llangollen in a sorrowful mood. Six years earlier, she had watched her lover Mariana enter an unhappy marriage, only for her unfaithful husband to give her venereal disease. Passing through Manchester on the way to Llangollen, Jack shared a hotel room with Mariana, where they enjoyed 'two kisses' but no more. Jack continued to Llangollen the following afternoon, clearly pining for her lost lover.

'Tell me if you think,' Mariana wrote eagerly to Jack following her visit, 'their regard has always been platonic.' Jack responded that an attachment as deep as theirs had to be secured by 'something more tender still than friendship.' They might not be lovers anymore, Jack wrote to Mariana, but what about in years gone by, during 'that feverish dream called youth'?

Jack was clearly moved by seeing the life Eleanor and Sally had created for themselves. Following her visit to Plas Newydd, she recorded in her diary, 'I could have mused for hours, dreamt dreams of happiness, conjured up many a vision of . . . hope.' Gentleman Jack never let go of that hope. Years later, she met a woman called Ann Walker, and they lived together for the last six years of her life. They even got married! Well, kind of. They had a same-sex wedding ceremony in a church in York, though it was not legally recognised. One cannot help but wonder whether the Ladies of Llangollen were Jack's inspiration.

By the end of their lives, Eleanor and Sally had become a much-loved fixture in the Llangollen community. They adopted the role of local squires, handing out charity to the poor and needy, and gracing civic events with their presence. In 1805, when a magnificent new aqueduct was opened over the River Dee, the Ladies of Llangollen floated above the river in a ceremonial barge, to the sounds of 8,000 cheering spectators and a volley of cannon fire (coming, as it happens, from the tiger-headed guns seized from Tipu Sultan's palace six years previously).

When the Ladies' faithful housekeeper, Mary Carryll, died in 1809, the people of the town swept the road clean for her passing coffin. She was the unofficial third member of the Ladies of Llangollen, but like so many domestic workers, her voice is lost to history. The epitaph on her memorial, however, gives some indication of her character:

> Patient, industrious, faithful, generous, kind,
> Her conduct left the proudest far behind;
> Her virtues dignified her humble birth,
> And raised her mind above this sordid earth.

Sally and Eleanor carried on for two more decades without Mary. Towards the end of her life, Eleanor lost her sight and became increasingly dependent on Sally to look after her. Proud and defiant to the end, Eleanor's personality lost little of its force. Then, on 2 June 1829, her tired eyes closed for the last time. She was ninety years old.

Eleanor's death brought the entire village of Llangollen to a standstill. All shops closed for the day, and her coffin was carried by twelve bearers. A local newspaper reported there was 'scarcely a dry eye to be seen'. The people of little Llangollen had taken this larger-than-life woman into their hearts, and were distraught to see her, seemingly so indestructible, go.

None were sadder than Sally Ponsonby, who was too grief-stricken to attend the funeral. She lived for two more years before being buried beside Eleanor in Llangollen's village church. After fifty-one years of happy cohabitation, their demi-paradise in a Welsh valley had come to an end.

In the village today, the local people still talk about the Ladies of Llangollen. By showing the possibility of finding love outside the conventional arrangement of husband and wife, they captured the imagination not just of a village, but of an entire generation.

What is more, they pioneered a simplified form of living, reducing their concerns to those which mattered most. As the German nobleman and garden designer Prince Pückler-Muskau put it following his own pilgrimage to Plas Newydd, 'a well-furnished library, a charming neighbourhood, an even-tempered life without material cares, a most intimate friendship and community amongst themselves – these are treasures . . . they must have chosen not quite badly.'

CHAPTER 8
LADY HAMILTON

The Georgian Celebrity Who Went from
Rags to Riches and Back

Georgian society had many rules. One of the most important was that the social class you were born into was the social class in which you were expected to stay. But not everyone played by the rules. Particularly not Lady Hamilton, the drop-dead gorgeous, superstar celebrity of Georgian Britain.

At the height of her fame, Lady Hamilton's face was reproduced across Europe in paintings and prints. Her fans wore Lady Hamilton badges, gambled with Lady Hamilton playing cards and drank out of Lady Hamilton tea sets. She lived in an Italian palace in the city of Naples, where she threw lavish parties for Europe's elite. Her affair with Lord Nelson, the greatest admiral in the Royal Navy, was an open secret, closely followed in the gossip columns of the day. How she dressed, danced and behaved was copied throughout fashionable society. She was the original influencer.

Lady Hamilton was a member of the English aristocracy, but this had not always been the case. She was born in 1765 about as far away from the life of an aristocrat as you could imagine, to illiterate parents in a small coal-mining village on the north-west coast of England. Her father was a blacksmith, and he died when she was two months old. According to local legend, she was sent out to work as a child selling coal from the back of a donkey on the side of the road to Chester.

It is sometimes said that truth is stranger than fiction. The story of how Lady Hamilton went from miserable rural poverty to glittering international fame could never be written as a work of fiction because no reader would find it believable. But her story is true, and is far more extraordinary than anything a novelist's imagination could create.

Aged only thirteen, Lady Hamilton escaped her life of poverty by travelling down to London in the back of a horse-drawn cart. After days of bumpy roads and sleepless nights she arrived in England's capital, a small girl in the big city, ready to make her name.

Her name, back then, was not Lady Hamilton, but plain and simple Emma Lyon. Emma's dream was to become an actress, and she found work backstage in the theatres of Covent Garden. From there she became a dancer, and word of her beauty spread amongst the aristocratic young men of the city. One such aristocrat was a disreputable love rat named Sir Harry Fetherstonhaugh, who invited Emma to come and party at his country house, located in a beautiful estate in the rolling Sussex countryside called Uppark. Let's put it this way: his intentions were far from pure.

The summer she spent at Sir Harry's estate was Emma's first introduction to the lives of the super-rich, and she was smitten. Sir Harry invited her to dine with his friends and taught her to ride on his horses. In return, she was to entertain his pals, who enjoyed hanging out with this beautiful, brassy northern lass. Rumour has it that she once danced naked for them on the table after dinner.

At some point during Emma's stay, she gave way to Sir

Harry's advances, and became pregnant with her first child. She was only sixteen. Was Sir Harry going to marry Emma and care for the child? You've got to be joking. Sir Harry was a baronet and Member of Parliament. How could he possibly marry the uneducated daughter of a Cheshire blacksmith?

For the first, but certainly not the last time, Emma's life was thrown into crisis, and she turned to a friend of Sir Harry's for support. Unlike most of Sir Harry's rowdy set of aristocratic friends, Charles Greville was a quiet and thoughtful man. His two great passions in life were collecting art and studying the history of ancient Greece and Rome.

Charles met Emma at Sir Harry's country estate, and like so many men, fell for her beauty and charm. In January 1782, six months pregnant with Sir Harry's child, she wrote to Charles pleading for help. You can hear poor Emma's desperation leap off the page: 'What shall I do? Good God! What shall I do? I have wrote 7 letters, and no answer . . . For God's sake, Greville write the minute you get this, and only tell me what I am to do . . . I am almost mad. Oh, for God's sake, tell me what is to become of me. Oh dear Greville, write to me.'

Charles Greville agreed to take care of Emma. She became his mistress, on the condition that her newly born daughter be sent up north to be raised by Emma's grandmother. Emma agreed, so Charles set her up in a small house in a village on the outskirts of London called Paddington Green. Here, he encouraged her to smooth out the rougher edges of her country-girl upbringing and become a respectable lady. Charles delighted in Emma's transformation, nicknaming her his 'fair tea maker of Edgware Row'. She learnt how to make polite chit-chat about the affairs of the day, how to dress in the latest fashions, and how to host Charles and his friends when they came to visit.

One such friend was an artist called George Romney. More than anyone else, Romney would set Emma on the path to fame. It was the fashion at this time for artists to paint figures from Greek and Roman mythology. To do so, they were always on the lookout for beautiful new models, and Emma was London's number one honey. Romney begged Charles to let Emma model for his paintings, and he agreed. Over the next few years Romney painted Emma obsessively, depicting her in dozens of paintings as one or other mythical figure from the ancient world. As the paintings spread around London and beyond, Emma's fame grew.

Three years into his relationship with Emma, Charles decided that he needed to move on and marry a respectable, wealthy wife, with the aim of bolstering his family fortunes. In order to find such a woman, he knew he had to leave his mistress, whose paintings were bringing her increasing fame and attention. But he also knew how much she adored him, and he did not have the courage to break up with her properly.

Instead, Charles played a trick on Emma. His 55-year-old uncle, Sir William Hamilton, was British ambassador to the Kingdom of Naples. Sir William had recently lost his wife, and Charles proposed to Emma that they visit him in Italy for the summer. The only snag was, Charles had some business to deal with in Scotland, so he suggested that Emma should travel to Naples early, and he would follow on a few months later. Only he never intended to do so. The coward.

Emma made the six-week journey from London to Naples in a coach, travelling through France, over the Alps into Switzerland, and down into Italy, arriving at Sir William's palace, the Palazzo Sessa, on 26 April 1786. That day was

Emma's twenty-first birthday. Sir William did his best to show Emma a good time, buying her gifts and taking her on trips to the theatre and the seaside. But it was not long before Emma realised that her beloved Charles had tricked her. He was not going to be following her to Naples, and – even worse – he expected Emma to start a new relationship with his elderly uncle Sir William.

Abandoned by her lover, stranded in a foreign city, and living with a lecherous older man who thought she was his mistress, what was Emma to do? At first she was distraught, writing fourteen tragic letters to Charles. Once again you can hear her desperation: 'I love you to that degree, that at this time there is not a hardship upon earth, either of poverty, hunger, cold, death, or even to walk barefooted to Scotland to see you, but what I would undergo. Therefore, my dear, dear Greville, if you do love me, for my sake try all you can to come here as soon as possible.' She did not receive a single reply.

What is remarkable about Emma is that throughout her life she turned a situation like this, which would have crushed many people, into a new and glittering adventure. After London and Paris, Naples was the largest city in Europe and its party capital. Set on a beautiful Mediterranean bay, the city was overshadowed by the huge volcano Mount Vesuvius. During the late eighteenth century, Vesuvius was highly active, erupting almost once every decade, and by night it would light up with fizzing bursts of fire. Naples was a heady mixture of danger and glamour, with visitors coming from all over Europe to experience its famous parties. Young, vivacious and beautiful, Emma fitted in well.

Sir William and Emma soon became friends. The old lord turned out to be a kindly and decent man, who worked hard to win Emma's trust. After five months of living together, she became his lover. Sir William was delighted to introduce his sexy young mistress to Naples high society, and Emma embraced the opportunity to charm the city's social elite, becoming fluent in French and Italian. Over the ten years that followed, she established herself as the most popular host, and honoured guest, in Naples society.

Emma adored entertaining the visitors who flocked to Sir William's Palazzo Sessa. She had a gorgeous singing voice, and learnt to play the harp. She even revived her early career as a dancer, inventing a captivating new form of dance which she called her 'attitudes'. On a simple, candlelit stage, Emma would appear in a loose-fitting dress and adopt the guise of different classical figures, gliding from one pose into another, with just a few shawls as props. The classically educated audience smiled in recognition as Emma embodied Athene, Medea and Cleopatra. It was like a greatest hits of the ancient world, performed in your living room. People flocked to see Emma's 'attitudes', and they were copied by fashionable young women across Europe.

Emma had a gift for friendships, and before long she was best pals with none other than Maria Carolina, the Queen of Naples. Emma became the Queen's closest confidante, and they spent long hours discussing politics and sharing gossip about the royal court. Queen Carolina's sister was the Queen of France, Marie Antoinette, and when she was executed during the French Revolution, it was Emma that Carolina turned to for comfort.

Just as they had in London, the greatest painters in Europe came to Naples to capture Emma's beauty on canvas. During this period, it was said that she became the most painted person of the age. Emma's image was reproduced all around the world, and her taste for loose-fitting, classically-styled dresses inspired a whole new fashion in women's clothes.

Then, after five years of life in Naples, Sir William decided it was time to make an honest woman of Emma and take her as his wife. The blacksmith's daughter from Cheshire was no longer Sir William's mistress. She was Lady Hamilton, the celebrated wife of Britain's ambassador to Naples. Emma still had her haters who enjoyed speculating about her past. Even her close friend, Queen Carolina, was rumoured to have expressed discontent that the English ambassador 'should live publicly with a prostitute taken from the very streets of London'. But the new Lady Hamilton took such gossip with humour and good grace.

Then, in 1798, a man who would set Lady Hamilton's life on a wholly different new course sailed into the Bay of Naples. His name was Horatio Nelson, and he was the bravest, most ass-kicking admiral in the entire Royal Navy. For the past six years Britain had been at war with France. The French army had invaded northern Italy and conquered Rome. Many in Naples, particularly King Ferdinand and Queen Carolina, were terrified that their city would be next. So, when news arrived in Naples that Lord Nelson and the British navy had destroyed or captured much of the French fleet off the coast of Egypt, the city erupted in celebration.

On the way back to England, Nelson arranged to stop off in Naples to repair and resupply his ships. Lady Hamilton wrote to Nelson encouraging him to stay at the Palazzo Sessa, and promised a hero's welcome. She wrote, 'The Neapolitans are mad, and if you was here now you would be killed with kindness. Sonnets on sonnets, illuminations, rejoicing. Not a French dog dare show his face. How I glory in the honour of my country and my countryman! I walk and tread in the air with pride, feeling that I was born on the same land with the victor Nelson and his gallant band.'

On arriving in Naples, Nelson was wounded and exhausted from six long months at sea. After a round of parties, he collapsed onto the soft pillows and clean sheets of his room in the Hamiltons' palace, where Lady Hamilton nursed him back to health on a diet of asses' milk.

Ten days after his arrival, Nelson had regained enough strength to celebrate his fortieth birthday. Lady Hamilton busied herself organising a spectacular bash for the war hero. That night, the warm Mediterranean air blew in from the Bay of Naples, and the palazzo was covered with decorations honouring the great Lord Nelson. Each of the 1,800 guests in attendance was given badges and ribbons to wear, emblazoned with the initials H.N.

Although both were already married, Nelson and Lady Hamilton could not take their eyes off each other. So much so that Nelson's stepson, who was also at the party, went off in a huff, angry at his stepfather's flirtatious ways. Two of the biggest celebrities of the day were falling in love.

Nelson cut an unforgettable figure at the Palazzo Sessa that night. Brave to the point of madness, he always led his men in enemy attacks, and had some brutal battle scars to prove it. He lost his right eye fighting the French in 1794 and his right arm three years later. Most of the top row of his teeth had fallen out, and chunks of hair were missing from his scar-scattered head. Short, wiry and weather-beaten from years at sea, Nelson's appearance was as shocking as Lady Hamilton's was beautiful. The one-eyed, one-armed Nelson even warned Lady Hamilton before he arrived in Naples of his 'mutilations', writing, 'I may now be able to show your ladyship the remains of Horatio Nelson.'

For Lady Hamilton, Nelson's mutilations simply added to his danger-loving sex appeal. Nelson, meanwhile, was captivated by his vivacious and caring host, and warmed to her humour. When the Admiralty back in London rewarded Nelson for his victory in Egypt by making him a baron, he was furious at not having been made a viscount. Emma soothed the admiral's wounded pride with a letter in October 1798, stating, 'If I was King of England, I would make you the most noble puissant Duke Nelson, Marquis Nile, Earl Alexandria, Viscount Pyramid, Baron Crocodile, and Prince Victory.'

Though they were in love, it was vital they kept their love a secret. Lord Nelson already had a wife, but it was an unhappy marriage that he had entered into for money, a situation exacerbated by his long periods away from home. Lady Hamilton genuinely loved her husband Sir William, but he was twice her age, and had become more of a father figure than a lover.

Despite Lady Hamilton's care, Nelson did not immediately warm to Naples, describing it as a 'country of fiddlers and poets, whores and scoundrels'. However, King Ferdinand and Queen Carolina were keen to put this hero of the seas to use during his stay. In return for Nelson's assistance, King Ferdinand agreed to ally with Britain against France. Lady Hamilton, with her fine command of French and Italian, acted as Nelson's interpreter in the ensuing negotiations, and became his unofficial political advisor.

Unfortunately, Nelson's scheming with King Ferdinand did not end well. In November 1798, Nelson agreed to help the Neapolitan army in an attack on French-controlled Rome, transporting 4,000 troops by sea. However, the campaign ended in disaster, and Ferdinand retreated to Naples even more unpopular than before.

The people of Naples had long disliked their king, and with good reason – he was a stubborn, dim-witted dolt, far more interested in hunting wild boar in the forests of southern Italy than ruling his kingdom. By December 1798, following Ferdinand's humiliation in Rome, the people had finally lost patience. On the city's streets, rumours were spreading that Neapolitan radicals were about to start a revolution, aided by the French forces stationed in Rome.

Naples was becoming more dangerous by the day. When a royal official was clubbed to death outside the palace by an angry crowd, the King and Queen realised it was no longer safe for them to remain in the city. Ferdinand and Carolina decided to flee to the island of Sicily, which they also ruled, and wait for the revolutionary fervour in Naples to die down.

To evacuate the entire royal household by sea, with their possessions and employees, during the dead of winter, was a pretty tough task. Harder still, it had to be done in secret. Queen Carolina, who had the political skill and intelligence her husband lacked, took charge of organising their escape. And who did she choose to help her? Her best friend, Lady Hamilton, of course. They also needed a trusted sea captain to sail them safely from Naples to Sicily through the rough winter seas. Who would that be? None other than the hero of the seas, currently residing in Naples: Admiral Lord Nelson.

Lord Nelson's ship, the *Vanguard*, was moored by the Naples harbourside. Night after night, Lady Hamilton arranged for the royal family's possessions to be loaded onto the ship. Food, clothing, King Ferdinand's hunting dogs, and £2.5 million worth of jewellery, money and silverware were taken to the harbourside under the cover of darkness.

Then, on the night of 21 December, Lord Nelson met the royal family in their palace. Armed with a lantern, cutlass and pistol, he led them through a secret passageway to the harbourside, and onto the *Vanguard*. From here, the royal family, Nelson and Lord and Lady Hamilton set sail for Sicily, along with a small group of courtiers, diplomats, ladies-in-waiting and the King's cook and gamekeeper.

For five days at sea, freezing winds and treacherous storms threatened to sink the *Vanguard*. At one point, Lady Hamilton found Nelson sleeping with a loaded pistol in his hand. When she asked why, the hard-as-nails admiral replied that if the ship were to sink, he wanted to blow his brains out before he drowned. Christmas Day came and went on board the ship with no celebrations, only tragedy: the King and Queen's six-year-old son Albert, who had already been ill before the departure, died at 7 p.m. that evening.

If Nelson had been in any doubts about Lady Hamilton's remarkable character before their escape, the voyage to Sicily removed them. She worked tirelessly, soothing the suffering of the *Vanguard*'s unhappy crew. Nelson later wrote that everyone on board the ship, including himself, owed a debt of gratitude to her ladyship. She made herself a 'slave' to the royal family, and did not go to bed once. On 26 December, the royal party arrived in Sicily.

Sicily had once been a powerful and wealthy medieval kingdom, but it was now a poor and forgotten corner of Europe. In this land that time forgot, the two lovers were free of the prying eyes of Naples society, which inevitably fed rumours back to the gossip columns of celebrity-obsessed London newspapers, and could finally pursue their love. While Sir William was preoccupied with the political situation in Naples, Lady Hamilton and Nelson explored Sicily's medieval castles and cathedrals, and wandered its famous lemon groves and rugged coastline.

By this point, Lady Hamilton was an established political figure in her own right, and from their new home in Sicily, she acted as a go-between for Nelson and the King and Queen of Naples. To help them regain control of their kingdom, Nelson and his British ships sailed back towards the city and blockaded it by sea, forcing the revolutionaries to surrender.

By the summer of 1799, Naples was once again in royal hands. As a reward for her help, King Ferdinand and Queen Carolina showered Lady Hamilton in diamonds, pearls, jewellery and silk dresses. Nelson was given a jewel-encrusted sword that had once belonged to the French King Louis XIV, and a Sicilian estate along with admission to the Italian nobility as the Duke of Bronte. In September, Ferdinand and Carolina threw a party at their Sicilian palace. Three life-size waxworks of Lady Hamilton, Sir William and Lord Nelson were placed in a temple for all the royal court to admire.

However, by then Lady Hamilton and Lord Nelson's Italian adventure was nearing its end. Sir William was approaching seventy years of age and wanted to retire to England. Nelson was also required back in London by the Admiralty. Before they left Italy, he suggested to Lord and Lady Hamilton that they go on a farewell cruise around Sicily, to Malta, and back to Naples. Sir William was under no illusion about his wife's relationship. As strange as it may sound, the Hamiltons and Nelson enjoyed living together as a threesome. Sir William rather liked the time he spent with the hero of the Royal Navy, even if it meant turning a blind eye to him shacking up with his wife.

It was during their farewell Mediterranean cruise that Lady Hamilton and Lord Nelson's love truly blossomed. In June 1801, Lady Hamilton bid farewell to Naples, the city that had made her. As she set sail for England, there was a new addition on board the ship. She was pregnant with Lord Nelson's child.

After five months travelling through Europe, the Hamiltons and Lord Nelson landed in Norfolk. Aside from one brief visit to marry Sir William, England was a land that Lady Hamilton had not seen in fifteen years. The bleak landscape of the Norfolk coast, coupled with the grey winter weather, must have made quite a contrast with the sun and glamour of Naples. Lady Hamilton was nervous: she did not know whether her relationship with Lord Nelson could survive the chillier social atmosphere of England. The carefree royal court in Naples had been relaxed about their affair, but English society was less forgiving. Men, of course, had mistresses. But they had to be private. In public, faithfulness in marriage had to be shown. Lady Hamilton could not even let anyone know she was now seven months pregnant.

Lord Nelson moved home with his wife, while the Hamiltons moved into a London townhouse. Despite endless speculation and rumours about their relationship in the newspapers, Lady Hamilton and Lord Nelson could not live together. When their daughter was born, Lady Hamilton had to invent a story that their daughter was an orphan she had agreed to take care of while living in Naples. However, she obviously wasn't too concerned about concealing the true identity of her daughter's father. She named her Horatia.

After they had passed a year in England, war with France resumed and Nelson went back to sea. The couple were frequently apart, but whenever they talked or wrote to each other, they dreamed of life together. Nelson was desperate to marry Lady Hamilton, but even though he had now separated from his wife, divorce was almost impossible. They even considered returning to Sicily, the island where their love had first flowered, so that they could be with one another.

In the summer of 1801, Nelson sent Emma a letter from the naval base in Portsmouth. He wrote, 'Now, my own dear wife, for such you are in my eyes and in the face of heaven, I can give full scope to my feelings . . . You know, my dearest Emma, that there is nothing in this world I would not do for us to live together, and to have our dear little child with us . . . I love you, I never did love anyone else.'

A few months later, they came one step closer to achieving their dream. Lord Nelson instructed Lady Hamilton to purchase a house where they could live together once the war was over. She bought a run-down farmhouse just outside London called Merton Place, and began turning it into 'Paradise Merton'. The house was surrounded by farmland, where Lady Hamilton kept pigs and hens. A stream with a pretty ironwork bridge ran through the gardens. The interior was made bright with large windows and verandas, and the entire house was covered with paintings and memorabilia celebrating Nelson's heroism at sea.

'Paradise Merton' was complete, and for a short while Nelson, Lady Hamilton and Horatia were able to live there as a family. When, in April 1803, Sir William died (albeit in Lady Hamilton's arms, with Nelson right beside them), the two lovers could finally be exclusive. But only a month later, Lord Nelson was sent back to sea. Now commander of the entire British fleet, he spent two years kicking the French navy around the Mediterranean, across the Atlantic, through the Caribbean and back.

For Lady Hamilton, these periods while Lord Nelson was away were agony. The constant fear of his death pushed her towards nervous exhaustion, and she lived in desperation for letters promising that he was alive and thinking of her. In the summer of 1805, Nelson was given leave to return home. He travelled immediately to Merton. But no sooner was he home than the French navy was sighted off the coast of Spain near the port of Cadiz, and Nelson had to leave. At 10 p.m. on 13 August 1805, he kissed his baby daughter Horatia goodbye and embraced Lady Hamilton. Later that night, he wrote in his diary: 'At half-past ten drove from dear dear Merton where I left all which I hold dear in this world to go to service my King and country.'

For the next three months Lady Hamilton waited and waited for news, but none came. Then, on the morning of 6 November 1805, a young Captain Whitby from the Admiralty arrived at the door of Merton Place. Lady Hamilton showed Whitby inside, and with a pale face and low voice he stated: 'We have gained a great victory.' Lady Hamilton demanded: 'Never mind your victory, my letters, give me my letters!'

Captain Whitby stood there unable to speak, and with tears in his eyes. Lady Hamilton immediately understood what news he had to deliver. She screamed, collapsed on the floor, and for ten hours could neither speak nor cry. Nelson had fought his last battle, shot through the chest on board HMS *Victory* as the British defeated the French navy at the Battle of Trafalgar.

Lady Hamilton received one final letter from her lover, written two days before he died: 'my name shall ever be most dear to you and Horatia, both of whom I love as much as my own life; and as my last writing before battle will be to you so I hope in God that I shall live to finish my letter after the Battle.' He never did get to finish the letter. Lady Hamilton later learnt that as he died, amongst Nelson's last words were, 'Take care of my dear Lady Hamilton.'

However, with Nelson gone, few people did take care of dear Lady Hamilton, for this is a love story without a happy ending. Throughout her life, Lady Hamilton had her enemies, who resented the fact that a blacksmith's daughter from Cheshire had been able to rise to the top of English society. After Nelson's death, these enemies ensured Lady Hamilton's fall from grace was swift. Their revenge began with Nelson's funeral. Before his death, Nelson had insisted that she should attend his funeral and sing at the service. But Nelson's family decided it would not be appropriate. Nelson was buried at St Paul's Cathedral with a crowd of thousands, but the love of his life had to remain at home.

Both Sir William and Lord Nelson left Lady Hamilton money in their wills. However, the Nelson and Hamilton families were entrusted with paying the money out, and often did so late, or not at all. One of Nelson's dying wishes had been for the British government to provide Emma with a pension, in recognition of the vital role she played in ensuring the Kingdom of Naples' support in the war against France. But the government ignored his request.

It must be said that after twenty years living among royalty, Lady Hamilton was not very good at reining in her high-spending ways. She frittered away money on her friends with excessive generosity, gambling at the card table, and – increasingly – drinking too much alcohol. Before long, she was bankrupt.

So began Lady Hamilton's sad and steady decline. Four years after Nelson's death, she sold Paradise Merton. She still could not control her spending, and in 1813 she was sent to debtors' prison with Horatia. Worse was still to come. On her release, she discovered that her private letters to and from Nelson were to be published. A friend to whom she had given the letters had betrayed her trust and sold them to a publisher. To make matters worse, the British people assumed that Lady Hamilton had sold the letters herself to pay off her debts.

Lady Hamilton and Nelson's innermost feelings were now laid bare for the nosy, gossipy British public to read. Lady Hamilton was humiliated. With her finances and reputation ruined, she fled with Horatia to France, hoping she could start a new life. But sadness and illness followed her there, and her dependence on alcohol grew.

Ten years on from Lord Nelson's death, Lady Hamilton lay dying in a cheap apartment in Calais. Bedridden and suffering from liver disease, she lay on her narrow bed in a cramped room with peeling wallpaper, Horatia by her side. The woman who had risen from poverty to become the greatest celebrity of her age, entertaining dukes, duchesses, princes and kings in the palaces of Europe, died, once again in poverty. She was buried in a simple grave, bearing the inscription 'Emma Hamilton, England's Friend'.

CHAPTER 9
HESTER STANHOPE

The Rebel Aristocrat Who Found Freedom
in the Syrian Desert

On the northern edge of the Holy Land, in what is today Lebanon, an elderly recluse and mystic lived in a sprawling fortress palace. Situated in the remote foothills of Mount Lebanon, her palace was surrounded by hills teeming with wolves and jackals. She never ventured outside its white walls, keeping only a small army of servants, a family of cats and the occasional visitor for company.

During the 1830s, guests to the hilltop palace told of the same routine. They would be welcomed inside by a servant, and invited to dine alone. Then, once the sun had dropped below the horizon, the mystic would appear. She wore long white robes, a turban of pale cashmere shawls, and leather slippers embroidered in silk. In her hand she held a staff topped with a carved ram's head. These were the clothes of an Arab holy man, but her white skin and blue eyes suggested she was born somewhere far away from Mount Lebanon.

Having greeted guests in her candlelit palace, she would take them for a moonlight walk around her gardens, where water flowed through marble fountains and the air was scented with jasmine and honeysuckle. Conversation flowed long into the night, fuelled by tobacco smoked from her bubbling water pipe. Wreathed in smoke, she regaled visitors with stories of her life, read their fortunes, and gave prophecies of two-headed serpents, rivers of blood and the coming of a new Messiah. Some guests said these were revelations of sublime power, others the ramblings of a mad old woman.

Who was she? There were tales that she was an aristocrat from England, born to one of its most powerful political families. That she had been a great beauty in her youth, who, having had her heart broken once too often, travelled East for a life of adventure. That she had been proclaimed Queen of the Desert in Syria, before retreating into a life as a recluse. Each one of these tales, and many others besides, were true.

Her name was Lady Hester Stanhope, and she lived a life like no other woman of her generation. Her grandfather was the legendary prime minister William Pitt the Elder, who died after collapsing on the floor of Parliament midway through an impassioned debate. Her uncle, William Pitt the Younger, would also become prime minister. Hester idolised her illustrious relatives, claiming that Pitt blood flowed through her veins 'like lava'. She always hoped to emulate their achievements, but rarely did it occur to her how difficult this would be for a woman.

Hester's mother was a Pitt, but she died when Hester was only four years old, leaving her in the care of her brilliant but mad father, the Earl of Stanhope. His political views were far-sighted, supporting causes such as democracy, the abolition of monarchies and an end to slavery. But while Citizen Stanhope (as he was known) wanted to bring hope and freedom to humankind abroad, he was a miserable old bastard at home. He banned his children from reading books or wearing 'pretty' clothes, and rarely let them leave the family home in Kent. To ensure that Hester learnt the virtue of a hard day's work, he gave her a small turkey farm to manage.

Strong-willed Hester rebelled against her father's authority, and her career as a wild child started young. When she was taken to the seaside in Kent at the age of eight, she sneaked away, found a boat and rowed out to sea, entirely sure of her ability to reach France. As the pebble beach drifted into the distance and the waves of the English Channel lapped around her boat, she felt no fear, and simply laughed at the horrified faces of those who came to save her.

Once she reached adulthood, Hester desperately wanted to break free from her father's prison and party with other aristocrats. At the age of twenty, she asked for permission to attend a glamorous bash at a neighbouring estate, to which the entire royal family had been invited. Hester's father, who despised the balls and banquets of English high society, refused. So, having borrowed a dress and carriage, she escaped and attended the party without a male companion – something unheard of for women at the time. Undaunted, she spent much of the evening amusing the King of England with stories about her bonkers father.

Hester's reputation for cheeky humour and daring behaviour began to spread. Now a young woman, she was tall and striking, and though not conventionally beautiful, her sparkling face had buckets of character. And she attracted men every bit as hot-blooded as herself.

Whilst most ladies at this time dedicated their early lives to finding a suitable husband, Hester's first romances were entirely unsuitable. Lord Camelford, a lieutenant in the Royal Navy, was tall, strong and ruggedly handsome, with tanned skin and dark curly hair – every bit Hester's type. He was also a scoundrel. Six years at sea had been enough to establish his reputation as the hardest drinker, brawler and womaniser in the Royal Navy. Having been dismissed from the navy in disgrace, he now walked the streets of London in a dirty brown coat with his collar turned up. He kept a pet bulldog named 'Trusty' and enjoyed bareknuckle boxing. In short, Lord Camelford was the poshest thug in London. And Hester found him completely irresistible. Before long, they were lovers.

You can probably guess what Hester's father made of the affair. When she returned home in the spring of 1800, he demanded that they break up, but Hester refused. In desperation, Stanhope pinned his daughter to the wall and held a knife to her throat, but even that did not scare her. Luckily for Stanhope, Camelford was not the sort of man to hang around. He promptly disappeared, only to be arrested a year later in Paris while on a solo mission to assassinate Napoleon Bonaparte, confirming many people's suspicions that he was, in fact, completely mad.

Around this time, Hester's uncle, Pitt the Younger, invited her to live with him. Pitt was a remarkable man. He went to the University of Cambridge aged only fourteen, and became Britain's youngest ever prime minister at the age of twenty-four. He was also very odd. His sole interest in life was politics, meaning that he had not the slightest interest in sexual relationships, male or female. However, he did need someone to help him entertain guests, and knew his cheeky, charming niece Hester could do the job well. It also gave him the chance to keep an eye on her increasingly wayward behaviour.

Hester, now aged twenty-six, adored life as the prime minister's 'hostess' at 10 Downing Street and Walmer Castle, his retreat on the Kent coast. At Pitt's dining table was a rotating cast of the most important politicians and military men of the day, who lavished young Hester with attention. Pitt enjoyed watching his sharp-tongued niece teasing these pompous politicians, and respected her political judgement. He liked to tell her she would have made an excellent military general: 'If you were a man, Hester, I would send you on the Continent with 60,000 men, and . . . I am sure that not one of my plans would fail.'

In February 1804, an ambitious young politician named Lord Granville came through the gates of Walmer Castle. Granville, it was said, was the most good-looking man in England, with blue eyes, dark curly hair and soft sensuous lips. Having recently returned from working as a diplomat in Paris, he also had exquisite taste in wine and women. Now aged 30, he was in the market for marriage. Pitt introduced Hester to Granville and in an instant she was smitten, making it her mission to win this devilishly handsome man as her husband.

At first, Granville seemed to return Hester's affections. She naively allowed him to become her lover, but could not see that she was being used. Granville was already in love with a married lady some years his senior, with whom he had two children. For him, Hester was simply a bit of a fun on the side, and a useful way to get closer to her uncle the prime minister. When Hester began spreading rumours around town that she and Granville were to become engaged, Granville went cold on poor Hester.

Pitt could see that Granville was bad news for his niece, so to get rid of him, he appointed Granville ambassador to the Russian court in St Petersburg. However, Granville continued his on-and-off affair with Hester right until his departure date, leading Hester to believe that Granville would change his mind, propose marriage and take her to Russia as his wife. When it became clear that this was never going to happen, Hester – shamed, humiliated and abandoned – tried to commit suicide.

The poison did not kill her, but it did cause horrible damage to her internal organs, leaving her unable to eat or sleep for twelve days. Pitt was devastated, blaming himself for both introducing Hester to the dastardly Granville and then sending him away. Two years later, Pitt died at the age of forty-six. Many claimed Hester's attempted suicide had hastened Pitt's own departure.

Before Pitt died, he arranged a parting gift for Hester. As a reward for serving as the prime minister's hostess, Parliament granted her a lifelong pension of £1,200 a year. This generous sum of money allowed her to rent a house in west London, where she lived alongside her two younger half-brothers – 'her boys', as she liked to call them. However, with Pitt dead, Hester no longer had a seat at the high table of British politics. She spent much of her time feeling bored and aimless.

What is more, Hester was now approaching thirty and her chances of finding a husband looked increasingly slim. When she met the Scottish army general Sir John Moore in the summer of 1807, she dared to think he could be the one. Moore, who had spent most of his forty-seven years fighting for the British army, had never married. He was handsome in a craggy, weathered sort of way, and beneath his rough military persona was a sophisticated, thoughtful man. Moore saw in Hester an intellectual match, and Hester saw in Moore a trusty, stable companion.

At this time, Britain was in the midst of a vicious war with Napoleon's France. Shortly after General Moore met Hester, he left to help the Spanish resist Napoleon's invasion with an army of 35,000 men (including Hester's two brothers). 'Farewell, my dear Lady Hester,' Moore wrote from the Spanish city of Salamanca, 'If I can beat the French, I shall return to you with satisfaction.' But it was a disastrous campaign, culminating in a cruel winter retreat from Salamanca to the port town of Corunna, where, in January 1809, Moore had his ribs shattered by a French cannonball. Knowing he was dying, he called Hester's brother to his side and breathed his last words, 'Stanhope, remember me to your sister.' For the rest of her life, Hester carried with her the bloodstained glove General Moore was wearing at Corunna.

News of the tragedy sent Hester spiralling into a deep, painful depression. With declining interest from men, and unable to have a career, she faced a future of boredom and irrelevance. But, as she later said, she would never give in to a future of knitting and sewing. There was only one alternative: take to the seas. For years, Hester had put up with politicians and military men telling stories of their great adventures. Now it was her turn. But where to go? A dashing South American freedom fighter named General Miranda, with whom she had a brief fling, suggested that she should set sail for Venezuela and help him start a revolution. But, deciding that was an adventure too far, she settled instead on a tour of the Mediterranean.

On 10 February 1810, Hester set sail for Gibraltar, the British colony at the southernmost tip of Spain. She intended to be away for a year. In fact, she would never return to England.

After years of boredom, the thrill of adventure brought Hester's vibrancy and sense of fun bubbling back to the surface. In Gibraltar, she met two young men, recent graduates from Cambridge University and now on their 'Grand

Tour'. Michael Bruce, a sensitive young man of twenty-three who hoped to become a politician, was trying to take his tour seriously. But his companion, an aristocratic playboy named the Marquis of Sligo, was far more interested in chasing women than expanding his cultural horizons.

Bruce and Sligo invited Hester to join them on their travels, and Hester accepted. She may have been encouraged to do so by the fact that Sligo was stinking rich, and had recently hired his own ship to take them across the Mediterranean. Sligo did not travel light, bringing with him tour guides, cooks, sailors, bodyguards, and even a painter to record his favourite moments. As part of this merry crew, Hester travelled from Gibraltar to Malta, then on to Greece, visiting Zante, the Peloponnese and Athens along the way.

Having escaped England with a broken heart, the last thing Hester planned to do was fall for another tall, dark, handsome toff. But that is exactly what happened next. From the moment they met in Gibraltar, Bruce and Hester felt a connection. Bruce, with his political aspirations, was drawn to Hester's intimate knowledge of government. While Hester saw in Bruce a young man of potential whom she could nurture to greatness. She was more than ten years his senior, and he knew she had something of a reputation. But away from the disapproving gaze of English society and under the warmth of a Mediterranean sun, Hester and Bruce were able to fall in love.

After six months touring the Mediterranean, Hester and Bruce arrived in the 'Golden City' of Constantinople (now Istanbul), capital of the Ottoman Empire. Divided by the mighty Bosporus strait, on one side of the waterway lay Europe, on the other lay Asia. As a crossroads between two continents, Constantinople hosted a kaleidoscope of different cultures, and its streets hummed with the babble of competing languages:

Arabic and Armenian, Persian and Greek. The narrow lanes of its bazaars sold the greatest array of carpets, textiles, silverware and jewellery found anywhere in the Middle East. And on the city's skyline, tall cypress trees and minarets stood guard around the magnificent Topkapi Palace, home to the Ottoman sultan. From this palace, he ruled a grand empire which stretched across southeastern Europe, North Africa and the Middle East.

Hester wasted no time making herself at home in the city, renting a beautiful house on the shores of the Bosporus where she could entertain the great and the good of Ottoman society. The combined spending power of Hester's government pension and a generous allowance from Bruce's father allowed the couple to live in considerable style.

Word quickly spread around Constantinople of this remarkable Englishwoman, and Hester caught the attention of Hafiz Aly, commander of the Ottoman navy. When Bruce went on a mission to find the remains of Troy with his pal Sligo, Hester was left on her own. Hafiz sent ships carrying Turkish delicacies sailing up the Bosporus to her home, and even proposed marriage, promising Hester that together they would produce a line of noble warriors. Hester politely declined. Perhaps she was put off by his decision, after returning from a military campaign in Iraq, to present her with the severed head of one of his enemies. 'The poor head was handed about on a silver dish', Hester later recalled, 'as if it had been a pineapple.'

Hester loved life in Constantinople. However, after a year spent exploring its mosques, bazaars and palaces, she was thirsting for more adventure. She wanted to travel deeper into the Ottoman Empire, to Egypt and the biblical cities of Damascus and Jerusalem.

So, on 23 October 1811, Hester and Bruce set sail for

Egypt. When a winter storm broke, they bitterly regretted their decision to save money by renting a small Greek fishing boat. Rain lashed down and waves crashed against the boat's sides, creating a hole in the hull where water came pouring in. Hester, who liked to laugh in the face of danger, passed around the last reserves of wine to calm everyone's nerves. But it was no good – the boat was sinking.

The crew escaped onto a life raft, and as Hester leapt on board, she managed to grab a small tin of her most treasured possessions, including a lock of Pitt's hair and General Moore's bloodstained glove. Those objects aside, every one of her possessions sank to the bottom of the sea: clothes, letters, diaries, books and jewellery. Some £3,000 worth of luggage, lost for ever.

However, instead of mourning the loss, Hester felt renewed. Deep down she knew how unlikely it was that she would ever return to England. Back home, she would have been shunned by polite society, condemned as a fallen woman to a life of seclusion. But her year in Constantinople taught her that as a European woman travelling independently through the Middle East, she could be welcomed with curiosity and amazement wherever she went.

Hester's past life disappeared beneath the waves that night, and when the life raft was washed ashore on the island of Rhodes the following morning, she began her reinvention. She bought calfskin boots, an embroidered jacket, cotton trousers and a silk sash, into which she tucked a pistol and knife. She shaved her head, so that she could wrap around it a turban of colourful silk. From that day onwards, she never wore European clothes again.

Dressed in their new Turkish attire, Hester and Bruce pushed on to Egypt. Here, Hester was received – as she had hoped – with fascination by Mehmet Ali, the Pasha who ruled Egypt on behalf of the Ottoman sultan. Originally a lowly soldier from Albania, Ali was a brawler who had worked his way to the top of the Ottoman army, and had conquered Egypt through both brilliance and brutality. A year before Hester's arrival, as a gesture of peace to Egypt's ruling class, Ali invited them to a grand reception in his Cairo palace. Once they had gathered inside, Ali's Albanian bodyguards began a massacre. When the guns fell silent, some 470 of his guests lay dead upon the palace floor. The message was clear: don't mess with Ali.

When Ali heard that a noble Englishwoman was travelling through his country dressed as a man, he wanted to meet this curiosity, sending seven liveried horses to bring Hester to his palace. Her charm worked wonders on the Egyptian pasha. He gave her the nickname Meleki, meaning 'angel', and invited her to sit by his side at a military parade. When he sent Hester a prize horse with a man's saddle, she rode it through the streets of Cairo as a man would, her legs straddling either side of the horse. Such behaviour was outrageous: the convention across Europe and Asia was for women to ride side-saddle. But Hester – it was now becoming clear – did not play by anyone else's rules.

Hester remained in Egypt for two months, improving her Arabic and planning the next leg of her journey. By this point, her relationship with Bruce was becoming strained. Bruce adored Hester, and had even proposed marriage – an idea she laughed off as absurd. However, he was frustrated standing on the sidelines as she wowed the Ottoman world, often introduced as her 'cousin'. Hester wrote regularly to Bruce's father, keeping him updated about their affair with a remarkable honesty. But her letters made it clear that their love was never going to last. Following an argument with Bruce, she wrote to his father: 'his taking it ill or well shall make no difference to me; I was not born to be any man's toady.'

On 20 April 1812, Hester and Bruce left Cairo and sailed for Palestine. As she travelled through the Holy Land with her convoy of camels and horses, and a small army of servants, Hester was frequently mistaken for a princess. At night, her grand procession slept in six enormous green tents, each decorated with images of flowers and jewellery, and topped with a brass star and crescent. Hester passed through the holiest sites of the Christian faith – Nazareth, Jerusalem, Bethlehem – and in each of them, a reception fit for a queen was ready to welcome her.

However, when Hester neared the Syrian capital of Damascus, she received a letter from the pasha telling her to continue no farther. Recently, a strict version of Islam had taken hold in the city, making it unsafe for those of other religions to visit. It was said that even the Christians who lived in Damascus did not venture outside after sunset, for fear of having their throats slit. When Hester insisted on visiting the city, the Pasha ordered her to arrive at night, unannounced, and with a veil covering her face.

What did Hester do? On 1 September 1812, she entered Damascus with her face unveiled for all to see, glowing in the amber sunlight of late afternoon. It was an astonishingly bold move, for which she might well have been killed. But, as Hester later put it, the Arab people did not see her as a woman or a man, but as a being apart. In fact, her pale face, her extraordinary self-assurance and her ability to speak Arabic led many to believe she was not human at all, but some sort of goddess.

The people of Damascus poured out to see her, covering

the streets with rosewater and coffee to scent her path through the city. As the days went on, the great figures in the city all held receptions in her honour. On the eve of Ramadan, the Pasha of Damascus himself invited Hester to a candlelit feast at his palace, with 2,000 guards and servants in attendance. And all the while, Hester kept on hearing herself compared to the same legendary figure from Syria's past: Queen Zenobia.

Zenobia was a killer queen of the ancient world. She was, and still is, an icon to the Syrian people, leading the region in a rebellion against the Roman Empire during the third century AD. She went on to rule a short-lived but magnificent Syrian empire from her capital city of Palmyra. To Hester, it was clear what the next step of her adventure must be. She would visit Palmyra, confirming the rumours that she represented nothing less than the second coming of Queen Zenobia.

The only problem was that Palmyra had to be reached via a dangerous 200-mile trek through the Syrian desert. During her travels, Hester had heard countless stories of the nomadic Bedouin tribesmen who controlled the desert, routinely robbing travellers and pilgrims, stripping them naked and leaving them for dead in the sands. What is more, the Bedouin were sworn enemies of their Ottoman overlords, so Hester had little to gain from her new-found friendship with the pashas of Egypt and Damascus.

However, as you must have realised by now, danger was what Hester lived for. From her new home in Damascus, she began cultivating an alliance with Sheikh Muhanna, a powerful Bedouin chief known as the 'Prince of the Desert'. It seems that the Bedouin tribes were just as keen as their Ottoman overlords to befriend the new Zenobia, and in late 1812 she set out to meet Muhanna in the desert. It was her most perilous journey yet, but still she felt no fear. 'I will take flight into the desert,' she wrote to Bruce's father. 'The universe is my country!'

Muhanna welcomed Hester into his Bedouin tribe with gifts of a gold-embroidered robe and a twelve-foot lance topped with black ostrich feathers. As she slept beneath the desert stars in a camel-skin tent, with nothing more than a straw mattress between her and the sand, Hester fell in love with Bedouin life. To her, these proud nomads looked impossibly romantic, dressed in their long woollen robes, daggers and pistols slung round their bodies, eyes smeared with black make-up to protect them from the sun. She looked at their weathered faces and untamed hair across the evening campfires, and considered them to be – in her words – 'the most singular and wonderfully clever people I ever saw'.

Hester's journey to Palmyra began the following spring. With her escort of seventy Bedouin warriors, she rode for twelve hours a day across the desert plain, which stretched to the horizon in a never-ending expanse of shimmering sand and rock. Her skin burnt, her throat cried out for water. Bruce begged that they turn back, but on Hester went.

It was during this journey that Hester experienced her toughest test yet. In the middle of the night, she woke to see her Bedouin warriors leaping on their horses and galloping away, screaming that enemy tribesmen were about to attack. Showing utter fearlessness, Hester leapt on her horse and rode straight towards the enemy. She stood upright in her stirrups, waved her pistol in the air and began a suicidal charge. But as she drew closer, she saw that the attackers were not enemies but her own Bedouin escort. They had faked the attack as a test of Hester's bravery, and she passed with honour. From then on, the Bedouins' loyalty to her was total.

When Hester finally reached the ancient city of Palmyra, it was even more magnificent than she had hoped. Most of the city was abandoned, but its colonnaded streets, holy temples, crumbling mansions and triumphal arch were all clearly visible. Gazing out across the ruins, Hester imagined a city of unsurpassed wealth and luxury, a trading hub with bazaars filled with goods from as far afield as India and China, and ranks of foot soldiers and cavalrymen, all ruled over by the magnificent Queen Zenobia.

The surrounding population were overjoyed to see the new Zenobia riding into their city. Dancing girls lined the central colonnaded street frozen in theatrical poses, and burst into life as Hester passed, bringing her procession to a climax as she reached the triumphal arch. The tribesmen shook their lances, the musicians banged their drums and the crowds sang out with joy as Hester was crowned with a wreath of flowers. Shortly afterwards, she wrote to her cousin, 'Without joking, I have been crowned Queen of the Desert under the triumphal arch of Palmyra . . . I am the sun, the star, the pearl, the lion, the light from Heaven . . . all Syria is in astonishment at my courage and my success.'

Sadly, Hester's rapturous reception in Palmyra would prove to be the high point of her adventure. From that day onwards, everything started to go downhill. When she returned to Damascus, a terrible plague was taking hold in the city. With people dying faster than their bodies could be buried, its inhabitants quickly lost interest in the second coming of Queen Zenobia. Soon she was yesterday's news.

Hester told Bruce it was not safe for him to remain in the plague-ravaged region, and after a heart-wrenching final goodbye, he returned to England. Then, in November 1813, Hester fell ill. It started with aching joints and a terrible headache, before turning into a fever, profuse sweating and violent shivers. Hester had caught the plague.

Over time, Hester would recover, but she was never the same. Her previously vibrant character became more withdrawn, more severe. She toyed with new schemes, pioneering an archaeological dig, attempting to establish a spy network and building her own army of Bedouin warriors. But as she grew older, these schemes became more and more far-fetched. Her grip on reality was weakening.

Hester retreated to a ruined monastery near Mount Lebanon, where she built her fortress palace, a crazed complex of trap doors, secret passageways and hidden rooms. She stopped reading books, claiming that she could gain 'sublime knowledge' through reading the stars. To those who visited her, she prophesied that a new Messiah would come to Earth and take her as his bride. In her palace grounds, she kept two white horses, named Layla and Lulu, on which she and her Messiah would conquer the Kingdom of Jerusalem. The vivid detail of these prophecies was no doubt helped by her fondness for datura, a local drug known for its hallucinogenic properties.

During the 1820s, as civil war engulfed Syria, Hester's monastery became a sanctuary for refugees. They believed her to be royalty, and Hester did not want to let them down, sparing no expense in providing them with care. In doing so her debts spiralled, and soon she owed money to almost every banker in Syria. Her lenders wrote to none other than Mehmet Ali, Hester's old friend from Egypt. Ali wrote to the British government; and in 1837 the government cut off Hester's pension. One year later, she died.

Hester's extraordinary life may well have been forgotten were it not for a man we have not yet encountered. For twenty years, a Scottish doctor named Charles Meryon accompanied Hester on her travels. He worshipped her, claiming, 'She is the best lady that ever breathed.' Following her death, he wrote a three-volume memoir of her life, ensuring her wild adventure lived on in people's memories.

Hester became an icon for other women who dreamed of adventure. Born with an instinctive, irrepressible desire for freedom, she refused to be bound by the expectations of other people. As she grew older, this drove her farther both from society and from her sanity, but perhaps that was inevitable. As she wrote to Bruce shortly after they parted, 'If nature has organised me so strongly I cannot help it. I can never be happy when pestered and when I feel I am not a free agent.'

CHAPTER 10

LORD BYRON

The Danger-loving Poet
Who Scandalised a Nation

On the night of 23 April 1816, the most famous poet in England sat down for dinner with two friends at the Ship Inn in Dover. Some local girls disguised themselves as maids so they could get a closer look at Lord Byron, the ultimate heart-throb of Georgian England.

Writers have spilt gallons of ink over the years trying to capture the combination of lust and loathing that Byron's looks inspired. He had wavy black hair and pale white skin. His jaw was strong, but his nose was fine, leading to blood-red lips which curled into a disdainful smirk. As he talked over dinner, his face would momentarily light up with a beautiful radiance – one friend compared Byron's smile to the gates of heaven. However, each time his face came to rest, it drifted back into the same look of cruelty and sorrow.

Like that of any good celebrity, Byron's personal brand was immediately recognisable. He wore leather boots, tight breeches, a black cloak, a white linen shirt open at the neck, and a gold chain. He walked with a sinister sliding limp, due to a right leg which had been deformed since childhood. If you think he sounds like Count Dracula, you are on to something. The first vampire story was written by Byron's own doctor, the character of a nocturnal, bloodsucking aristocrat based on his patient.

At twenty-eight years of age, Byron appeared more than usually troubled that April evening. Over the past year, his life had fallen apart. His wife had left him, taking their newborn child with her, and he was distraught, drinking ever larger doses of laudanum to dull the pain.

Byron was spending the night in Dover ready to set sail for France the next day, abandoning his broken family and debts of some £30,000. But there was another, more serious reason for his flight. Behind his haunted look were rumours, spread by former lovers, of a dark past. The word on the street was that Byron had been indulging in a sin so heinous, and so obscene, that most dared not speak its name. He had to flee Britain or risk social oblivion and imprisonment, perhaps even death.

'I awoke one morning and found myself famous.' That is how Byron described the fame that greeted him following the publication of his poem, *Childe Harold*, four years earlier in the spring of 1812. It was a style of poem in which Byron would become the master: long stories, told in verse, about damaged heroes in distant lands. 'Childe' was an old-fashioned word for a young knight, and Harold, like most of Byron's heroes, was a thinly disguised version of himself.

Byron based the poem on his own Grand Tour around 'the East', following his graduation from Cambridge University. For two years, he rode through Turkey, Albania and Greece, a land he came to adore. He drank in everything he saw: Ottoman palaces; Greek bandits; Jewish merchants; Turkish baths; the evening call to prayer from a mosque's minaret; fragrant pomegranate and lemon trees; embroidered waistcoats; turbans; daggers; and silver-mounted pistols tucked into silken sashes. He swallowed it all, and spent the next four years pouring these memories into his work.

Byron followed *Childe Harold* with his 'Eastern Tales', a series of five exuberant poems which left his readers breathless. The most popular tale, *The Corsair*, told the story of a dashing but cruel Greek pirate named Conrad, a man of 'one virtue and a thousand crimes'. It sold 10,000 copies on its first day of publication.

Byron was a literary superstar, able to do things in verse that no other poet could dream of. He could transport a maiden aunt from a drizzly Sunday afternoon in Bath to the divan of a sultan's palace or the bloodstained deck of a pirate ship. Intensely vivid and emotional, Byron's poems were not subtle, but they were sensational. His future wife coined a term for the frenzied adoration which greeted his work: 'Byromania.'

Young women seemed particularly vulnerable to Byron's poems, and helpless fangirls flooded his mailbox with declarations of love. The ultimate Byron fangirl was a young aristocrat named Lady Caroline Lamb, with whom he began a fiery affair during the summer of 1812.

Beautiful, brilliant and unhinged, with a slight, boyish figure, large dark eyes and a low, sexy voice, Caroline was in many ways the female mirror of Byron – as a child she had been nicknamed 'the young savage'. She had literary ambitions of her own, and would go on to write a series of successful novels. And like Byron, she was from the cream of English society. Her father was an earl, and her husband was a prominent politician who would later become prime minister. They had a son, but it was an open marriage.

During the summer of 1812, Byron began visiting Caroline's London mansion. In fact, fiery doesn't quite do justice to the intensity of the affair. The first time they made love, Byron asked Caroline to rest her head on a skull, with a case of loaded pistols beside her. Byron was also into role play, so Caroline would visit him dressed as a servant boy. It was Caroline who first described Byron as 'mad, bad and dangerous to know'.

The relationship did not end well. When Byron tried to break it off, Caroline attempted suicide and had to be taken to her family's home in Ireland to recover. That winter, she built a bonfire to burn an effigy of Byron, along with all the letters, chains, rings, flowers and feathers he had sent her. She even paid girls from the nearby village to dance around the flames in white dresses.

However, years later, Caroline was still bombarding Byron with letters. One of them included a cutting of Caroline's hair, not from her head, but somewhere altogether more intimate. And they were stained with blood, as she explained in her letter: 'I cut the hair too close and bled.' Meanwhile, on the rebound, Byron had a dalliance with one of Caroline's friends, a busty forty-year-old aristocrat named Lady Oxford, whose charms Byron described as 'autumnal'.

You could write a whole book on the women Byron loved at the height of his fame, a period he would later call 'his reign'. However, by 1814, he had become entangled in a particularly dangerous love affair with a close relative and needed an escape route. Marriage to a wealthy young woman could provide that escape, as well as some much-needed cash to pay off his debts.

Byron found his target in Annabella Milbanke. Born to a wealthy family of provincial aristocrats, innocent little Annabella was raised in County Durham on England's wild and remote northeast coast, far from the naughty world of

London high society. Pretty but not beautiful, Annabella had a stout figure and simple manners. She was intelligent, with a calm, analytical mind and a love of mathematics – Byron called her 'my Princess of Parallelograms'. In truth, she was in no way Byron's type, but after crazy Caroline, he probably found Annabella's plainness reassuring. To rub salt into his ex-lover's wounds, Annabella also happened to be the niece of Caroline's mother-in-law.

Sensible Annabella, who knew of Byron's bad-boy reputation, refused his first proposal of marriage. But when he proposed again a year later, she said yes. She was naïve enough to believe she could fix his wayward character. How wrong poor Annabella was.

Their wedding in January 1815 was a total disaster. The couple chose to have a small, private ceremony at Annabella's parents' house, Seaham Hall, on the windswept North Sea coast. Byron approached the day with the quiet despair of a convicted man, arriving so late that Annabella's mother refused to greet him. The night before the wedding, his own best man tried to call the whole thing off, and Annabella's mother spent the following morning in tears. Nevertheless, the marriage went ahead. That evening, Byron made love to Annabella for the first time on a sofa before dinner. He then woke her up early the next morning, crying out, 'Good God, I am surely in hell!'

When Lord and Lady Byron moved to their new London home, matters only deteriorated. Married life brought out the worst in Byron. In drunken rages, he would tear around their house, breaking and burning their belongings. Having taken a job on the management committee of a theatre, he spent his evenings lounging around theatre lobbies, drinking brandy and seducing young actresses. As he left for the theatre he would taunt Annabella, telling her, 'I am looking out to see who will suit me best.'

In December 1815, Annabella told Byron she was going into labour with their first child. His response was to go out, get drunk and come home late. He then started throwing glass bottles at the ceiling to disturb his wife as she gave birth in the room above. By this point, Byron's sadistic bullying had become too much for his poor wife to bear. However, she did not take her husband's behaviour personally, concluding instead that he must be under the influence of a mental disorder.

Annabella was probably correct. Generations of Byron men had earned a reputation for being irresistible to women and impossible to marry, romping through life with a trail of heartbroken lovers, illegitimate children and unpaid bills in their wake. The Byron family motto was 'Crede Byron', meaning 'Trust in Byron'. It is difficult to think of a more unsuitable instruction: the Byron men were some of the least trustworthy in Britain, and as mad as march hares.

Byron's own father was called 'Mad Jack' Byron. He was a dashing and danger-loving officer in the British army who gambled away the fortune of his first wife, herself a baroness, before stealing the heart of another wealthy young woman, Byron's mother, Catherine. He gambled away her fortune in a matter of years, then fled to France where he died aged thirty-five of tuberculosis. Though Byron never knew his father, he idolised him, always imagining (incorrectly) that Mad Jack had left the world by slitting his own throat.

Nobody was that surprised when, a month after giving birth, Annabella left London with her child, telling Byron they needed time apart. A few weeks later, he received a letter from her lawyer requesting a formal separation. Byron would never see his wife, or his daughter, again.

Prior to leaving London, Annabella rifled through Byron's private papers, looking for the evidence she needed to separate from her husband while keeping custody of their daughter. She suspected that Byron had committed a heinous sin, and her lawyer urged her to find proof. Byron's vengeful ex-lover Caroline was only too happy to help out, sharing her own suspicions of his scandalous past. Before long these stories had escaped the lawyer's office and entered the London rumour mill.

Annabella had kicked a hornet's nest, creating a swarm of gossip that would chase Byron away from his family and his country of birth for good. But what was the heinous sin had he committed? Well, there was not one, but two.

The first was sodomy. Byron enjoyed having sex with women, but he gained his truest, most profound pleasure from men. Georgian Britain had a well-established homosexual underworld, particularly among the aristocracy, to which society had – for much of the period – turned a blind eye. However, as the nineteenth century dawned, a tougher and less tolerant national culture was taking root, leading to a violent crackdown on homosexuality. Five years previously a well-known gay hangout in London, the White Swan on Vere Street, had been raided. Twenty-seven men were arrested, eight were tried, and two were executed.

Byron was caught out by this change in the moral climate. He knew sodomy was punishable by death, but had never been that good at keeping his liaisons with men a secret. In fact, he quite enjoyed shocking friends and family by hinting at them, particularly when he was drunk, which was often. In these moments, with his filter switched off, who knows what conquests Byron had bragged about?

To start with, there were the boarding-school boys he had

flirted with at Harrow, and the handsome young chorister named John with whom he fell in love at Cambridge. And then there were his travels in the East, where homosexuality was practised much more freely. This was one of the main reasons Byron had chosen to travel there in the first place, and he was not disappointed. He kept a young Greek lover named Niccolo, enjoyed a gay orgy in Athens, and revelled in the homosexual subculture of Turkish baths – 'those marble palaces of sherbet and sodomy', as he described them.

But sodomy was not the worst of Byron's sins. More scandalous still were the accusations of incest.

Byron's childhood had been deeply unhappy, brought up as the only child of his depressed single mother, Catherine. She submitted him to a series of painful treatments on his right leg, intended – unsuccessfully – to cure his deformity, and he grew up overweight and anxious, with a lifelong habit of biting his nails.

Byron longed for a large, loving family, so when he met his half-sister Augusta for the first time aged fifteen, he felt an immediate connection. She was the product of 'Mad Jack' Byron's first marriage to the baroness, a remnant of the father Byron never knew. This connection turned into an obsession, and before long Byron was in love with Augusta. He saw her as the only person in the world with whom he could behave without a mask.

Ten years later, Augusta and Byron reconnected. By now he was twenty-five and at the height of his fame, while Augusta was married to a cavalry officer in the British army, with whom she had three children. However, during her husband's long absences, Byron would visit her country house in the Cambridgeshire village of Six Mile Bottom. Sometime in the summer of 1813, they became lovers.

Byron must have known that what he was doing was wrong, but he could not help himself. In fact, he always found it easiest to fall in love when there was some terrible danger involved. They were not even concerned about keeping their relationship a secret, and had pet names for each other: she called him 'baby Byron', while he called her 'Goose'.

Two months into their marriage, Byron and Annabella went to stay with Augusta at Six Mile Bottom. Byron submitted both his wife and his sister to a week of unbearable torture, teasing his sister, humiliating his wife, and forcing both of them to participate in kissing competitions. When angry with Annabella, he would order her upstairs to leave him with Augusta, telling her, 'we can amuse ourselves without you, my dear', or with nasty sarcasm, 'my charmer'. When angry with Augusta, he openly threatened to tell Annabella of their secret.

Heaven knows what Annabella must have thought, lying in bed on her own, as she listened to her drunken husband canoodling with his half-sister in the room below. When Byron finally did make it upstairs, the worse for wear after a night on the brandy, he would taunt her, 'Now I have *her*, you will find I can do without *you*.'

Running around the house at the time was Augusta's fourth child Medora, named after the heroine of *The Corsair*. Byron was Medora's godfather, and delighted in calling her 'my child'. What could he have meant? Many still wonder today whether Medora was, in actual fact, Byron's child.

By the spring of 1816, rumours of Byron's incest and sodomy were all over London. Overnight he was transformed from the darling of English society into a symbol of all that was wrong with England's sinful, aristocratic elite. Those newspapers which had built him into a national hero now tore him down as a depraved pervert. The hatred was so fierce that

Byron feared assassination, and threatened to blow his own brains out with a pistol. There was no other option but exile.

Byron did manage to fit in one last affair before he left for France, another helpless Byron admirer named Claire Clairmont. Brought up in a bohemian London household of authors and philosophers, Claire was raised to be a woman of independence and initiative. Now approaching adulthood, she arranged to lose her virginity to Byron in a secretive hook-up somewhere on the edge of London, and he obliged. He was pretty relaxed about the whole affair, later writing, 'I never loved nor pretended to love her . . . but a man is a man – and if a girl of eighteen comes prancing to you at all hours – there is but one way.' Byron left with his passions sated, and Claire left pregnant with her first child. She was, in fact, seventeen.

A few days later, Byron sailed from Dover for France. He may have been a disgraced social outcast in exile, but that did not stop him from travelling in style. Before leaving London, he purchased a magnificent black carriage, drawn by four horses and emblazoned with his family crest of a mermaid holding a mirror, and that motto *Crede Byron*. It was a miniature palace on wheels, containing full dining equipment, a library and a bed.

Byron modelled his carriage on that of the French Emperor Napoleon Bonaparte, which had carried him on his military campaigns around Europe. He had always idolised Napoleon, seeing him as a modern-day hero sweeping away the old order of monarchies and aristocracy, installing liberty and progress in their place. However, only a year before, Napoleon had been defeated at the Battle of Waterloo and removed from his imperial throne in Paris, much to Byron's disappointment.

As he travelled through Belgium, Byron made a pilgrimage

to the battlefield of Waterloo, its plains still strewn with the bullets and broken swords of the dead. From there he travelled to Germany, and along the River Rhine, before spending the summer in the Alps. That autumn he descended into Italy, reaching his final destination, Venice, in November.

There was one stop on Byron's 1816 European tour which deserves further mention, as it led to one of the most famous nights in the history of English literature. In the Swiss city of Geneva, Byron ran into none other than Claire Clairmont, now three months pregnant with his child. She was travelling with her half-sister, the author Mary Godwin, and her lover, the poet Percy Shelley. No doubt at Claire's insistence, the literary trio decided to make the most of Byron's arrival and rented a villa on the edge of Lake Geneva. Byron rented another, grander villa nearby, and together they planned to spend the summer relaxing, writing, and enjoying the fortuitous coming together of four brilliant young minds.

However, the weather that summer was awful, an unbroken spell of mists, fogs, rain and eerie deadness. They spent much of their holiday stuck indoors with nothing to do. So, one night, Byron suggested a competition. They would see who could tell the most blood-curdling, horrifying ghost story imaginable.

Mary spent the next few weeks developing the story of a German scientist who creates a living creature from dead matter, which becomes a monster and turns on its creator. Two years later, her story was published with the title *Frankenstein*. Byron told the story of a nocturnal, blood-sucking aristocrat. His doctor stole the story, and had it published three years later as *The Vampyre*. Thus, gothic literature was born that stormy night in Geneva in 1816.

When Byron reached Venice at the end of the year, he was

greeted with that strange sensation of having arrived somewhere new, but feeling instantly at home. Venice in 1816 was not the bustling tourist trap of today. English visitors flocked to Naples and Florence, the 'Ramsgate and Margate' of Italy, as Byron snobbishly put it. Venice, meanwhile, was a half-derelict backwater, ruled by a foreign power, the Austrian Hapsburgs.

Once a proud independent city state, Venice was now in decline, its people so poor that even noblemen begged on the streets. However, Byron loved the eerie, dreamlike quality of its canals, the romance of its inhabitants, and its lazy, seductive atmosphere. He saw in Venice's faded glamour a reflection of himself, a ruin amidst ruins.

Venice may have been poor, but its people knew how to party. Byron took a lease on the Palazzo Mocenigo, overlooking the Grand Canal, and set about turning it into the headquarters of an epic two-year binge. It was here that Byron's behaviour reached peak debauchery. Having sold his family estate, and with his poems flying off the shelves, he was flush with cash and spent wildly, submerging himself in the pleasures of the flesh. Byron once claimed to have slept with 200 women during these first two years in Venice.

Byron in Venice was like an overgrown child, living out his every fantasy. Having always loved animals, he kept a private zoo on the first floor of his palazzo, containing dogs, birds, monkeys, a fox and a wolf. In the midst of the summer heat, the smell must have been pretty special.

Presiding over Byron's mad palazzo was his housekeeper and lover. Named Margherita, she was anything but plain. A feisty working-class Italian, she had beautiful eyes, a foul mouth and a strong body – 'fit to breed gladiators from', was Byron's verdict. He found her exaggerated emotions hilarious, and seems to have employed her mostly for comic value. Of particular amusement for Byron was her habit of crossing her body while making love whenever she heard a church bell ring. Despite being a poor baker's wife, she took on the role of lady of the house, bossing around the other servants in an aristocratic gown and feathered hat.

As fun as it may sound, Byron's man-child behaviour in Venice did become a bit embarrassing. He wrote poems here and there, but failed to produce anything on a par with *Childe Harold* or the 'Eastern Tales'. When Percy Shelley visited the palazzo in summer 1818, he was saddened to see his hero sacrificing his literary gift to a prolonged, self-destructive bender. Other friends reported that the poet, once so gorgeous, had put on weight and was looking pale and tired. Endless tales of late-night debauchery seemed rather sad coming from a has-been writer the wrong side of thirty, with bad breath and a receding hairline.

Byron did, eventually, straighten himself out. He became a regular attendee at Venice's *conversazioni*, civilised gatherings where the city's elite discussed literature, art and politics. His favourite was hosted by a countess known as *el fumento* (the oven), due to her habit of keeping a slab of warm polenta between her breasts, ready to nibble on whenever she felt hungry. There, in the spring of 1819, Byron met a beautiful young countess named Teresa.

A well-educated and fiery young woman, Teresa was stuck in a loveless marriage to a count three times her age. Although Byron had vowed to take no new female acquaintances, he was struck by her flowing blonde hair and 'uncommonly good' bust, and excited by her passion and volatility. According to Teresa's recollections later in life, the moment her and Byron's eyes met at *el fumento*'s party was to 'seal the destiny of their hearts.' The following year, she abandoned her count for the English poet.

For the next four years, Byron and Teresa lived together, by far his longest single relationship. One of Byron's friends later recalled that Teresa was the 'only *real* love of his whole life.' They ended up settling in Pisa alongside a circle of English adventurers and artists, including Percy Shelley. These were perhaps the happiest and most productive years of Byron's life, during which he wrote his greatest poem yet, the satirical masterpiece *Don Juan*.

However, Byron had always been preoccupied by thoughts of death, and settling down with Teresa gave him a renewed fear of his own mortality. In 1822, the daughter Byron had with Claire died aged five. Three months later, Shelley was caught in a storm while at sea and drowned, his body washed up on the sands. Shelley's boat, which had sunk to the bottom of the sea, was called the *Don Juan*.

The death of Byron's daughter and friend in quick succession sent him into a spiral of depression and self-examination. He had always worshipped the great men of history, men like Napoleon, who had left their mark on the world in actions, not words. Compared to such men, what had he achieved? After thirty-four years on this earth, all he had to show for it were a few pretty poems and endless tales of his stories of bedchamber shenanigans. Hardly heroic. Some work of noble note, he hoped, might yet be done.

The answer came in April 1823, with the arrival at Byron's house of two messengers – a British naval officer and a Greek revolutionary. For the past 400 years, Greece, once the greatest civilisation on Earth, had been ruled by the Turks of the Ottoman Empire, its people oppressed, its culture buried. However, in 1821, the Greeks had risen up against their

Turkish overlords and taken control of their southern heart-
land, the Peloponnese.

Across Europe, idealistic young men, raised on the myths
of ancient Greece, volunteered to join the Greek Revolution.
The London Greek Committee was formed to organise the
British contribution, and sent messengers to see whether
Byron was willing to lend his celebrity power to their cause.
Perhaps a donation? Or a few poems? They had little idea
how enthusiastic his response would be.

Since the Grand Tour he had taken as a young man, Byron
had been obsessed with the thought of Greek independence.
In *Don Juan*, Byron imagines a Greek poet singing a song of
freedom for his nation:

> The mountains look on Marathon,
> And Marathon looks out the sea;
> And musing there an hour alone,
> I dream'd that Greece might still be free.

This was Byron's chance to help make that dream a reality.
There and then, he promised to join the cause and fight
alongside the Greek rebels. Teresa was devastated, but she
knew that once made up, her lover's mind could not be
changed. He planned to leave in three months, and became
a whirlwind of energy, ordering a scarlet and gold military
uniform from Genoa's best tailor, and an ornate brass helmet
modelled on those of the heroes of ancient Greece. It had
great feathered plumes and was stamped with the Byron family
crest and motto.

In July 1823, dressed in his glittering new uniform and
helmet, Byron set sail for Greece on his own chartered ship.
Its name? Why, *Hercules* of course! Byron had always loved

dressing up, but this time his soldier's uniform was for real. It was as if Lord Byron was stepping onto the page of one of his poems, the hero of his newest, most epic tale yet.

After a stop off on the island of Cephalonia, Byron sailed for the Greek port of Missolonghi in December. Missolonghi was right in the thick of the action, guarding the border between the newly independent Greek nation and its foe the Ottoman Empire. The town's inhabitants gave Byron a hero's welcome of artillery and musket fire, overjoyed to witness this world-famous poet joining their cause.

However, in truth, there was little that was heroic about Missolonghi. It was a poor, war-ravaged town on a swampy lagoon, teeming with mosquitoes and malaria. Two years after their glorious uprising, the Greek armies were tired and disillusioned. Infighting and stalemate had taken hold.

But Byron was desperate for action. He struck up an alliance with a group of colourfully dressed warriors known as the Souliotes, originally from the mountains of Albania, but now fighting with the Greeks. Byron loved these dashing, roguish soldiers, and took 500 of them into his pay, forming the core of a force that became known as the 'Byron Brigade'. Other soldiers soon joined, attracted by Byron's large quantities of cash. Equipped with his own small army, Byron assumed the role of general, and began planning an attack on a Turkish-held port to the east of Missolonghi named Lepanto. Bursting with excitement, he declared, 'Glorious Apollo! No General had ever before such an army!'

However, Byron spoke too soon. Poems about war rarely cover the tedious tasks of gathering ammunition supplies, recruiting officers and resolving pay disputes, but this – Byron soon found out – was the reality of war. Worst of all, his brave Souliote warriors treated their leader, the noble

Lord Byron, like a cash machine. Many enlisted twice in the Byron Brigade under different names, tricking him into giving them double pay.

In February 1824, Byron's attack on Lepanto was called off. The Byron Brigade had become a laughing stock, and its general was left humiliated. As the weather turned, day after day of pouring rain left Byron trapped in this remote, worn-out town, with little prospect of seeing action. His hopes of glorious war were now on hold, and he was constantly pestered for money, or expected to resolve the petty squabbles of his troops.

Byron found some distraction by falling in love with his Greek servant, a handsome young man called Lukas. Byron came on strong, but Lukas was having none of it. The great seducer had, it seems, lost his touch. It sounds pathetic, but Lukas's rejection hit Byron hard. Nobody said no to Lord Byron! But now, it seemed, they did. He was clearly past his prime.

Then, while on one of his daily horse rides outside Missolonghi that April, Byron was caught in a ferocious downpour. Returning home, he was deathly pale and shivering uncontrollably. The chill turned into a fever, and for the next ten days Byron lay in bed, suffering from spasms, vomiting, and a rattling, choking cough.

Byron told his doctor not to bother treating him. 'Die I must,' he claimed, 'for to terminate my wearisome existence I came to Greece.' In circumstances a bit less heroic than he perhaps hoped, his wish was granted. On 19 April 1824, Byron died, his last words being 'I want to sleep now'. A bit of a let-down for the most celebrated English poet since Shakespeare.

However, there was no disputing the brilliance of Byron's

life. *The Times* called him 'the most remarkable Englishman of his generation'. The love for his poems only grew in the years that followed his death, but today, it is the legend of his life that has implanted itself most firmly in the public imagination. He is one of the few writers in English history whose name has become an adjective: 'Byronic', used to describe any tale of heroism over which some dark shadow looms.

'The great object of life,' Byron once wrote, 'is Sensation – to feel that we exist – even though in pain – it is this "craving void" which drives us to Gaming – to Battle – to Travel – to intemperate but keenly felt pursuits of every description.' Today, in every doomed celebrity, irresistible rogue and live-fast-die-young rock star who disdains public convention while seducing public affection, there remains a trace of the Byronic.

Not only did Byron live this life, he wrote it, leaving behind volumes of exuberant verse which capture the imagination of Byromaniacs to this day. Such a life, some would say, can never die.

CHAPTER 11
MARY ANNING

The Dorset Fossil Hunter
Who Helped Discover the Origins of Life

In 1812, many people still believed that the world was 6,000 years old. Well, 5,816 years old, to be precise. In 1650, an Irish bishop studied all the descendants of Adam and Eve listed in the Bible, and estimated that the Earth was created on Sunday 23 October, 4004 BC. For those who saw the Bible as the ultimate source of truth, this remained the best guess going for the age of the Earth.

Life on Earth had always been seen as static, with a straight line from the creatures God made during the seven days of creation to those that exist today. No extinction. No evolution. It came as quite a surprise, therefore, when a young girl and her brother dug the skeleton of an enormous, unknown sea creature out of the cliffs beside Lyme Regis, Dorset, sometime in 1812.

Strange findings were common in this part of the world. Local people would scour the beaches for neatly coiled spirals known as 'snakestones', said to help women become pregnant, or long, pointed rocks known as 'devil's fingers', said to cure blindness. Where did these rocks come from? Nobody knew. One popular theory was that they were decorations planted below the Earth's surface by God, like the flowers planted above its surface.

However, nothing like this sea creature had ever been found before. The brother, Joseph Anning, uncovered the skull in 1811. At first it looked like a crocodile, but its sockets held enormous eyes the size of dinner plates. Joseph wanted to keep digging, but he had to start work in town as an apprentice to a furniture maker. So he left his younger sister to finish the job.

For month after month, Mary Anning chipped away at the cliff, the bitter sea winds biting through her layers of skirts and shawls. One year later, she had uncovered an entire, intact skeleton. This extraordinary creature was seventeen feet long, with the mouth of a crocodile, the eyes of a fish, the body of a lizard and the flippers of a dolphin. Now known as an ichthyosaur, it was not a dinosaur, as dinosaurs do not live at sea, but it did date from the Jurassic era, some 200 million years ago.

Mary's ichthyosaur was the first in a series of discoveries she would make over the next thirty years, transforming humankind's understanding of life on Earth. Most remarkable of all, when she finished chipping away at that Lyme Regis cliff and excavated the ichthyosaur, she was only twelve years old. But then again, there had always been something about Mary.

She was born in Lyme Regis, a small fishing town on the southwest coast of England, in 1799. Lyme was once a thriving medieval port, but as trade moved north the town went into decline, leaving a population of 1,000 inhabitants to eke out a living from fishing and smuggling, and a smattering of summer tourists.

Not much ever happened in Lyme, so when a troupe of performing horsemen came to visit one summer's day in 1800, most of the town turned out to watch. A friendly neighbour named Elizabeth took one-year-old Mary to the show, but it was a washout. Clouds rolled in from the sea, rain poured down, and loud thunderclaps rumbled overhead. Looking for shelter, Elizabeth ran beneath a tree with baby Mary in her arms. Bad idea. A lightning fork burst through the clouds, sending branches and leaves in every direction. Moments later, Elizabeth lay motionless on the floor, her body blackened and charred, her hair matted, and smoke rising from her shoes.

Elizabeth was dead, but somehow Mary was still alive. She was seized from Elizabeth's arms and rushed back to the Annings' cottage, where a doctor bathed her in a tub of warm water. After an agonising wait, the doctor announced that Mary's breathing had steadied and she would survive. A crowd that had gathered around the cottage erupted in cheers. From that day onwards, the people of Lyme often said that being struck by lightning was the making of this young girl. As she grew to be an adult, she always kept her spark: a strong-willed young woman with a fine mind and a sharp tongue.

During Mary's fight for survival, her mother must have looked on in horror, thinking she was about to lose her second daughter called Mary in as many years. In 1798, the first Mary Anning had been keeping warm beside the fire on a cold winter's day, aged just four. Mrs Anning left her unattended for five minutes. She returned to find that a spark from the fire had set light to a pile of wood shavings, burning her daughter to death.

Mary's parents, therefore, were no strangers to hardship. Her father was a well-known figure in town: a tall, bushy-bearded carpenter with thick workman's arms, he was a natural rebel, once leading a local protest against high food prices. Though he owned a small carpentry workshop, his real passion was searching for fossils in the cliffs beside Lyme Regis and selling them to tourists from a table outside his cottage.

This passion consumed the entire family. Whenever storms hit the Dorset coast, new layers of cliff would fall away, revealing more hidden treasures. The Annings would wait patiently inside their cottage until the storm passed, at which point Mr Anning would stride out to the beach with his tools, Mary and Joseph running behind him in their wooden clogs, ready to help bring home the harvest.

Mr Anning taught his children to spot a fossil from the slightest changes in a rock's colour or texture. Mary adored her father, and her fossil-hunting skills were legendary. It was said that from looking at a pile of fifty rocks, she could pick the exact one which – with a tap of her hammer – would crack to reveal a beautiful snakestone or smooth devil's finger. Back in the cottage their mother Molly, in her white apron and bonnet, would scrub the fossils clean, ready to be sold.

Unfortunately, fossil hunting did not bring in a steady income, and the Anning family always struggled with money. In 1804, none other than Jane Austen holidayed in Lyme Regis, and visited Mr Anning's poky little workshop to have the lid of her jewellery box valued. He put it at five shillings, a price – Austen observed in a letter to her sister – 'beyond the value of all the furniture in the room together'.

In 1807, Mr Anning set out to flog some of his fossils at the Pilot Boat Inn, a popular stopping place for coaches travelling to London. As he began the three-mile walk along the cliffs, a mist drifted in from the sea. He lost his footing on the clifftop path, fell to the beach and was knocked unconscious. Somehow, he came to and stumbled home, but he was never the same man again. In 1810, bedridden and coughing up blood, he died.

Two years later, Mary uncovered her ichthyosaur. Perhaps it was the memory of her fossil-mad father which kept her chipping away through those long winter months. She sold the skeleton for £23 to a local landowner, who had it exhibited in London. This diabolical monster of the Dorset coast caused quite a sensation, and people travelled from across Britain and beyond to see it.

Twelve-year-old Mary was now a legend in Lyme. Early most mornings, she could be seen walking to the cliffs, her cheeks reddened by the cold sea winds. Never that bothered by her appearance, Mary wore homemade dresses, layers of shawls, and her hair tied roughly in a bun.

Mary also took to wearing a top hat stiffened with tree resin to protect against rockfalls and mudslides. Fossil hunting was dangerous work. She escaped from being swept out to sea countless times desperately trying to uncover a fossil before the tide came in. There was also the danger of rival fossil hunters stealing her finds, especially when Mary had to visit the local quarry to find men who could help her shift the bigger rocks. Later in life, she took on an assistant called Tray – a beloved black and white terrier whom she trained to guard her finds from thieves until she returned.

Although Mary was a loner, she did form strong friendships with those who shared her love of fossils. Elizabeth Philpot lived at the posh end of town and was a keen fossil hunter. Though Elizabeth was twenty years older than Mary and belonged to a different social class, the pair became firm friends. As an educated woman, Elizabeth encouraged Mary to nurture her scientific interest.

Before long, Mary was able to hold her own in discussion with some of the greatest scientists of the day. In 1815, an Oxford professor named William Buckland came to visit her cottage. A jovial figure with a round face and a cheeky sense of humour, Buckland was famously eccentric. He was obsessed with the natural world, and his rooms at Oxford teemed with snakes, frogs, guinea pigs and birds. An invitation for dinner with Buckland could mean dining on hedgehog, ostrich, porpoise or crocodile. It was his stated ambition in life to 'eat my way through the animal kingdom'.

In 1815, Buckland's obsession with geology, or 'undergroundology' as he called it, was taking off, and he was in Lyme Regis to pick Mary's brains. He and Mary must have made a strange sight fossil-hunting together, the sixteen-year-old country girl in her scrappy old dress chatting away with the professor from Oxford, dressed in a suit and formal academic gown (which he insisted on wearing even for the most inappropriate of tasks).

Buckland had grown up just six miles away in the village of Axminster, where his father was a clergyman. Since he first saw them on holiday as a child, Buckland had been fascinated by the mysterious cliffs of Lyme Regis. The cliffs are made up of layers of the muddy rock known as shale, compressed on the seabed over millions of years, then pushed above the Earth's surface to resemble the pages of a scrunched-up book. To those who learnt to read these pages, the secret history of life on Earth could be found. However, Buckland did not always like what he read.

Like his father, Buckland was a committed Christian, and he desperately wanted to reconcile what was found in those cliffs with the Bible stories he had memorised as a child. How could an ancient sea creature have ended up encased in a

Dorset cliff? Easy, Buckland would answer. It must have been as a result of Noah's flood.

Across the Channel in France, another scientist was struggling with similar questions, but coming up with very different answers. With his shock of red hair and piercing blue eyes, Georges Cuvier was said to be the cleverest man in Europe, the 'Napoleon of the intellect'. His theories of life on Earth were all-conquering, and in 1819 the French state made him a baron for his contributions to science.

Baron Cuvier's specialism was animal anatomy, and it was said that he could identify an entire animal from being shown a single bone. However, some of the bones that had recently been dug up in France did not fit with any animals known to exist today. Could Noah's flood explain why elephant skeletons were being found in the Alps? And why did these elephants have enormous tusks and woolly skin?

Cuvier was the first scientist to establish the woolly mammoth as a separate species from the elephant, and one that had become extinct. In doing so, he developed a theory that the Earth passes through phases of creation and extinction. Unlike Buckland, this theory made no reference whatsoever to the Bible.

By the start of the nineteenth century, geology was the most exciting new science in Europe. Due to the Industrial Revolution, the ground was being dug up like never before, making way for canals, coal mines and factories. And where you dig, you find fossils. In Britain, a whole new species of 'gentlemen geologists' had emerged to study these findings. And the emphasis was on gentle*men*. Their headquarters was the London Geological Society, a men-only club where members could discuss their theories late into the night over dinner and wine.

How ironic it was that their theories would come to be so influenced by the findings of a poor, uneducated young woman living on the west coast of England.

At this time, Mary and her family were becoming poorer. When he died, Mr Anning left them £120 in debt, and these were hard times for the working people of Dorset. War with Napoleon robbed Lyme of what little trade it had left and tripled the price of bread. In 1811 the Annings applied for parish relief, an early form of benefits paid out by the wealthier people of the town. Claiming parish relief would have filled a proud, working family like the Annings with shame.

In March 1820, a retired army officer and fossil hunter named Colonel Thomas Birch paid a visit to the Annings' cottage and was distressed by what he saw. He regularly visited the Annings, but now saw the family responsible for some of the most important geological findings in Britain reduced to selling off their family furniture, just to pay the rent.

The following month, Birch put his entire collection of fossils up for auction in London. There were buyers from as far afield as Germany, Austria and France, including the great Baron Cuvier, who purchased an ichthyosaur for his museum in Paris. Overall, Birch raised £400, all of which he donated to the Annings.

This remarkable show of kindness gave Mary the financial security to keep on hunting fossils, and she did so with gusto. Three years later, Mary made her greatest discovery yet. It was a December morning in 1823, and winter storms had once again caused the cliff face to collapse. Scouring the rubble, Mary began uncovering a new skeleton. What emerged was almost too extraordinary to be believed.

The nine-foot sea creature had the head, paddles and body of a turtle. However, separating its head from its stout little body was an almost comically large neck, making up half its length. Such a neck defied belief: today's reptiles have up to eight separate bones in their necks, but this creature had thirty-five. It would have made the creature unable to swim underwater, and an impossibly easy target for sharp-toothed predators.

Mary, who was excellent at drawing, made sketches of her finding and sent them to various gentlemen geologists. The Duke of Buckingham purchased the skeleton for £110, the highest price ever paid for a fossil.

Then, disaster. One of Mary's sketches ended up in the hands of Baron Cuvier in Paris, and he promptly declared Mary's finding a fake. As an expert anatomist, he simply refused to believe the length of the creature's neck. Instead, he suggested that this Dorset peasant girl had fixed the skeleton of a snake onto the body of a sea creature in a vain attempt to make a few more quid from its buyer.

The accusation could have destroyed Mary's career. Thankfully, her old pal Professor Buckland was not going to let that happen. Having recently been made President of the Royal Geological Society, he arranged for a special meeting on 20 February 1824 to discuss her latest finding.

Anning's discovery was set in concrete and shipped from Dorset to London. When it arrived at the Geological Society in Covent Garden, it was too large to fit into the meeting hall and had to sit in a dark corridor, where visitors could inspect it by candlelight. Two geologists presented a paper to the assembled guests, arguing that Mary's plesiosaur (as it had been termed) was genuine. They reasoned that its neck must have stayed above water, curling downwards like an ancient, reptilian swan. The assembled guests were convinced, and when news of their paper reached Cuvier, he quietly dropped his accusation. It was a remarkable victory: poor uneducated Dorset girl 1, esteemed French scientist and nobleman 0.

The next few years were the most exciting of Mary's career. By 1826, she had saved enough money to buy a shop at the posh end of town, near her friend Elizabeth Philpot. Its large white sign read 'Anning's Fossil Depot': how proud her father would have been.

That same year, Elizabeth and Mary landed upon an ingenious new way to make money. Looking at the squid caught by the local fishermen of Lyme Regis, Mary suspected that the long, pointed devil's fingers found on the nearby beach were in fact the fossilised remains of ancient squid. True enough, when they cracked one open, they found a tiny chamber of dried-up ink.

Elizabeth then had an idea. They could add warm water to the fossilised ink, make a brown paint, and use that to create images of Jurassic Dorset. Soon, a painting made from 100-million-year-old fossilised squid ink became the must-have souvenir for any wealthy visitor to Lyme Regis.

During the Christmas holidays of that year, Buckland turned up at Mary's cottage asking about some smooth, curled stones he had found on the beach in Lyme. Having noticed these stones in the intestines of fossilised sea creatures, Mary already had an answer: they were lumps of fossilised faeces. Dinosaur poop.

Most gentlemen geologists thought this an indelicate subject of study, but the eccentric Buckland and plain-speaking Mary positively revelled in the comedy of crapology. Buckland became obsessed with dinosaur poop, which he termed coprolites. He even had a table made for his drawing room with polished coprolites inlaid into the wood.

To analyse them further, Mary and Buckland would heat

coprolites in warm water until they began to soften, releasing into her kitchen a foul stench that had been locked up for millions of years. They were then able to study the small bones and scales that lay inside the coprolites, thus determining the diets of Jurassic creatures, and building a prehistoric food chain which separated the eaters from the eaten. Today, coprology is widely practised amongst geologists, but it was Buckland and Mary who pioneered the discipline in her small Dorset home.

Two years later, Mary made another thrilling discovery. Once again, December storms had been battering the cliffs outside Lyme, and searching through the rubble Mary saw what looked like a wing. As she began chipping away, the creature that emerged looked like the stuff of nightmares: it had the body of a lizard, the snout of a crocodile and the pointed wings of a bat, out of which protruded long hooked fingers. Mary had made the first ever discovery, outside Germany, of a pterodactyl.

As soon as he heard the news, Buckland raced to Lyme Regis to see Mary's pterodactyl, and he bought it from her there and then. This gave him the privilege of presenting it to the Royal Geological Society in February 1829. He described it with his trademark flair, setting the public imagination on fire by declaring it to be 'a monster resembling nothing that has ever been seen or heard-of upon earth, excepting the dragons of romance and heraldry'.

However, as Britain went pterodactyl mad, Mary received very little recognition for her work. Buckland had taken official credit for her discovery. This was a frustration that plagued Mary throughout her career, but now it was her old pal Buckland who was writing Mary out of her own story. Perhaps it was Buckland she was thinking of when Mary said, some years later, that the great men of learning had taken advantage of her. They 'sucked her brains' of her knowledge, and stole the glory of her discoveries for themselves, leaving her with nothing.

For the gentlemen of the Geological Society, this was an easy trick to play. Scientific research was still seen as pastime of the upper classes, carried out by men with sufficient private income not to have to work for a living, and thus able to dedicate their minds to scholarly pursuits. Such men had no trouble portraying Mary as an uneducated beach scrounger, who stumbled across fossils but did not really understand their significance. This was unfair. Though Mary had only spent a few years at her local school, she was an avid self-educator. From her cottage in Lyme, she corresponded with individuals and museums across Britain, gathering whatever scientific books and articles she could. She even attempted to learn French to better understand the works of Baron Cuvier. Throughout her life, she kept notebooks into which she carefully copied passages from the books and scientific articles she read.

According to Lady Harriet Sylvester, who visited Mary in 1824, only God's favour could explain how 'this poor, ignorant girl' had acquired such an extraordinary knowledge and understanding of geology. 'Professors and other clever men', she wrote, 'all acknowledge that she understands more of the science than anyone else in this kingdom.'

However, the gentlemen geologists never felt the need to give Mary her due. They would have found it hard enough to be lectured on Jurassic geology by a woman, let alone one in a ragged dress who spoke in the rural burr of a West Country girl. Instead, they found it most convenient to just ignore her.

Most of Mary's notebooks and letters were lost following her death. One of the few sources that does remain is a hand-copied version of an article on the ichthyosaur by two gentlemen geologists. Mary clearly thought the authors waffled too much, as she added her own footnote at the end of the article, reminding herself, 'When I write a paper there shall not be but one preface.' Mary never did write her own paper, but if she had, there was no doubt in her mind that it would be better than anything these men could write.

Not all gentlemen geologists treated Mary badly. Roderick Murchison was another army officer who took up fossil hunting following his retirement. He and his wife Charlotte were regular visitors to Lyme and became close friends with Mary. In 1829, they invited her to stay at their London town-house. Mary wrote back excitedly, confiding that at thirty years of age, 'I have never been out of the smoke of Lyme.'

That summer, high on the success of her recent discoveries, Mary boarded a passenger ship at Lyme harbour which trav-elled along the English Channel, then up the Thames to London. The Murchisons hosted Mary at their home on the edge of Regent's Park, and took her around town, visiting the Geological Society and the British Museum. No evidence remains of Mary's feelings towards London, but it is a telling fact that she never returned. Perhaps the teeming streets and smoking factories of the city and the formal drawing rooms of Regent's Park were too much for a country girl raised in a carpenter's cottage on the Dorset coast. Or perhaps it was too depressing to stand in the rooms where men took the credit for the discoveries that she had worked so hard to find.

Mary spent the rest of her life in her cottage in Lyme. As the gentlemen geologists rose to become university professors, museum directors and knights of the realm, Mary continued to scour the cliffs and beaches for fossils to sell in her shop, with little public recognition.

In 1829, Mary's brother Joseph married, leaving just Mary and their mother Molly living together. Then, in October 1833, when Mary was working on the beach with Tray – as ever – by her side, a mudslide came thundering down the cliff. The falling rocks narrowly missed Mary but dropped directly on Tray. By the time she had dug him from the debris, her beloved dog was dead. Mary was distraught, as she wrote to Charlotte Murchison: 'Perhaps you will laugh when I say that the death of my old faithful dog has quite upset me . . . it was but a moment between me and the same fate.'

Mary's life in Lyme was becoming increasingly lonely. It did not help that she was by now something of a social misfit: too educated to mingle with the class from which she came, but never welcomed by Lyme's more educated inhabitants. However, she was able to form strong friendships with anyone who shared her love of fossils. Anna Maria Pinney was a teenage girl from a wealthy family who moved to Lyme Regis in 1831. When she walked through the door of Anning's Fossil Depot, she was besotted by the cluttered piles of ancient objects. She and Mary instantly became friends.

Together, they went out fossil hunting for days on end, and Anna Maria kept detailed records of their conversation in her teenage diary. It offers a fascinating glimpse of Mary as she approached middle age, and her proud, defiant character: 'She glories in being afraid of no one,' Anna Maria wrote, 'and delights saying everything she pleases. She would offend all the world.' Years of watching others build successful careers on the back of her discoveries had built up a well of resentment in Mary's heart. She described to

Anna Maria how she 'stands still and the world flows by her in a stream'.

If loneliness and resentment were not enough to contend with, the Annings' financial worries returned during the 1830s. In 1835, Mary met a banker from London who offered to invest her life savings of £300 for an excellent return. Mary handed over her money, never to hear from him again. He was a conman who left Mary with nothing.

Mary was facing the prospect of spending her last years in the workhouse, when her old sparring partner Professor Buckland came to the rescue sometime in 1838. He wrote to all his friends in the scientific community, and raised a fund of £200, which the British government then bolstered with a donation of £300. This sum of money gave Mary a pension of £25 per year for the rest of her life, enough to keep her from the workhouse door. Finally, she had been given some recognition for her contributions to science.

Four years later, her mother Molly Anning died aged 78. Now Mary was truly alone. She spent more and more time indoors, reading science, poetry and religious texts. Her notebooks from this period have survived, and the poems she chose to copy are revealing. Lord Byron's verse about approaching middle age clearly moved her:

> My days are in the yellow leaf
> The flowers and fruits of love are gone –
> The work, the canker and the grief
> Are mine alone!

So too did Thomas Gray's 'Elegy Written in an Country Churchyard', which points out how many remarkable lives go unnoticed by society:

Full many a flower is born to blush unseen,
And waste its sweetness in the desert air.

Towards the end of her life, some geologists enjoyed poking fun at the prickly spinster, laid low by misfortune. In 1832, a fossil hunter visited Mary and described her in his journal, rather sarcastically, as a 'geological lioness', presiding over a 'little dirty shop, with hundreds of specimens piled around in the greatest disorder'. In 1839, the famous biologist Richard Owen, who first coined the term 'dinosaur', paid her a visit. Before he left, he joked in a letter to a friend that he would 'take a run down to make love to Mary Anning at Lyme'.

Mary must have known people were laughing at her behind her back, but she never lost her pride. King Frederick Augustus of Saxony (now part of Germany) visited Anning's Fossil Depot with his personal doctor in 1844. They were on the lookout for items to take back to the King's own natural history museum in Dresden. After he purchased a six-foot ichthyosaur skeleton for £15, the doctor handed Mary his pocketbook and asked for her name and address. 'Mary Anning, Lyme Regis,' she wrote, before adding, 'I am well known throughout the whole of Europe.'

Mary was now entering the last few years of her life. She was sometimes seen stumbling out of her cottage looking lost and confused, so unpleasant rumours began to spread around Lyme that she had taken to drink. In fact, she was taking laudanum to ease a dull ache in her breast. It was breast cancer, to which she finally succumbed on Tuesday 9 March 1847.

Despite all her discoveries, Mary never lost her Christian faith, and was buried in St Michael's Church in Lyme. The Geological Society paid to have a stained-glass window celebrating her life put up in the church. It was a memorial for the woman who, starting at the age of twelve, had provided them with three decades of peerless discoveries. Nevertheless, it was only in 1904 that the Geological Society finally began admitting women. If there is a heaven, you can be sure that Mary was looking down smiling, thinking about the path she had beaten, along which other female scientists could now follow.

During the first few decades following her death, Mary faded from public memory. Her findings could be found in museums across Europe, but their discovery was always attributed to the man who purchased them, not the woman who dug them up. By the start of the twentieth century, Mary was all but forgotten, save for the popular tongue twister she inspired, 'she sells seashells by the seashore'.

However, in recent years there has been a sustained effort to revive Mary's legacy. She leaps from the pages of Georgian history as a total one-off: the uneducated carpenter's daughter who became an expert fossil-hunter and could hold her own in a debate with an Oxford professor.

What is more, the sea creatures that Mary discovered changed for ever the way we look at the world. They gave scientists the courage to start thinking about the age of the Earth not in thousands of years, but in millions. Such a time-span made it possible to consider whether life forms were not created, but instead evolved over time.

Today, you can still visit Mary's grave in Lyme Regis. It is normally covered with fossils, gifts left there by her legions of young fans. On the beach, you will see a steady stream of tourists from all over the world, with fossil hammers in their hands, chipping away at the same cliff face where Mary once worked. Each time there is a major storm, new finds are still being discovered.

What more exciting prospect could there be for a young scientist than to discover a creature from that more ancient Dorset, where the ichthyosaur once swam and the pterodactyl swooped.

CHAPTER 12

JAMES WATT

The Mechanical Magician
Who Turned Steam into Power

Look around the room in which you are currently sitting. Try to find a single object which was not, at some point during its manufacture, made by machinery powered from fossil fuels. Can you find anything? I doubt it.

Two hundred and fifty years ago, the opposite was the case. Everything, from the chair on which you are sitting to the book in your hands, was made by hand. If machines were involved, they were usually powered by human or animal muscle. For a small number of processes, such as grinding flour or spinning cotton, the power of wind and water could be harnessed to drive the wheels of industry. But for the most part, it was human sweat that made the objects people owned.

The same was true of travel. On land, people travelled either on foot or on the backs of animals. At sea, it was the wind in the ships' sails that allowed travellers to cross oceans. This was the pre-modern, pre-industrial world. A world of windmills, craftsmen's cottages and horse-drawn carriages that had existed for millennia.

On Friday 8 March 1776, a new world was born. In the small

town of Tipton, some eight miles west of Birmingham, the era
that we inhabit today – of power stations, cars, factories and
aeroplanes – saw its first signs of life. That morning, a large
crowd of businessmen, reporters and labourers gathered to
watch a coal-fired steam engine complete its first day's work.
This thirty-foot-tall monster guarded the entrance to a coal
mine. It powered a water pump, designed to drain the mine
and stop the workers from drowning. The furnace was lit, the
valves were opened, and the cylinder filled with steam. Slowly,
the great beast groaned into life.

Once it was running at full speed, the beam on top of the
engine completed fourteen strokes a minute, pumping sixty
feet of water out of the mine in under an hour. A reporter
from the *Birmingham Gazette* estimated it was four times
as efficient as any previous engine. He concluded his report,
'by this example the doubts of the inexperienced are
dispelled, and the importance and usefulness of the invention is finally decided.'

Standing beside the engine that day was its inventor, a
shy, gloomy Scotsman named James Watt. He looked older
than his forty years, his greying hair and stooped shoulders
telling of a life dogged by difficulty. But after years of hard
work and struggle, Watt finally had something to celebrate.

His invention would entirely transform the way in which
people lived and worked. Over the next century, steam engines
would spread into every corner of the world. They would
pump water, spin cotton, power factories, saw wood, print
newspapers and hammer metal. They would drive trains
across continents, and power ships across oceans.

The wheel may have come first, and Edison's light bulb might
be better known, but James Watt's steam engine is, perhaps,
the single most important invention in human history. And

Watt, an anxious man prone to long bouts of depression, very nearly abandoned the project before it was completed.

James Watt was born in 1736 in the Scottish port of Greenock, which was growing wealthy from Britain's trade with its American colonies. Watt's father was a shipbuilder, carpenter and merchant. He owned a number of trading vessels, and built Greenock's first crane, designed to lift hefty bales of American tobacco onto the docks.

At their family home, Watt's father ran a workshop, where a team of craftsmen repaired and manufactured instruments needed at sea, such as telescopes, compasses and quadrants. Watt was a shy young boy who disliked school, so his father gave him his own bench at the family workshop. Here, young Jamie (as he was known) engrossed himself for hours with his chisels and hammers, creating miniature models of pulleys, pumps and musical instruments.

Surrounded by his father's tools, and ready supplies of metal, wood and glass, the young Watt became a skilled craftsman. Watching him at work, one of his father's employees was said to have remarked, 'Jamie has fortune at his fingertips.'

In 1753, Watt's family was struck by a double tragedy. His mother died, and his father's business was ruined following a shipwreck. So Watt set out to make his own way in life, ending up (via London) in Glasgow where he became a scientific instrument maker to the university. From a shop in central Glasgow, Watt put his skills as a craftsman to use, making intricate objects such as microscopes, compasses, scales and syringes.

Glasgow University was modern and forward looking, and Watt thrived in the company of its philosophers and professors. He seemed to become an expert in whatever he touched, quickly gaining a reputation as something of a local genius.

He invented a new pocket-sized tool that enabled artists to draw in perspective. He pioneered new methods for manufacturing pottery. When he wanted to read a book on machinery by a German scientist, he taught himself German. According to one story, Watt was asked to build an organ for Glasgow's Masonic Lodge, even though he knew nothing about music. Accepting the job, he immersed himself in the design of organs and the theory of harmonics, until the organ he built was better than any other in the city.

Although he was always shy, Watt's restless mind made him fascinating company. The professors of Glasgow University flocked to his workshop to discuss their latest theories and ideas. They must have been quite surprised to discover that this craftsman was the most gifted scientist in Glasgow! One professor of chemistry recalled, 'Whenever any puzzle came in the way of any of us, we went to Mr Watt. He needed only to be prompted – everything became to him the subject of a new and serious study.' In 1763, Watt was presented with a puzzle that would change not only the course of his life, but of world history.

Watt did not invent the steam engine. That had been achieved in 1712 by an ironmonger from Devon called Thomas Newcomen. To understand Watt's genius, you need to understand how the Newcomen engine, on which he based his invention, worked. So here comes the scientific bit. Bear with me . . .

Coal was burnt to boil water, which created steam. The steam filled a cylinder which drove a piston upwards, and then cooled back into water, creating a vacuum which pulled the piston down. The piston's up-and-down motion drove a beam, which in turn powered a machine. In this fashion, the Newcomen engine became the first machine in human history to turn fossil fuel into power. For thousands of years, fossil fuels had been used to create heat and light, but never power.

Since its invention, the Newcomen engine had mostly been used to pump water out of coal and tin mines. However, the engines were horribly inefficient. A vast quantity of coal had to be burnt to produce only a tiny amount of power. For this reason, fifty years after its invention, the steam engine had made little impact on the world.

The Natural Philosophy department at Glasgow University owned a model of a Newcomen engine, but it no longer worked. In 1763, they asked Watt to repair it. Tinkering with the engine, Watt became fascinated by its technology. He observed that the entire cylinder had to be heated and cooled every time the piston completed one up-and-down motion. This, he observed, was the main reason the engine was so inefficient. If he could design an engine where the cylinder remained permanently hot, while still allowing the steam to cool, he could provide cheap, efficient power. For the next two years, the search for a solution obsessed Watt.

Outwardly, his life carried on as normal. He opened a new shop, married his beloved wife Margaret, and bought a family home. But inwardly, he could not stop thinking about steam engines. Away from work, he spent evenings and weekends desperately trying to square the circle of how to cool steam in a hot cylinder.

Then, one Sunday afternoon in the spring of 1765, Watt had his eureka moment. Reminiscing as an old man, his memory of how this happened remained as vivid as ever. He was walking through Glasgow Green, past an old washing-house, 'when the idea came into my mind . . . as steam was an elastic body it would rush into a vacuum, and if a communication were made between the cylinder and an exhausted vessel, it would rush in to it, and might be there condensed without cooling the cylinder.' Before he reached the other side of Glasgow Green, Watt recalled, 'the whole thing was arranged in my mind.'

Watt's inspiration was to build something he called a 'cold condenser'. Here comes another scientific bit . . .

Once the engine's cylinder has filled with steam, a valve is opened to let the steam fill a separate vessel surrounded by cold water: the 'cold condenser'. Here the steam condenses, creating a vacuum in both the condenser and the adjoined cylinder, forcing the piston back downwards. Then the valve closes, and the cylinder refills with steam.

The very next day, Watt rushed to his workshop, put on his leather apron and started building a model. He used a large brass syringe for the cylinder, onto which he soldered a rectangular tin to act as the cold condenser, and his wife's sewing thimble as a miniature lid. When he filled the cylinder with steam and opened the valve, the model worked. Watt was overjoyed, writing to a friend: 'I can think of nothing else but this machine. I hope to have the decisive trial before I see you.'

However, it was one thing making a miniature model. It would be quite another turning it into a full-sized, working steam engine, capable of pumping water or powering a machine. And here lies the fundamental challenge faced by inventors throughout history. Watt had a genius idea, which stood to make him very rich. But that was in the future. To prove his engine worked, he needed cash now, in order to rent a workshop, buy materials, pay workmen and build his prototype. But who would invest in something that did not yet exist?

Watt found his answer in John Roebuck, a wealthy indus-
trialist who had recently purchased a coal mine outside
Edinburgh. Roebuck's mine kept flooding, and Watt convinced
him that, given enough time and money, he could build an
engine powerful enough to drain the mine. So in 1768
Roebuck lent Watt a barn in the grounds of his large house
in Kinneil outside Edinburgh, and agreed to fund his research.

Watt found the work lonely and frustrating. None of the
local ironmongers could manufacture parts accurate enough
for his needs, and the steam kept leaking from his cylinders.
Twice he overhauled his design to solve the problem, but with
no success. After two years, Watt's invention had got nowhere,
and he was running out of money.

It was during this period that Watt began suffering from
severe depression, something he called 'the mulligrubs'. He
abandoned his work, and stayed in bed for hours. Even when
he got up, he would sit alone with his head in his hands,
plagued by headaches and stomach pains. Roebuck, who was
losing money every day that his mine remained flooded, could
not understand Watt's lack of motivation. In a letter he pleaded
with Watt, 'You are letting the most active part of your life
insensibly glide away. A day, a moment, ought not to be lost.'

But it was of no use. Watt had lost hope. In a letter to his
friend in 1769, he wrote, 'of all things in life, there is nothing
so foolish as inventing.'

Watt's lack of money caused him particular anxiety,
perhaps a legacy of seeing his father's business collapse as
a young man. To make ends meet, he took a job as a surveyor
for canals. A century before the invention of the train, canals
were heralded as the newest, most efficient form of industrial transport, and they began carving through the British
countryside. To many this was exciting work, but Watt hated

it. He was a slight, delicate man, and could not bear spending long days outside in the wind and the rain. Having only taken the job to save his wife Margaret and two young children from poverty, it now kept him away from his family for months on end. Without their company, Watt was miserable.

On his thirty-fifth birthday in 1771, Watt had a particularly bad attack of the mulligrubs. He sent a letter to his friend, stating: 'It is rather curious but I really think that on the whole I grow less inventive as I grow older . . . Today I entered the 35th year of my life and I think I have hardly done 35 pence worth of good in the world but I cannot help it. I do as much as indolence and ennui permit.'

Two years later, Roebuck was declared bankrupt, ruined in part by his investment in a flooded coal mine which Watt's engine failed to drain. It looked less likely than ever that Watt's engine, rusting away in Roebuck's barn in Kinneil, would be completed.

Things could not get much worse for Watt, but they did. In September 1773, while surveying for a new canal in the Highlands, he received a letter from his family doctor telling him that Margaret – pregnant at the time with their third child – was dangerously ill. Watt immediately set out for home, travelling for three days through driving rain. He arrived in Glasgow on 29 September, only to find his wife and unborn child were already dead. In fact, they had died before the letter even reached him. With Margaret gone, Watt wrote in his journal, 'I lost the comfort of my life.'

Widowed, in debt, and with two small children to raise, Watt's life was in tatters. He wrote an anguished letter to a friend confessing, 'I have lost much of my attachment to the world, even to my own devices. I long much to see you . . .

but so many things are in the way, and I am so poor.' In his letters from this time, Watt sounds almost suicidal.

However, there was a saviour on the horizon. Many of the great achievements in human history have been carried out by partnerships, where each individual has qualities which compensate for the other's flaws. Watt's genius was for inventing, but he was a hopeless businessman. He once wrote to a friend, 'nothing is more contrary to my disposition than hustling and bargaining with mankind.' He needed someone with the pushy determination to make his invention a reality. That someone was Matthew Boulton.

Born and bred in Birmingham, the bombastic Boulton could not cross the street without spotting a business opportunity. He learnt to be a metalworker from his father, and at the age of 17 created a new process for inlaying steel belt buckles with enamel. He then shipped his colourful belt buckles to France, so that they could be imported back into England at inflated prices as the latest French fashion. Like the city that made him, Boulton was brash, hardworking and ambitious.

Over the past thirty years, Birmingham had doubled in size, driven by its thriving trade in metalwork. From morning to night, the city rang out with the sound of hammers on anvils, as skilled craftsmen fashioned jewellery, locks, guns, swords, cutlery and countless other metal objects. An inventory from the 1770s shows the city had 39 bucklemasters, 46 brassfounders and 129 buttonmakers. During the eighteenth century, there was no better place for a businessman to make his fortune. Birmingham was the boom town of Georgian England.

Watt first met Boulton in 1769 while travelling back to Glasgow from London. Boulton had heard rumours of Watt's engine and wanted to show the budding inventor around his Soho Manufactory. One of the first modern factories in Britain, the Soho Manufactory was Boulton's pride and joy. It had been built from scratch to look like a country mansion from the outside. But inside there toiled some 700 metal-workers, creating all manner of objects, from belt buckles to coat buttons, corkscrews to candlesticks. Boulton was an incurable show-off, and delighted in showing the great and the good around Soho. Visitors came from as far afield as Germany, Russia and Turkey to marvel at this wonder of the modern world.

Boulton reinvested every penny he made into new ventures, taking larger and larger loans from Birmingham bankers such as the wealthy merchant Sampson Lloyd (founder of Lloyds Bank). In Watt's steam engine, Boulton saw the most exciting venture of them all. He spent years trying to persuade Watt to move to Birmingham and build his engine there. When Roebuck offered Boulton the right to manufacture Watt's engines for the West Midlands, Boulton's response was typical: 'It would not be worth my while to make for three counties only, but I find it very worth my while to make for all the world.'

So Boulton waited. When Roebuck went bankrupt, he saw his chance. Boulton bought a two-thirds share in Watt's invention from Roebuck's auditors, and the Kinneil engine was dismantled and sent to Soho. A year later, after the death of his wife, Watt followed.

Boulton was a snappy dresser, with curly brown hair, lively eyes and a mischievous grin. He was as comfortable talking to the King and Queen of England about their order for a new tea set as he was bantering with workmen on the factory floor – all of whom he knew by name. Forever ready with a joke, the buoyant Boulton lifted Watt out of his mulligrubs and breathed new life into Watt's engine. Within six months of arriving at Soho, Watt was once again fired with enthusiasm. In a letter to his elderly father, he wrote that his work was becoming 'rather successful', adding, 'I expect the invention will be very beneficial to me.' For the dour, self-doubting Scotsman, this comment was almost boastful.

The move to Birmingham also placed Watt at the heart of industrial England. His inability to find an airtight cylinder, which had caused such problems in Scotland, was solved by an ironmonger working thirty miles west of Birmingham, beside the River Severn in Shropshire. His name was John 'Iron-Mad' Wilkinson.

Something of a celebrity, 'Iron-Mad' Wilkinson claimed to produce the best-quality iron in the world. His life was guided by a conviction that anything could, and therefore should, be made out of iron. He worked at an iron desk, overlooking the iron coffin in which he planned to be buried. He paid his workers with iron tokens, and amazed the people of Shropshire by building an iron boat which floated on the River Severn. Wilkinson also invented a precision tool for boring holes in iron, allowing him to manufacture cannons for the British army with perfectly smooth barrels. Could this boring machine make perfectly smooth engine cylinders? 'Iron-Mad' Wilkinson said it could, so Boulton and Watt placed an order.

By 1776, Watt's first steam engine at the Bloomfield coal mine in Tipton was almost complete. He spent January and February supervising its construction, and its March debut – as the *Birmingham Gazette* reported – was a triumph. That afternoon, Boulton and Watt attended a celebratory dinner hosted by the mine owners. As Watt's wine glass was refilled and toasts were made in his honour, he must have cast his mind back over the gruelling journey that had brought him there. Eleven years on from his eureka moment on Glasgow Green, through all of the frustration and despair, he had achieved his dream.

Watt's second steam engine was installed at a Shropshire foundry belonging to none other than 'Iron-Mad' Wilkinson. It powered bellows, which blasted air into a furnace, feeding the coal fire with oxygen. This sustained an immense heat of 1,300 °C in the blast furnace, the best temperature for making cast iron. Wilkinson purchased another eighteen steam engines over the next twenty years. It was a mutually supportive relationship: Watt's engine allowed Wilkinson to make better iron, and Wilkinson's iron allowed Watt to make better engines.

As word of Watt's invention spread, orders poured in. Later, in 1776, a gin distillery in east London ordered an engine to pump water to its copper pans. In 1778, a French businessman ordered two engines to provide the people of Paris with running water. In 1783, the largest flour mill in the world was built in London, with two of Watt's engines powering its millstones. Positioned beside the River Thames, the Albion Mill ground 150 bushels of wheat an hour. Watt's engines also unloaded wheat from boats on the Thames, and loaded them back up with flour.

The writer James Boswell visited Boulton's Soho Manufactory in 1779. As Boulton showed Boswell the engine-making rooms, he gestured to the factory floor and boasted, 'I sell here, sir, what the world desires to have – POWER.' He was not wrong. In the space of twenty-five years, Boulton and Watt had sold 448 steam engines.

Their greatest source of business was the tin and copper mines of Cornwall. Here on the southwestern tip of England, thousands of labourers toiled underground in unimaginable hardship. Descending hundreds of metres below the Earth's surface, with just a candle in the brim of their hats to light the way, they chipped away at the Earth's core for six hours at a stretch. The greatest threat to Cornish miners was flooding, and here Boulton and Watt's engine could help. Over ten years, they constructed thirty-nine steam-powered water pumps for Cornish mine owners, saving countless lives in the process.

Boulton enjoyed his visits to Cornwall, and bought a pretty cottage in the picturesque village of Cosgarne. Watt was less impressed, ordering waxed linen coats to be sent from Birmingham so that he could cope with the incessant rain. He disliked dealing with the rough-and-ready Cornish engineers, complaining that 'all of them love drinking too much.'

When it came to making money from their engines, none of Boulton and Watt's customers were charged upfront. Instead, Boulton devised a novel payment scheme, charging an annual fee for an engine's use, based on the savings it brought to the customer's business. While calculating this saving for Samuel Whitbread's brewery in Brick Lane, London, Watt estimated a horse could raise 33,000 lb of water, one foot per minute. By that estimation, Watt calculated that Whitbread's engine provided the power of 200 horses. Or to put it another way, 200 horsepower. Watt's measurement of engine power survives to this day.

Historians often debate the reasons why Britain became such a hive of invention during the early Industrial Revolution, and a strong contender is Parliament's system for granting patents. Dating back to the reign of Queen Elizabeth, a Parliamentary patent gives an inventor the exclusive right to make money from their invention for a set amount of time. In January 1769, Watt received his first patent for 'A new method of lessening the consumption of steam and fuel in fire-engines' (no. 913). This gave him the financial incentive to develop his idea, knowing it wouldn't be stolen the minute it was revealed.

Such theft was a very real threat. When a group of Cornish mine owners visited the Soho Manufactory for a tour in 1776, one of them saw a copy of Watt's designs lying on a table and pinched it. The culprit, it turned out, was a fiery mine owner named Richard Trevithick. Though he did return Watt's papers, he must first have studied them closely: twenty-five years later, his son, also named Richard Trevithick, became the first inventor to attach Watt's steam engine to a moving vehicle, thereby creating the steam train.

Patents could only be awarded by an Act of Parliament. When Boulton went into partnership with Watt in 1774, he told Watt to ask Parliament for an extension to his patent, but Watt was reluctant. He despised dealing with pompous politicians. After his first visit to Parliament, he promised never to return, stating that '[I] never saw so many wrong-headed people on all sides gathered together . . . I believe the Devil has possession of them.' However, Watt received a letter from a friend, telling him to stop his incessant worrying: 'come and lick some great man's arse and be damned to you.' Watt did as he was told, and his patent was extended for twenty-five years.

In the years to come, Watt's patent proved controversial. Rival engineers complained that his exclusive right to manufacture steam engines until 1800 prevented competition and delayed industrial progress. When a group of Cornish mine owners threatened to stop paying their fees, Watt was furious. In a letter to Boulton, he fumed that 'the invention has been the product of my own active labour and of God knows how much anguish of mind and body.' He owned his invention, Watt argued, as much as any aristocrat owned their land.

In 1787, Boulton thought of a new application for their steam engine. For hundreds of years, coins had been struck at London's Royal Mint using screw presses, stamping each metal coin, one after another, by hand. It was an inefficient, expensive process which the government undertook rarely, causing regular shortages of metal coins. So Boulton designed the world's first steam-powered coin press. The circular machine looked not unlike a child's merry-go-round, and as it spun, it churned out 120 coins per minute.

Boulton promised the British government he could produce new coinage for half the price of the Royal Mint, but the politicians dithered. So Boulton looked elsewhere. He manufactured coins for use in the Americas, West Africa and India. Then, in 1797, Boulton finally landed the contract he craved. The British government ordered the Soho Mint to create some 1,266 tons of penny pieces, totalling a cool £40,000, over the next two years. Foreign orders duly followed, and Boulton supplied steam-powered coin presses to the royal mints of Spain, Russia and Denmark. Today, it is a journalistic cliché to describe inventions with runaway success as a 'licence to print money'. However, for Boulton and Watt's steam engine, this became quite literally true.

Boulton died in 1809, fondly remembered by all who knew him. Watt lived for another ten years. Having finally achieved financial security, his happiness blossomed in old age. In 1790, he built Heathfield Hall on the edge of Birmingham, where he lived out his days with his second wife and children.

In an attic above the kitchen at Heathfield, Watt built his workroom. Lit by a skylight and sash window, it contained a lathe and workbench, and shelves for his collection of rocks, fossils, chemicals and tools. Here, Watt recreated his happiest childhood memories, losing himself for hours in the thrill of discovery. The attic even contained a frying pan, so he did not have to leave his workbench to eat. Hidden away in his attic, Watt continued inventing. He created a successful machine for copying letters, and worked for years on a process for duplicating sculptures. His last great invention, in 1810, was a flexible water tunnel running along the bed of the River Clyde, modelled on a lobster's tail. When the Glasgow Corporation Water Works offered him payment, Watt refused. It was a gift to the town that had made him.

By the end of his life, Watt was famous around the world, celebrated as a hero of scientific progress. The British Prime Minister, Lord Liverpool, offered Watt a baronetcy, but he was not going to be seduced into the aristocracy. He did, however, accept an honorary degree from Glasgow University, and membership of the French Academy.

Watt died at Heathfield House in 1819. A few years later, the Scottish novelist Walter Scott described having met the 85-year-old Watt as he neared the end of his life. Scott wrote of a kindly old man whose benevolent exterior hid extraordinary mental powers: 'This potent commander of the elements – this abridger of time and space – this magician, whose cloudy machinery has produced a change in the world the effects of which, extraordinary as they are, are perhaps only now beginning to be felt.'

We are still feeling the effects of that magician's invention today. However, having been hero-worshipped during his lifetime, Watt is now largely forgotten. Why is this? Maybe it is because in bringing us the modern world, Watt's invention also brought us fossil fuel consumption, global warming and ecological destruction. Watt's invention has gone from being a gift to humankind to perhaps its greatest threat.

Nevertheless, Watt's name shines on. Literally, in fact. In 1882, the British Science Association wanted to devise a new unit for measuring electricity, and the president suggested they call it the 'watt', in recognition of the great inventor. Today, all bulbs have written on them their brightness in watts, so the name of this gloomy Glaswegian is illuminated every time you turn on a light.

Conclusion

The End of the Party

On 26 June 1830, the sun was setting on Georgian Britain. King George IV lay dying in Windsor Castle, a morbidly obese, opium-addicted recluse, mocked and despised by the nation he ruled. One month later, *The Times* reported from his funeral with what must be one of the most brutal take-downs of a monarch in British history:

> There never was an individual less regretted by his fellow-creatures than this deceased king. What eye has wept for him? What heart has heaved one throb of unnecessary sorrow . . . If George IV ever had a friend – a devoted friend – in any rank of life, we protest that the name of him or her has not yet reached us.

He was, the editorial concluded, 'of all known beings the most selfish'.

George IV's infamy had begun early. As a young Prince of Wales, he infuriated his parents by hanging out with a rowdy set of aristocrats who – it was claimed – corrupted his morals entirely. By 1795, the 33-year-old prince's debts amounted to a staggering £630,000 (at a time when a successful shopkeeper might make £200 a year) and would take Parliament eleven years to pay off. Much of this money was spent on his lavish London home at Carlton House, where he entertained a string of mistresses – singers, actresses, wives of important noblemen – leaving a trail of illegitimate children in his wake. He even married one of his mistresses in secret. She was, to his family's absolute horror, a Catholic, so the marriage was declared invalid.

In 1795, a new marriage was arranged for Prince George, to a Protestant princess from Germany named Caroline of Brunswick. Never one to cast out the beam from his own eye before recognising the splinter in another's, George complained on meeting Caroline that she was crass, ugly and smelly. On their wedding night, he was so appalled at the prospect of sharing a bed with her that he hit the brandy, drank himself unconscious and collapsed in the fireplace. The next morning, he steeled himself to make love to her for the first and only time. Nine months later, a daughter was born, but by then George and Caroline were separated.

Prince George's distaste at his wife's appearance was a bit rich, considering that he was fat enough for the press to dub him the 'Prince of Whales'. In 1820, he was crowned George IV, and in order to stop the press from mocking him, he tried to pay them off, but to no avail. Unable to face the hatred and ridicule of his subjects, he became more and more reclusive, spending his days in Windsor Castle or on board the royal yacht. But he never stopped eating.

By the end of his life, George IV weighed in at twenty stone, with a fifty-inch waist (just two inches short of Henry VIII). Trussed up in his tight-fitting clothes, as was the fashion, one observer said he looked 'like a great sausage stuffed into the covering'. Two months before George's death, the Duke of Wellington joined him for a meal at Windsor Castle, and recorded with astonishment what this king of gluttony could put away: a pigeon and beef pie, most of a bottle of white wine, a glass of champagne, two glasses of port and a glass of brandy, followed by a large dose of laudanum to ease his digestion. The meal in question? Breakfast.

The sad thing is, George IV was no dolt. As a young man he was good-looking, charming and intelligent. He had a much-admired eye for art and architecture, rebuilding part of the West End while he was Prince Regent (hence Regent Street) and starting work on Buckingham Palace. However, his personality was poisoned by the loose morals of his day, and in old age he became a drunken, lecherous tribute act to the age of libertinism. As he lay dying in Windsor Castle in the summer of 1830, his breathless bulk demonstrated the unpleasant consequences of all that Georgian merriment.

Libertines had once been celebrated for their heroic self-indulgence, but by the time of his death, George IV was roundly despised. The Duke of Wellington, who served as his prime minister, called him 'the worst man he ever fell in with his whole life, the most selfish, the most false, the most ill-natured, the most entirely without one redeeming quality'. Ouch!

King George IV's abysmal reputation had been sealed by the changing moral climate of late Georgian Britain. Between his birth in 1762 and his death in 1830, a remarkable revolution in manners took place. The traumas of war and rapid social change combined to bring the eighteenth-century's air of carefree hedonism to an end, ushering in a strict new code of respectability. The Victorian age was looming.

In 1828, a society fencing-master and sometime celebrity

named Henry Angelo wrote his memoirs. As a young man, Angelo had been no stranger to the vulgar pleasures of Georgian London. Looking back at his 'gay days' hanging out in boisterous drinking clubs and Jacob's Well tavern by the Barbican, he blushed at his folly, and reflected on how far times had changed. 'In no period of our domestic history', he wrote, 'has so universal a change in the manners and habits of the people generally taken place, as within the last half-century.' He concluded, 'we may be said to be no longer the same people.'

Georgian Britain, tired of its wild living, had checked into rehab. As the great historian G. M. Young wrote, 'By the beginning of the nineteenth century, virtue was advancing on a broad, invincible front.' Raucous living was roundly disparaged. Respectability now ruled.

Some historians have argued that the first national trauma to trigger this sea change in moral attitudes began in 1775. In that year, thirteen British colonies on the North American mainland rose in rebellion against King George III. In response, the King's government sent 32,000 troops across the Atlantic to quell the rebellion. They could never have imagined that, six years later, the British army would surrender at Yorktown, ensuring independence for the United States of America, and humiliation for the British Empire. On hearing the news from Yorktown, the exhausted Prime Minister, Lord North, collapsed with relief as if he had taken a bullet to the chest, exclaiming 'Oh God: it is all over.'

The American War left Britain traumatised. It was not so much a foreign war as a civil war, fought against their own kith and kin, who spoke English and worshipped a Protestant God. What is more, the colonial rebels successfully defeated their mother country with the support of her arch enemy:

France. The loss of her American colonies sent Britain into a period of prolonged soul searching. Many concluded that it was the loose morals and amateurism of Britain's ruling class which were to blame for this national humiliation.

The next great trauma was the French Revolution, and the subsequent Revolutionary and Napoleonic Wars, which lasted almost unbroken from 1793 to 1815. At £1.7 billion, these wars cost more than three times as much as all the previous wars Britain had fought since 1688 put together. For almost a decade, Britain held its breath, expecting the French army to cross the Channel and invade at any moment. From 1803 to 1805, anyone in Dover with a telescope could watch the 200,000 troops in Napoleon's 'Army of England' completing their drills on the French coast.

For Britain's politicians, the strain of pursuing this war was unbearable. Pitt the Younger worked himself into an early grave, drinking heavily and finally succumbing to death when he heard of yet another barnstorming Napoleonic victory in Europe. His desperate last words were 'My country! How I leave my country.' Spencer Perceval took over as prime minister in 1809 and fared little better. Like an increasing number of people in late Georgian Britain, he was an evangelical Christian, and came to believe that Napoleon Bonaparte was the harbinger of the Apocalypse, the seven-headed beast from the book of Revelation. Such a belief was not uncommon as apocalyptic fears pervaded Britain. From their pulpits, evangelical preachers declared that only by ridding themselves of sin could the people of Great Britain save themselves from imminent national destruction.

Sadly, Perceval did not live to see his Satanic Majesty Napoleon Bonaparte finally defeated at the Battle of Waterloo in 1815. Three years earlier, he had been shot dead in the lobby of the House of Commons by a lone assassin, a former businessman who had lost his mind having gone bankrupt while trading with Russia.

Over the course of Britain's war with France, one in ten men served in the army, one in six if you count the home defence militias. This militarisation of national life triggered perhaps the most visible change in late Georgian Britain: male clothing. During the early 1790s, men still pimped themselves out in silks, satins, embroidered velvet, gold lace and powdered wigs. However, to a nation at war, such clothing was far too effete. A more manly national outfit took hold, of plain blue and black coats, high white collars, long trousers and leather boots, with short-cropped hair in place of powdered wigs. This was honest, practical clothing, befitting a more serious age, and would persist for the rest of the nineteenth century.

The third national trauma was industrialisation. Watt's steam engine was invented in 1776, the same year that the American Declaration of Independence was signed. However, its true impact was felt only a generation later, from the turn of the century onwards. The rapidity of this change can be seen in the spiralling consumption of coal – the wonder fuel of industrial Britain – used to power factories, pump water, smelt iron and drive trains. In 1800, 10 million tonnes of coal were mined in Britain. By 1853, the figure was 72 million tonnes.

Those born in the year of George IV's death entered a Britain where life was largely stationary, and the fastest anyone could travel on land was the speed of a galloping horse. However, once they reached their twenty-first birthday in 1851, they would see 6,000 miles of railway track laid across the country, linking every major town and city in Britain.

That year, for the first time, more than half of Britain's population lived in urban areas. The easy stability of Georgian Britain was over, and a new age of anxious unpredictability had begun.

Victorian writers looked back at the dying embers of Georgian Britain as a simpler, more certain time, untroubled by the stresses and strains of modern life. In her 1859 novel *Adam Bede*, the author George Eliot wrote that 'Leisure is gone – gone where the spinning wheels are gone, and the pack-horses, and the slow waggons, and the pedlars, who brought bargains to the door on sunny afternoons.' She offered a nostalgic description of the typical eighteenth-century gentleman:

> He was a contemplative, rather stout gentleman, of excellent digestion – of quiet perception, undiseased by hypothesis: happy in his inability to know the causes of things, preferring the things themselves. He lived chiefly in the country, among pleasant seats and homesteads, and was fond of sauntering by the fruit-tree wall, and scenting the apricots when they were warmed by the morning sunshine.

Such a leisurely existence was harder to maintain in the Age of Steam. Far away from the squire's fruit-tree wall, Britain's growing industrial cities were creating a new order. Take Manchester, which by the start of the nineteenth century had become the global capital of cotton production. Cotton factories turned this small town, with a population of 70,000 in 1801, into a global city of 300,000 people, known as 'Cottonopolis', by 1860. People flocked from across the British Isles to work there, often crowding into atrocious slum housing, with whole families in a single room. In this city of the future, great fortunes were made by the few while horrible suffering was endured by the many. As a French visitor to industrial Manchester recorded,

> A sort of black smoke covers the city. Under this half-daylight 300,000 human beings are ceaselessly at work. The homes of the poor are scattered haphazard around the factories. From this filthy sewer pure gold flows. In Manchester civilised man is turned back almost into a savage.

While rural workers were still brought up in a culture of deference towards their local landlord, factory workers developed a flinty hostility to their masters. They did not think much of their complacent, aristocratic government either. However, working-class people in cities such as Manchester had no political voice. In 1832, Manchester may have been one of Britain's largest cities, but it still had only two Members of Parliament. When 60,000 workers gathered in St Peter's Field on the edge of Manchester in 1819 to demand political reform, magistrates unleashed the local militia, leading to the deaths of eighteen innocent people. Many in Britain were outraged by the Peterloo Massacre, as it became known, and the country felt closer to revolution than at any other point in its history.

It was during these dark days of war, social change and fear of revolution that the whole mode of behaviour in Georgian Britain was transformed. In this newly nervous nation, an energetic campaign against immorality and sin gathered pace, and the bounds of acceptable behaviour changed for ever.

The groundwork for this campaign had been laid by a religious revival during the previous century. In 1738, a young Church of England priest named John Wesley attended a small religious meeting in Aldersgate Street, London, where – at a quarter to nine in the evening – he felt the warmth of Christ enter his heart, and underwent a conversion. There and then, Wesley committed his life to preaching a more energetic form of Christianity, to combat the sleepy complacency of the Church of England. He did so with astonishing enthusiasm. By the time of his death at the age of eighty-seven in 1791, Wesley had ridden 250,000 miles on horseback and preached no fewer than 40,000 sermons. In doing so, he founded a new faith, known as Methodism.

In the year that Wesley died, there were 72,000 Methodists in Britain. It was most popular among working-class groups who felt uninspired by the traditional Church of England, such as London artisans, Lancashire factory workers and Cornish tin miners. Olaudah Equiano was one such convert. Methodism thrived in remote rural areas such as Lincolnshire and north Wales, where worshippers were electrified by its open-air services, charismatic preachers, communal eating (known as 'love feasts') and stirring hymns – many of which were written by Wesley's brother Charles.

With their faith in Christ reborn, Methodists embraced a new way of life bound by self-discipline. They rejected the rowdy popular culture of Georgian Britain, turning against alcohol, cruelty to animals and violent sports. Instead, they dedicated their lives to personal salvation through clean living and good deeds. By the end of the Georgian period, the number of Methodists in Britain had reached 250,000.

Methodism's impact, however, went far beyond its believers. As the eighteenth century drew to a close, evangelical worship was seeping into the established Church of England, where clerics began copying its emotional services and emphasis on salvation. Importantly, the evangelical revival of the late eighteenth century won followers among the cream of British

society: aristocrats, businessmen, bishops and prime minis-
ters. None were more influential than William Wilberforce.

The wealthy son of a Yorkshire merchant, Wilberforce was
intelligent and ambitious, becoming elected to Parliament as
MP for Hull at the age of twenty-one. Like many a sociable
young Georgian, he was fond of singing, drinking and
gambling. However, in 1785, he underwent a religious conversion. From that day onwards, he later wrote, God had set him
two great objectives, the first of which was to end the slave
trade in the British Empire.

Britain's campaign to end the slave trade lasted for two
hard-fought decades. On one side were freed slaves, evangelical Christians, and reformers who stressed the common
humanity of African people. On the other side was a wealthy
collection of plantation owners and merchants, known as
the West India lobby. They opposed abolition on the basis
that African people were naturally inferior and suited to
enslaved labour, giving rise – some historians have argued
– to the poisonous racial discourses that thrived over the
following centuries. They also predicted the economic
collapse of the British Empire if her colonies stopped trading
slaves, while other European powers – namely the French
and Portuguese – continued.

The abolitionists responded with an enormous campaign
consisting of speeches, books, pamphlets, petitions and
boycotts. Finally, in 1807, Parliament abolished the slave trade
throughout the British Empire. The abolitionist campaign had
injected a new moral seriousness into British public life, and
abolitionists – delighted with their victory – looked for new
evils to slay. When the House of Commons voted in favour
of the 1807 Act, Wilberforce turned to a fellow evangelical
MP and asked, 'What shall we abolish next?' Not sensing the

rhetorical nature of Wilberforce's question, his friend replied, 'The lottery, I think.'

The second objective that God set Wilberforce at the time of his conversion was a reformation of manners in British society. Wilberforce remains most famous for his role in the abolition of the slave trade, but it was his second objective which – arguably – had the greater impact on British society in the century that followed.

In 1785, Wilberforce's conversion to evangelical Christianity was seen as rather eccentric among the well-to-do. By 1807, it was much more mainstream. He was now at the centre of a wealthy and powerful group of evangelical politicians, social reformers and businessmen, nicknamed 'the Saints', who committed their lives to overturning what he called 'the universal corruption and profligacy of the times'. The Saints were also known as the Clapham Sect, as many worshipped at Holy Trinity Church on the edge of Clapham Common. But their influence spread far beyond southwest London.

The Saints strived to put religion at the centre of their daily lives, with Christ's work pervading all that they did. This led to a burst of new philanthropic and reforming societies. In 1823, the politician and future historian Thomas Macaulay dubbed his era the 'age of societies', writing: 'There is scarcely one Englishman in ten who has not belonged to some association for distributing books, or for prosecuting them; for sending invalids to the hospital, or beggars to the treadmill; for giving plate to the rich, or blankets to the poor.'

Macaulay was not wrong. One historian has counted over 150 such societies formed between Wilberforce's conversion in 1785 and his death in 1833. There was the Society of Universal Good Will (1786), the Society for Promoting the Religious Instruction of Youth (1800), the London Society for the

Suppression of Mendacity (1818), and the – very precisely named – Friendly Female Society, for the Relief of Poor, Infirm, Aged Widows, and Single Women, of Good Character, Who Have Seen Better Days (1802). However, few had more impact than the Society for the Suppression of Vice, formed in 1802.

The Vice Society (as it became known), co-founded by a fiery London barrister named John Bowles, was dedicated to rooting public obscenity and disorder out of Georgian Britain. Its members campaigned against swearing in public, inns and taverns of ill-repute, publishers of obscene books and images, nude bathing, brothels and gaming houses. To aid their cause, they printed and distributed a book, named *The Constable's Assistant*, which listed long-forgotten statutes under which such sins could be prosecuted. It ran to four editions over two decades.

A particular obsession of the Vice Society was the need to keep the Sabbath holy. This infuriated many working people, for whom Sunday provided their only chance to get a haircut, buy meat for a roast or enjoy a leisurely pint. That diehard rake Byron mocked the society's Sabbath campaign in a poem from 1809:

> Raise not your scythe, Suppressors of our Vice!
> Reforming Saints! too delicately nice!
> By whose decrees, our sinful souls to save,
> No Sunday tankards foam, no barbers shave

Some may have laughed along with Byron's mockery, but the tide of public opinion seemed to be with the society, not with him. In the nervous atmosphere of war and social upheaval, the Vice Society was an agent of national renewal. Byron was a relic of the previous century's ways.

Byron's generation of Georgians could be remarkably foul-mouthed. Their private letters, as well as bawdy songs and poems, contain enough four-letter words to rival any modern potty mouth. One German visitor quipped that while standing on the streets of Georgian Britain, one might assume that everyone was called 'Damme'. However, by the end of the century, colourful language was drying up. In Sheridan's 1775 play *The Rivals*, the gentleman Bob Acres observes of genteel society, 'Dams have had their day.'

By the new century, language was being policed like never before. London's Codpiece Row was renamed Coppice Row, while 'bellies' became 'stomachs', smocks became 'shifts', and 'bitches' became 'mother mastiffs'. At a dinner party, referring to a chicken thigh could now risk acute embarrassment. In 1807, a writer and member of the Vice Society named Thomas Bowdler published *The Family Shakespeare*, in which he removed all words and phrases 'which cannot with propriety be read aloud in a family'. This bizarre publication gave rise to the verb 'to Bowdlerise': to castrate a classic text by removing all possible offence.

Many did laugh at the prudishness of this new morality. In 1811, the journalist Hewson Clarke joked that society would soon ban 'every object that seems to bear a *Phallic* outline', worrying that obelisks would be taken down, pokers removed from fireplaces, and rolling pins 'burnt without mercy'. He was not far wrong. Eleven years later, when the grateful women of England raised a fund for a statue of Achilles to be erected in Hyde Park in honour of the Duke of Wellington, they instructed the sculptor that Achilles might be carved in the classical style (nude), provided a fig leaf covered his tackle.

There was also a visible change in life on Britain's streets.

New Vagrancy Acts in 1822 and 1824 widened the definition of vagrancy to include, essentially, any undesirable individual. Zealous local magistrates used the Acts to prosecute disreputable taverns, theatres and gambling dens. Surrey magistrates instructed the manager of Vauxhall Pleasure Gardens, a favourite Georgian nightspot, that public dancing was no longer permitted. If the public were to start dancing, he was told, the band should immediately launch into a slow march until such behaviour ceased.

During the 1810s, there were still eighty-six fairs held in and around London between Easter and October. These events were much loved for their rowdy fun, as all walks of life gathered to enjoy jugglers, ballad singers, freak shows and fortune-telling pigs (always known, for some reason, as Toby). However, revellers did have a tendency to get drunk and frisky, something disapproved of by the local authorities, and a clampdown began. Thirty years later, most of them had gone. Some hung on, such as the historic Bartholomew Fair, a three-day spectacular which had taken place in Smithfield every September since 1133. However, from the 1820s, the City Corporation began regulating and restricting the fair, until it was squeezed out of existence in 1855. The poet and critic Leigh Hunt had a point when, in 1817, he foretold the 'Death of Merry England'.

This moral revolution meant the older generation of Georgians were often told off for their crude manners by their prim and proper children, a trope in many plays and novels from the period. An 1826 magazine called *The English Spy* tells the story of an upwardly mobile cockney named Mr Marigold who moves his family to a fashionable new square, but pines for the rowdy London streets of his youth. When Mr Marigold's priggish daughter Biddy complains about his vulgar tastes, Mr Marigold launches into a rant against the new morality. 'Give me the society where I can eat, drink, laugh, joke, and smoke as I like,' he demands, 'without being obliged to watch every word and action, as if my tongue was a traitor to my head, and my stomach a tyrant of self-destruction.'

By that year, however, such a society was hard to find. This generational shift can be seen in the offspring of some of our Georgian heroes. Byron's one legitimate daughter, Ada, was brought up to renounce her hell-raising father. She married, had three children, and – like her mother – developed a passionate interest in mathematics. She spent her life writing about the possible design of an 'Analytical Engine', something that foreshadowed the birth of the computer, and is credited with writing one of the earliest computer codes. Today, Ada Lovelace (as she became known) is remembered as a pioneer in the field of computer science.

Mary Wollstonecraft's daughter Mary Shelley may have eloped with Byron's buddy Percy Shelley and married him at the age of nineteen, but she brought up their son to be a very different sort of man. When, having sent her son to Harrow, she was asked how he would learn to think for himself, she exclaimed, 'Oh God, teach him to think like other people.' It seemed to work. The only grandchild of that great radical Mary Wollstonecraft, Percy Florence Shelley, became a baronet, a family man, a High Sheriff of Sussex and a keen yachtsman.

In a word, he became respectable. This term, first used in 1785, was the nineteenth-century's watchword of social approval. It was used endlessly to describe not just those who were polite, but those whose politeness spoke of a deeper goodness of character. Respectability meant drinking in moderation, staying faithful to your partner, and suppressing your wilder human urges.

Respectability also meant taking charge of your emotions. Eighteenth-century Georgians admired authentic, sincere emotion. Women shrieked with laughter in public, while male politicians were praised for sobbing on the floor of the Commons. Abroad, the British were famous for their emotional incontinence: addicted to quack medicines for imaginary ailments and descending into a fit of the vapours at the slightest provocation. England was believed to be a suicide hotspot, while excessive soppiness was known as the 'English malady'. All this changed at the start of the nineteenth century, as the British formed a new reputation for the buttoned-up suppression of emotions: 'Keep a stiff upper lip!' and so on. It just did not do any longer to sob in public.

The church was a great beneficiary of these changes, as the sleepy Anglicanism of the eighteenth century gave way to the vital religion of the Victorians. In 1790, the *Annual Review* reported on the recent upswing in religious attendance, writing: 'churches were well attended, and sometimes even crowded. It was a wonder to the lower classes, throughout all parts of England, to see the avenues to the churches fill with carriages.'

This trend continued for decades. The number of Sunday Schools built or founded in Britain rose from 2,290 between 1780 and 1801 to 11,910 between 1822 and 1831. In 1804, the British and Foreign Bible Society was founded to distribute a Bible to every home in Britain, then extended its mission abroad. Many of the great and the good became patrons, including gentry, aristocracy and even (difficult as it is to believe) the Prince of Wales. By 1825, they had distributed 4,252,000 Bibles in 140 languages throughout Britain and her colonies. One of the most influential writers of the early nineteenth century was an evangelical moralist named Hannah More, whose guides to Christian living sold in their millions. In 1813, she wrote to a friend: 'my heart rejoices at the progress of religious society – wide, and more wide the blessed circle spreads in the elevated walks of life.'

Some Georgians took a stand against all this moralising. In 1824, the *Brighton Gazette* reported that forty fellows had established a 'Society for the Encouragement of Vice' in their louche seaside town. But most Georgians changed with the times. Francis Place was one of them. Born to a poor family in Drury Lane in 1771, his father was a typical eighteenth-century man. First a prison keeper, then an innkeeper, he was, according to his son, 'governed almost wholly by his passions and animal sensations', and spent his time 'drinking, whoring, gaming, fishing and fighting'. For a time, Francis seemed set to follow in his father's footsteps, until he trained as tailor, educated himself about politics, and set himself on the path to respectability.

Place became an influential working-class radical, supporting campaigns for universal male suffrage, greater powers for trade unions, and popular education. However, like many radicals of the time, he combined left-wing politics with conservative moral values, preaching the virtue of hard work, discipline and restraint.

During the 1820s, Place began recording in fine detail the London of his youth, in order to demonstrate how far society had progressed. He recalled the obscene lyrics of popular ballads sung in rowdy taverns, known as 'blackguard' or 'flash' songs. One that stuck in his mind was a not particularly romantic love song about a certain lady named Sally:

Why blast you, Sall, I love you!
And for to prove what I have said,
This night I'll roundly fuck you.
Why then says Sall, my heart's at rest.

Place observed that by the 1820s, even London's prostitutes would disapprove of such vulgarity. For every 100 singers of such songs in the 1780s, he estimated, you might find one today. Place saw this as evidence of British society's improvement. By the end of the Georgian period, he claimed, far fewer people were wasting their money, and ruining their lives, in taverns and brothels. Instead, he wrote, 'The people are better dressed, better fed, cleanlier, better educated in each class respectively, much more frugal, and much happier.'

Francis Place died in 1854, with no doubt in his mind that the Victorian era from which he departed was better than the Georgian era into which he was born. Was he correct? From today's perspective, to claim that one historical period is better or worse than any other is a bit simplistic. We cannot make monolithic moral judgements about millions of people, spanning an entire country, over generations.

Compared to the Victorians, the Georgians were no better nor worse. They were different. As I hope this book has shown, they were more colourful, entertaining, humorous, and – perhaps – free-thinking than those that came after. But they were less morally serious, less industrious and less committed to improving the world in which they lived. Perhaps – like the Roundheads and Cavaliers in Sellar and Yeatman's comic history *1066 and All That* – the Victorians were 'right but repulsive' while the Georgians were 'wrong but wromantic'.

For all its preachiness, the moral revolution that began in late Georgian Britain, and peaked in the Victorian period, led to humanitarian breakthroughs which we still celebrate today. On 26 July 1833, the House of Commons abolished slavery throughout the British Empire, freeing 800,000 Africans from bondage. Three days later, at the age of seventy-three, William Wilberforce died, no doubt believing his life's work was complete. However, we should not be too rosy-eyed about this great moral triumph: infamously, it was the slave owners, and not the enslaved, who received compensation.

As well as abolition, late Georgian Britain also saw campaigns for religious toleration, political and civil rights, the reform of prisons, and the humane treatment of animals – a cause to which an Irish Member of Parliament named Richard Martin dedicated his life. In 1824, he (along with Wilberforce) helped to establish the Society for the Prevention of Cruelty to Animals. His contemporaries roundly mocked him, with George IV nicknaming him 'Humanity Dick', but he was a man ahead of his time. In 1835, Parliament finally outlawed cockfighting and bull-baiting, those favourite blood sports of Georgian Britain. Today, the society he formed still exists as the RSPCA.

As with all cultural shifts, it is hard to determine how much actually changed on the ground. How large was the gulf between rhetoric and reality? For all their moral campaigns, countless Victorians still drank too much, gambled away fortunes, had extra-marital affairs and visited prostitutes. However, whereas the Georgians were open and honest about such indiscretions, the Victorians shrouded them in guilty secrecy. This led to the accusations of Victorian hypocrisy which bedevil this most argued-over and misunderstood era of British history to this day.

As the Georgians faded from view, did the Victorians bring an age of socially courageous reformers, remarkable inventors and brave explorers? Or were they just a band of priggish, hypocritical, empire-building nasties? You will have to meet the Victorians to find out.

Further Reading

Introduction

The best introduction to Georgian society I have read remains Roy Porter's *English Society in the Eighteenth Century* (1982), a classic of scrupulous but readable historical scholarship. Porter had an eye for telling detail and wrote with a pace and humour befitting the age he covered. For London specifically, Jerry White's monumental *London in the 18th Century* (2012) is a cracking read, as is Lucy Inglis's *Georgian London* (2014). A thorough account of the lives of Black Georgians can be found in David Olusoga's *Black and British* (2016), a fascinating corrective to the often whitewashed image we have of Britain's past. The emergence of a new British national identity is a story told in Linda Colley's *Britons* (1992), a book I first read while studying A-level history and have revisited with increasing enjoyment ever since. For the Royal Navy, such an integral part of Georgian Britain, I relied on Ben Wilson's excellent *Empire of the Deep* (2013).

Chapter 1: Anne Bonny and Mary Read

There is tantalisingly little evidence about the lives of Anne Bonny and Mary Read, therefore much that has been written about them is shrouded in conjecture. What we do know is almost all taken from *A General History of the Pyrates* (1724) by Captain Charles Johnson, generally considered a pen name and thought by some to have been Daniel Defoe (author of *Robinson Crusoe*). The only other source that testifies to Anne and Mary's existence is a Jamaican pamphlet from 1721 entitled *The tryals of Captain John Rackam and other pirates*. For background on the 'Golden Age' of Caribbean piracy, David Cordingly is one of Britain's leading experts. In 1992, he curated the 'Pirates: Fact and Fiction' exhibition at the National Maritime Museum in Greenwich, which I still remember visiting as an excitable young child. His book *Life Among the Pirates* (1995) brings the story of Caribbean piracy right up to the modern day, via Victorian novels and Hollywood films. Colin Woodard's *The Republic of Pirates* (2007) is a well-researched and rip-roaring profile of the pirates who made Nassau their base, and of Governor Rogers' campaign to bring them to heel.

Chapter 2: Bonnie Prince Charlie

There is no shortage of Bonnie Prince biographies to choose from. For a page-turning, swashbuckling account, Carolly Erickson's *Bonnie Prince Charlie* (1989) is a good place to start. For a more academic account of his life, Frank McLynn's *Charles Edward Stuart* (1988) remains one of the best available. Jacqueline Riding's recently published *Jacobites* (2017) has earned its place as the authoritative account of the '45 uprising and is particularly good at sorting romance from reality in this much mythologised tale. For primary sources on the uprising, *The Lyon in Mourning* (1895) is a collection of letters, memoirs and speeches, compiled in the three decades following the events by Robert Forbes, a Scottish bishop and Jacobite. It was later published in three volumes by the Scottish History Society.

Chapter 3: John Wilkes

I first encountered the eighteenth-century political phenomenon that was John Wilkes in Linda Colley's *Britons*, in which she retells the story of his Middlesex campaign as an early example of patriotic populism in British politics. The most recent full biography is *John Wilkes* (2006), an authoritative account written by Arthur Cash with real affection for his subject. As an American, Cash is particularly good on Wilkes's transatlantic impact, which included being the namesake of Abraham Lincoln's assassin. Helpful accounts of Wilkes's political campaigns can be found in two essays from *History Today*, 'Wilkes and Liberty' (1957) and 'John Wilkes and the Middlesex Election' (1961), both written by the esteemed historian of eighteenth-century radicalism George Rudé.

Chapter 4: Tipu Sultan

Tipu Sultan is long overdue a full-length biography. The most recent offering was *Tiger of Mysore* (1970) by Denys Forrest. It is a lively, detailed account, but having been written from the India Office on Blackfriars Road half a century ago, it does retain some glow of imperial nostalgia. A more recent account of his life can be found in *Tipu's Tigers* (2009) by Susan Stronge, published by the Victoria and Albert Museum to provide the historical context behind one of their most popular exhibits: Tipu's mechanical, redcoat-mauling tiger. For background detail about the rise of British power in India, I had the benefit of writing this chapter shortly after the publication of William Dalrymple's masterly history of the East India Company *The Anarchy* (2019). In terms of primary sources from Tipu's palace, many of his documents were seized following the Siege of Seringapatam and translated by members of the East India Company for publication. Thus, where we do hear Tipu's voice, it is frustratingly through the filter of his colonial interpreters.

Chapter 5: Olaudah Equiano

The most recent academic biography of Equiano is the meticulously researched *Equiano, the African* (2005) by Vincent Carretta, an American professor of English and expert on Equiano's work. Carretta edited and wrote the introduction for the Penguin Classics edition of *The Interesting Narrative and Other Writings* (2003), still in print 230 years after its original publication, and the source for much of the detail in this chapter. For the wider story of the struggle for abolition in Britain, *Bury the Chains* (2005) by Adam Hochschild is an authoritative account. The aforementioned *Black and British* by David Olusoga contains an excellent account of how freed slaves such as Equiano could expect to be treated in Georgian Britain.

Chapter 6: Mary Wollstonecraft

The two best Wollstonecraft biographies remain *The Life and Death of Mary Wollstonecraft* (1974) by the renowned historical biographer Claire Tomalin, and *Mary Wollstonecraft: A Revolutionary Life* (2000) by Janet Todd, a leading expert on Wollstonecraft's life and works. Todd is the editor of *The Complete Works of Mary Wollstonecraft* (7 vols, 1989), and of *The Collected Letters of Mary Wollstonecraft* (2003), which contains her candid, and often tragic, love letters to both Imlay and Godwin. The account of Mary's Scandinavian travelogue, so celebrated in its time but now largely forgotten, is from Richard Holmes' *Sidetracks: Explorations of a Romantic Biographer* (2001). For further background on the lives of women in Georgian England, Amanda Vickery's *The Gentleman's Daughter* (1998) and *Behind Closed Doors* (2009) both show how women found freedom and even prominence within the confines of eighteenth-century society. In terms of Wollstonecraft's own works, *A Vindication of the Rights of Woman* and *Letters Written in Sweden, Norway, and Denmark* remain in print today.

Chapter 7: Ladies of Llangollen

Sally and Eleanor are increasingly cited in historical surveys of Georgian society, in particular those that focus on gender and sexuality, but there are few dedicated biographies. Much of this chapter is based on *The Ladies of Llangollen* (1971) by Elizabeth Mavor, a tasteful and readable account of what Mavor describes as their 'romantic friendship'. For more on Anne Lister, or 'Gentleman Jack', *The Secret Diaries Of Miss Anne Lister* (2010) edited by Helena Whitbread shows the potential in early nineteenth-century Britain for a strong-willed woman to pursue her unconventional love affairs with surprising candour.

Chapter 8: Lady Hamilton

I first became aware of quite how extraordinary Lady Hamilton's life was in 2017 at an exhibition at the National Maritime Museum in Greenwich. A book published to accompany the exhibition, *Emma Hamilton: Seduction and Celebrity* (2016), recounts in fine detail her impact on eighteenth-century Europe, particularly in art, fashion and material culture. In addition, this chapter was greatly aided by two excellent biographies of Lady

Hamilton, *Beloved Emma* (1986) by Flora Fraser, and *England's Mistress* (2006) by Kate Williams. Much of Emma's heart-wrenching correspondence with her various lovers and betrayers can be read in *Life and Letters of Emma Hamilton* (1963) by Hugh Tours.

Chapter 9: Lady Hester Stanhope

I first encountered the character of Hester Stanhope while reading William Hague's biography *William Pitt the Younger* (2005), in which she plays a bit part. Fortunately, there are two recent biographies of Lady Hester. *Star of the Morning* (2008) by Kirsten Ellis and *Lady Hester* (2005) by Lorna Gibb both tell her globetrotting story with authority and verve. As mentioned towards the end of her story, the most important primary source for Hester's life is *Memoirs of the Lady Hester Stanhope* (1845) by Charles Meryon. However, having been written by such a devoted admirer, some of Meryon's recollections of Hester do contain a touch of fantasy.

Chapter 10: Lord Byron

There is no shortage of Lord Byron biographies. For this chapter, I relied on Fiona MacCarthy's *Byron: Life and Legend* (2002), which does an inestimable job of condensing such a well-documented life into a single volume. For Byron's poetry, the Penguin Classics *Selected Poems* (1996) is excellent, though you have to look elsewhere for his late-in-life masterpiece *Don Juan*.

Chapter 11: Mary Anning

Much of the recent interest in Anning can be traced back to the work of Hugh Torrens, former president of the British Society for the History of Science. His presidential address,

'The Greatest Fossilist the World Ever Knew', was recorded in the *British Journal for the History of Science* (1995) and is an excellent first port of call for those wanting to learn more about her. Tracy Chevalier's novel *Remarkable Creatures* (2009) also brought Anning to much wider acclaim, and is a well researched work of historical fiction. In terms of full-length biographies, *The Fossil Hunter* (2009) by Shelley Emling does a good job of marshalling a detailed narrative on Anning's life from the sparse records that remain. For the wider context of the early nineteenth-century mania for geology, *The Dinosaur Hunters* (2001) by Deborah Cadbury is a rip-roaring piece of historical storytelling.

Chapter 12: James Watt

It is a mark of how far Watt has fallen from popular acclaim that, despite his life being a favourite topic of Victorian biographers, no standard biography has been published for almost a century. The best available remains *James Watt: Craftsman and Engineer* (1936) by H. W. Dickinson. For more technical detail on his invention, there is *James Watt and the Steam Engine* (1927) by H. W. Dickinson and R. Jenkins. An enormous help in creating this chapter was Jenny Uglow's group biography, *The Lunar Men* (2002), which brilliantly evokes the intellectual firmament of the so-called 'Midlands Enlightenment' from which Watt's completed steam engine was born.

Conclusion: The End of the Party

One of the best available accounts of George IV's life remains Christopher Hibbert's two-volume biography *George IV* (1973). *A Mad, Bad, and Dangerous People?* (2006) by Boyd Hilton is an excellent survey of the late Georgian period, and is particularly strong on the upswing in religious enthusiasm at the turn of the century. The remarkable reformation in manners to which this religious revival contributed is the subject of Ben Wilson's fascinating social and cultural history *Decency and Disorder* (2007). A fitting companion to Wilson's work is Vic Gatrell's *City of Laughter* (2006), a jaw-dropping account of the seamier side of London life, whose later chapters address the rise of so-called 'Victorianism' and the end of Georgian libertinism. Published more recently, *The Time Traveller's Guide to Regency Britain* (2020), by Ian Mortimer, contains all you might wish to know about everyday life in the late Georgian period. For more on Britain's Industrial Revolution, *Iron, Steam & Money* (2013) by Roger Osborne is one of the best general introductions available.